EMERGING MULTIDISCIPLINARY PROCESSES IN E-BANKING

Emerging Multidisciplinary Processes in E-banking

Editor:

Jacinta Austin

ArclerPress

www.arclerpress.com

Emerging Multidisciplinary Processes in E-banking
Editor: Jacinta Austin

708 3rd Avenue, 6th Floor
New York
NY 10017
United States of America
www.arclerpress.com

ISBN: 978-1-68094-491-4

Library of Congress Control Number: 2016951345

About the Editor

Jacinta Austin

Jacinta obtained her International Business degree from Griffith University 2012 and a Postgraduate Certificate in Business from University of Southern Queensland in 2014. Her interested is in business and marketing. Jacinta is currently studying a Master of Business (Marketing) from Queensland University of Technology.

Contents

List of Contributors

Cabriella Pravettoni
Department of Social and Political Studies, University of Milano

Salvatore Nuccio Leotta
Department of Social and Political Studies, University of Milano

Claudio Lucchiaiu
Department of Social and Political Studies, University of Milano

Raffaella Misuraca
Department of Psychology, University of Palermo

Regaieg Essafi Raida
Institute of Management Sciences, Tunisia Faculty of Economic Sciences and Management, Tunis, Tunisia

Bouslama Néji
Institute of Management Sciences, Tunisia Faculty of Economic Sciences and Management, Tunis, Tunisia

R. K. Uppal
D.A.V. College, Malout (Punjab)

Bishnupriya Mishra
Academy of Management Studies, Krupajal Group of Institutions, Kausalyaganga, Bhubaneswar

A. Sima Emadi
Department of Computer, Islamic Azad University, Meybod Branch, Iran

B. Somayeh MehriArdestani
Department of Computer, Science and Research Branch, Islamic Azad University, Yazd, Iran

Mazanai Musara
University of Fort Hare South Africa

Guendalina Capece
University of Rome "Tor Vergata", Department of Enterprise Engineering, Rome, Italy

Domenico Campisi
University of Rome "Tor Vergata", Department of Enterprise Engineering, Rome, Italy

Charles K. Ayo
Dept of Computer and Information Sciences, Covenant University, Ota, Ogun State Nigeria

Wilfred Isioma Ukpere
Department of Industrial Psychology and People Management, Faculty of Management, University of Johannesburg South Africa

Xiangfeng Chen
School of Management, Fudan University China

Chenxi Hu
School of Management, Fudan University China

Amparo Marin de la Barcena
Group for Automation in Signals and Communications, Technical University of Madrid, Madrid, Spain

Derya Birant
Dokuz Eylul University Turkey

Stefano Tennina
CISTER Research Unit, ISEP/IPP Rua Dr. António Bernardino de Almeida, Porto Portugal

Luigi Pomante
Dept. of Electrical and Information Engineering and Center of Excellence in Research DEWS, University of L'Aquila, Poggio di Roio, L'Aquila (AQ) Italy

Francesco Tarquini
Dept. of Electrical and Information Engineering and Center of Excellence in Research DEWS, University of L'Aquila, Poggio di Roio, L'Aquila (AQ) Italy

Roberto Alesii
Dept. of Electrical and Information Engineering and Center of Excellence in Research DEWS, University of L'Aquila, Poggio di Roio, L'Aquila (AQ) Italy

Fabio Graziosi
Dept. of Electrical and Information Engineering and Center of Excellence in Research DEWS, University of L'Aquila, Poggio di Roio, L'Aquila (AQ) Italy

Fortunato Santucci
Dept. of Electrical and Information Engineering and Center of Excellence in Research DEWS, University of L'Aquila, Poggio di Roio, L'Aquila (AQ) Italy

Marco Di Renzo
Laboratory of Signals and Systems (L2S), CNRS - SUPELEC - Univ Paris-Sud 3 rue Joliot-Curie, Gif-sur-Yvette (Paris) France

Philip Chan
Institute for Quantum Information Science, and Department of Electrical and Computer Engineering, University of Calgary Canada

Itzel Lucio-Martínez
Institute for Quantum Information Science, and Department of Physics and Astronomy, University of Calgary Canada

Xiaofan Mo
Institute for Quantum Information Science, and Department of Physics and Astronomy, University of Calgary Canada

Wolfgang Tittel
Institute for Quantum Information Science, and Department of Physics and Astronomy, University of Calgary Canada

Albrecht Enders
University of Erlangen-Nürnberg, Germany

Tawfik Jelassi
École Nationale des Ponts et Chaussées, Paris

Andreas König
University of Erlangen-Nürnberg, Germany

Harald Hungenberg
University of Erlangen-Nürnberg, Germany

Ismail M. Romi
College of Administrative Sciences and Informatics, Palestine Polytechnic University, Palestine

Stephen Kent Callaway
Assistant Professor of Management, University of Toledo

Sandeep Bhailalbhai Jagani
Candidate PhD Candidate, Manufacturing and Technology Management, University of Toledo

Elsa Shokrollahpour
Department of Industrial Management, Science and Research Branch, Islamic Azad University, Tehran, Iran

Farhad Hosseinzadeh Lotfi
Department of Mathematics, Science and Research Branch, Islamic Azad University, Tehran, Iran

Mostafa Zandieh
Department of Industrial Management, Management and Accounting Faculty, Shahid Beheshti University, G.C., Tehran, Iran

Dr. Ala`Eddin Mohd Khalaf Ahmad
Assistant Professor, Department of Marketing, Applied Science University, Amman 11192, Jordan

Dr. Hasan Ali Al-Zu'bi
Associate Professor, Department of Business Administration, Applied Science University, Amman 11192, Jordan

Mahdi Salehi
Accounting and Management Department, Zanjan University, Iran D.N. 1, Nagilo Alley, Emam Street, Hidaj City, Zanjan Province, Iran

Mehrdad Alipour
Management Department, Islamic Azad University, Zanjan Branch, Zanjan City, Iran

Dr. Mohsen Rasoulian
Islamic Azad University, Naragh Branch ,Iran

Monire Safari
Islamic Azad University, Naragh Branch ,Iran

Kwame Annin
Kumasi Polytechnic, Kumasi, Ghana

Maurice Omane-Adjepong
Garden City University College, Kenyase-Kumasi, Ghana

Sonita Sarpong Senya
Central University College, Miosto, Ghana

Sana Haider Sumra
Department of Management Sciences, The Islamia University of Bahawalpur, Pakistan

Mohammad Khurram Manzoor
Lahore School of Economics, Pakistan

Hassan H. Sumra
Management Sciences, COMSATS Institute of Information & Technology, Pakistan

Momina Abbas
MCB Bank Circle Office, 4-A Qasim Road, Dubai Chowk, Bahawalpur

Xiao Ling Qiu
Keller Graduate School of Management of Devry University

Preface

The way consumers have done banking has dramatically changed in the last 20 years since with the introduction of e-banking. With this there has been changes within the banking industry in ways of the implementation of multidisciplinary processes within individual banking organisations. This book with be looking at a wide range of published research looking at different areas of e-banking, ranging from how it effects consumers to different processes that this form of banking influences both in developing and developed countries. The chapters will be looking at the usability and trust of e-banking, determining if the consumer see e-banking as an important role and if they trust the banking security measures and how security models and architecture electronic banking; looking at the how they have adopted the system and still provided the banking services. Also, having a look at how this new making system has been implemented into different countries including developing countries, this includes behaviour models. With relation to management, how the supply change is different or changed in finance and how banks are determining risk management. Then looking at how e-banking and if market research has been influenced and how banks have used this data within management.

Editor

Jacinta Austin

INTRODUCTION

Online banking, also known as internet banking, e-banking or virtual banking, is an electronic payment system that enables customers of a bank or other financial institution to conduct a range of financial transactions through the financial institution's website. The online banking system will typically connect to or be part of the core banking system operated by a bank and is in contrast to branch banking which was the traditional way customers accessed banking services. To access a financial institution's online banking facility, a teacher with internet access would need to register with the institution for the service, and set up a password and other credentials for customer verification. The credentials for online banking is normally not the same as for telephone or mobile banking. Financial institutions now routinely allocate customers numbers, whether or not customers have indicated an intention to access their online banking facility. Customer numbers are normally not the same as account numbers, because a number of customer accounts can be linked to the one customer number. Technically, the customer number can be linked to any account with the financial institution that the customer controls, though the financial institution may limit the range of accounts that may be accessed to, say, cheese, savings, loan, credit card and similar accounts.

The customer visits the financial institution's secure website, and enters the online banking facility using the customer number and credentials previously set up. The types of financial transactions which a customer may transact through online banking are determined by the financial institution, but usually includes obtaining account balances, a list of the recent transactions, electronic bill payments and funds transfers between a customer's or another's accounts. Most banks also enable a customer to download copies of bank statements, which can be printed at the customer's premises (some banks charge a fee for mailing hard copies of bank statements). Some banks also enable customers to download transactions directly into the customer's accounting software. The facility may also enable the customer to order a cheese book, statements, report loss of credit cards, stop payment on a cheese, advice change of address and other routine actions.

Precursors

The precursor for the modern home online banking services were the distance banking services over electronic media from the early 1980s. The term 'online' became popular in the late 1980s and referred to the use of a terminal, keyboard and TV (or monitor) to access the banking system using a phone line. 'Home banking' can also refer to the use of a numeric keypad to send tones down a phone line with instructions to the bank. Online services started in New York in 1981 when four of the city's major banks (Citibank, Chase Manhattan, Chemical and Manufacturers Hanover) offered home banking services. Using the videotext system. Because of the commercial failure of videotex these banking services never became popular except in France where the use of videotex (Minitel) was subsidised by the telecom provider and the UK, where the Prestel system was used.

First online banking in the United Kingdom

Almost simultaneously with the United States, online banking arrived in the United Kingdom. The UK's first home online banking services known as Homelink was set up by Bank of Scotland for customers of the Nottingham Building Society (NBS) in 1983. The system used was based on the UK's Prestel view link system and used a computer, such as the BBC Micro, or keyboard connected to the telephone system and television set. The system allowed on-line viewing of statements, bank transfers and bill payments. In order to make bank transfers and bill payments, a written instruction giving details of the intended recipient had to be sent to the NBS who set the details up on the Homelink system. Typical recipients were gas, electricity and telephone companies and accounts with other banks. Details of payments to be made were input into the NBS system by the account holder via Prestel. A cheese was then sent by NBS to the payee and an advice giving details of the payment was sent to the account holder. BACS was later used to transfer the payment directly.

Stanford Federal Credit Union was the first financial institution to offer online internet banking services to all of its members in October 1994.

What is Electronic Banking?

Also known as online banking or e-banking, electronic banking allows people to manage their bank accounts over the Internet. In most cases, an account can be set up at the time a customer opens a checking or savings account. Some banks give their customers the ability to create budgets, send checks, and view months of statements. A major advantage to electronic banking is that people who use it no longer need to keep a checkbook because most transactions are uploaded to the bank's website within one business day. It is important to practice good judgment when using electronic banking services because money can usually be spent if a user name or password comes into the possession of another person.

Electronic banking accounts are available only to people who have an account with a bank that offers this service. The customer must usually acquire a log-in and temporary password from a bank employee. Both user names and passwords can often be changed to more secure letter and number combinations. Electronic banking accounts are rarely limited to people who have checking and savings accounts; those with credit cards, vehicle loans, and mortgages may also qualify. On the other hand, a bank might not have this feature available to people with certain kinds of accounts, but it all depends on the bank.

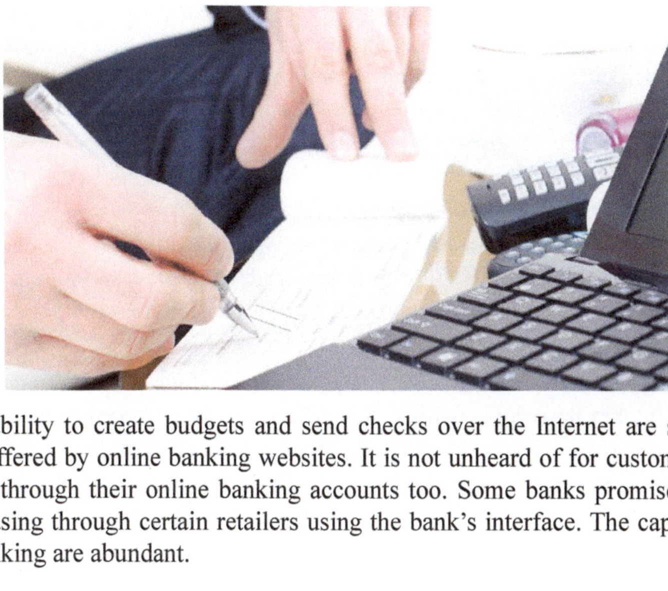

The ability to create budgets and send checks over the Internet are some basic services offered by online banking websites. It is not unheard of for customers to buy insurance through their online banking accounts too. Some banks promise discounts for purchasing through certain retailers using the bank's interface. The capabilities of online banking are abundant.

One advantage to electronic banking is that the software typically keeps track of all expenses related to the account. This means the customer can put less effort into doing this herself. Another advantage to this type of banking is that some banks allow customers to open and close connected accounts, like savings. It is sometimes possible to also upgrade an account.

Many online banking accounts allow customers to view their banking account and routing numbers. This is very personal information that could be used to purchase things online. Letting this kind of information be accessed by a stranger can lead to theft. Although there is a similar risk with carrying around banking checks, online merchants do not ask for identification before withdrawing money from an account.

Emerging Multidisciplinary Processes in E-banking

The traditional mode of delivering products and services by banks to the consumers is through a single distribution channel and that is physical bank branches. Financial services industry is metamorphosing due to the advent of Internet, rapid technological evolutions, deregulation, globalization, as well as the impact of changing competitive and regulatory forces. In order to cope with the quick changes in the business scenario, banks started to rely on distribution channels as an alternative strategy for differentiation and gaining further competitive advantage. The abovementioned paved way for the development of the e-banking phenomena.

It provides a comprehensive explanation of what e-banking is, the evolution of e-banking, existing trends of e-banking in developed, developing, and newly industrialized nations, future directions for further possible research, and concluding remarks.

There are many proposals offer anonymous and non-repudiation e-payment protocols. But they have the drawbacks that the anonymity can be misused by fraudulent to perform a perfect crimes. Currently, the hot research concentrates on the accepting of e-payment protocols where the anonymity of the coins is cancelable via a trusted authority in the case of criminal entities. We suggest an efficient protocol for e-payment scheme that offers a good level of security with appreciate to its efficiency.

The proposed protocol prevents the blind office and the bank from impersonate an entity, so that the entity could not repudiate it when the entity misused a coin. Another benefit is that it is constructed from efficient cryptography schemes so that its security can simply be analyzed. The strength of this scheme is in its easiness. So, we claim that the suggested protocol is more efficient than the existing schemes, since it allows to both a blind office and a bank to impersonate an entity to find and to spend a coin without to be noticed. It might cause a repudiation difficulty where the entity can repudiate his bad activities by proposing that both the bank and the blind office acted inaccurately. Other relevant issues related to the new protocol will be discussed in the section of the security of the scheme.

E-banking services especially in the developing economies, highlighting the major challenges of e-banking in the developing economies with a guideline or recommendations to address those challenges. Technology has introduced new ways of delivering banking to the customer. Developed countries (DC) customers of the e-banking services are fully aware of the services but the customers in the developing economies are still lag behind. It is clearly seen that delivery channels are lacking in meeting the demands of the customer by not making them aware of e-banking and using obsolete or not too up-to-date technology.

The other issue is that there are very few or no banking facilities in the rural areas and furthermore, access to the Internet is close to impossible in these areas therefore awareness and utilization of these services is very little or none at all. At last but not the least is that banks must adapt to the electronics age. Consumers demand it. Economics drives it. Banks must exploit it.

In today's business environment, knowledge is increasingly recognized as the most important and valuable asset in organizations and a key differentiating factor in business. Therefore, many organizations are positioning themselves strategically based on their tangible and intangible internal resources, and their capabilities rather than on their products and services. However, in order to an organization to be successful in the exploitation of knowledge assets to drive competitive advantages, a holistic approach that spans Knowledge Management (KM), business strategy, and organizational and human factors should be used. The aim of this study is to investigate the effect of some factor on KM Strategic Alignment between KM and business strategy in the banking sector at Persian Gulf Countries. The results have indicated factors such as knowledge sharing, trust, openness to change, IT infrastructure and skills, and existence of CKO are strongly correlated to the strategic alignment between KM and business strategy. Thus, managers in the Persian Gulf banking sectors should adopt new rules using flexible organizational culture, reforming and redesigning their organizational structure, and incorporating an advanced information technology in their operations for competitive advantage.

Internet banking strategy can be generally very challenging, but more challenging in an economic environment infested with high degree of corruption, insecurity, bad governance, poverty, and financial system instability. Due to its global nature, Internet banking, under such situation, is threatened by the easiness at which off-line crimes are transmitted into online businesses, and the difficulty in building trusts and confidence in online business relationships.

Internet is not simply one more distribution channel among the multi-channel strategies used by the financial industry; it is fostering new "e-Business Models" such as Internet-primary banks. However, in spite of its strong development potential, this type of bank has often achieved a weak breakthrough onto this market and shows modest financial results.

Nowadays, e-banking plays an important role in e-society and human life. Imagine an e-society without e-banking is not possible. The e-banking is considered as an enabler factor to e-business, e-commerce, e-government, and other e-initiatives. Despite the pivotal role of e-banking in our lives, yet a comprehensive conceptual model of electronic banking success factors has not been provided by the researchers.

It provides comprehensive conceptual model by categorizing factors affecting implementation of electronic banking. In this regard, the factors affecting implementation of electronic banking was classified based on Co-structural factors, Content factors, and Context factors.

We called this conceptual model as the Tri-Category (3C) Model. The questionnaire used for gathering data. The results showed that there is a positive relationship between successful implementation of E banking and attention to Co-structural, Content, and Contextual factors.

It introduces Banking Technology as a confluence of several disparate disciplines such as Finance (including risk management), Information Technology, Computer Science, Communication Technology and Marketing Science. It presents the evolution of banking, the tremendous influence of information and communication technologies on banking and its products, the quintessential role played by computer science in fulfilling banks' marketing objective of servicing customers better at a less cost and thereby reap more profits. It also highlights the use of advanced statistics and computer science to measure, mitigate, and manage various risks associated with banks' business with its customers and other banks. The growing influence of customer relationship management and data mining in tackling various marketing related problems and fraud detection problems in banking industry is well documented. RFID enabled bank notes, Antiphishing techniques that make Internet banking secure, and the applications of Web 2.0 in banking.

Nowadays, the banks are using new technologies to provide better services to customers. One of these new technologies is RFID. Then, some applications of RFID in banking sector such as RFID applications in the cheese between banks, reducing the manual operation, customer relationship management, tracking and tracing, money transferring system, countering counterfeiting, contactless smart cards, people identification, phone banking, establishing security, checking purpose, and so on are explained. Finally, some of the barriers to 'technology acceptance by the customers and some methods to data protection and increasing security in RFID systems are described.

The emergence of e-banking has created a significant transformation towards the services provided by the banks. E-banking provides alternatives for faster delivery of banking services to a wider scope of customers, hence creating a major impact towards e-society. Nowadays, e-banking has gained increasing popularity in delivering online services for e-society. However, prior to the implementation of e-banking, several factors and best practices must be identified to ensure a more efficient execution of e-banking services towards the development of e-society. E-banking factors are found to have a significant effect on the success of e-societies.

What are the different types of banking transactions?

Among the various types of banking transactions are wire transfers, online bill payments and credit card transactions. Other financial transactions that may occur through a bank include mortgage loans and small business loans. Several different types of banking transactions can take place in person, by telephone or online.

Various payment transactions make doing business easier. Among these options is a payment method known as a wire transfer. Essentially, transactions utilizing this method involve the transfer of funds from one party's banking account to another party's banking account. These business transactions are a routine way of doing business in some parts of the world and help make international business transactions more effective.

Online transactions are also an effective way of handling banking transactions. By establishing a checking account that allows online transactions, account holders are able to schedule bills to be paid automatically each month or are given the option of manually paying bills online from a personal computer. Online banking also allows account holders to monitor funds in an account without having to call or visit a bank in person to obtain transaction records.

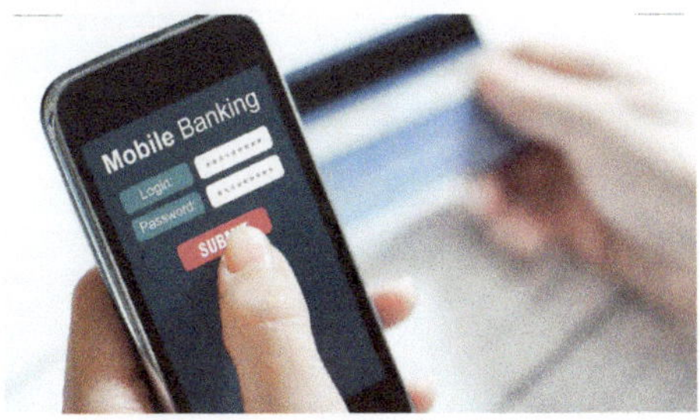

Individuals or businesses approved for bank credit cards are also able to initiate credit card transactions for purchases. These banking transactions present the user with a convenient way to purchase items, pay bills, rent cars or perform a variety of other financial transactions without using cash. Credit card holders also do not have to pay for an item's entire amount at the time of purchase, but are able to repay the amounts charged in smaller increments, instead. Credit card transactions are, however, accompanied by additional interest charges and other fees may apply.

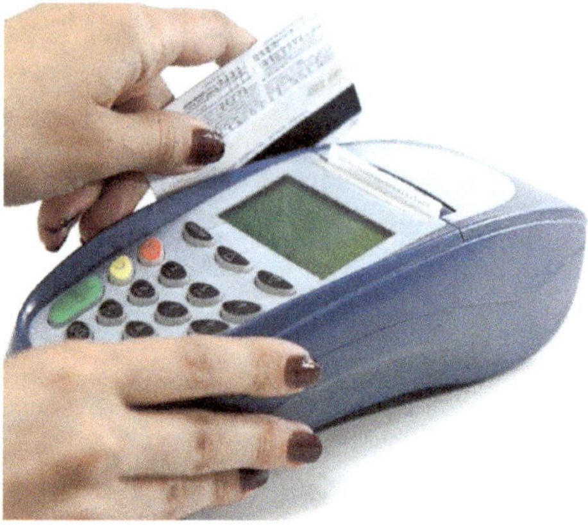

When purchasing a home, starting a new business, expanding a business or when in need of funds for a variety of different interests, banking transactions that lend money to borrowers are often sought. These transactions do not require the borrower to be a current banking customer, but upon credit approval individuals and businesses can receive financial loans. The amounts and terms of each loan vary, and a borrower may even have more than one loan from more than one banking institution. While most other banking transactions may transpire online or by phone, the process of obtaining a bank loan most often requires an in-person visit to a bank to discuss options, submit an application and sign for the release of funds if a loan is approved.

1

CHAPTER

USABILITY AND TRUST IN E-BANKING

Cabriella Pravettoni, Salvatore Nuccio Leotta, Claudio Lucchiaiu and Raffaella Misuraca

INTRODUCTION

In the last decade of the twentieth century, new types of economic transactions have become increasingly more prevalent. The most widespread is e-business (electronic business), which derives from a feature of IBM's marketing strategy: organizing customers and company business generally through electronic equipment and software. In e-business, information and communication technologies are used to enhance the business, including any process that an organization conducts over a computer network. In e-commerce (electronic commerce), information and communication technologies are used in interorganisational transactions and in business-to-consumer transactions. E-commerce eliminates the middleman between the producer and the consumer. The real novelty for the consumer is the continuous and ubiquitous availability of service.

E-banking is a particular branch of e-commerce. It allows bank clients to obtain information and carry out transactions online, and much more. Transactional home banking systems can be used to carry out online fund transfers, to make tax, invoice, and bill payments, and to check and change personal data. It is also possible to trade on the stock exchange in real time, to participate in public share offerings, to access detailed financial analyses, and to buy and sell shares with lower commissions than in traditional banking or phone banking (Cusamano & Yoffie, 1998). These characteristics alllow e-banking to be considered by researchers as a promising new technology (Gunasekaran & Love, 1999; Yousafzai, Pallister, & Foxall, 2003) and as a potentially infinite universe of information (e.g., Page-Thomas & Uncles, 2004) wherein decisions can be more informed (e.g., Alba, Lynch, Weitz, Janiszewski, Lutz, Sawyer, & Wood, 1997; Mishra & Olshavsky, 2005).

Citation: Cabriella Pravettoni, Salvatore Nuccio Leotta, Claudio Lucchiaiu and Raffaella Misuraca, Usability and Trust in E-Banking, Doi: 10.2466/PRO.101.4.1118-1124.

E-banking had relative fast growth in the last 10 years. However, there is a great difference across geographical areas. In the U.S. the average use of online banking is 44%, higher than the European (E.U.) average of 36% (Deutsche Bank Research, 2006). Across Europe the use of e-banking varies from 70% in northern countries (such as Finland, Iceland, etc.) to 20% in southern countries (such as Italy and Greece). There are several factors limiting or slowing the growth of e-banking in some countries. One of these is lack of trust (Aladwani, 2001; Sillence, Briggsa, Harris, & Fishwick, 2006). Online transactions and relationships do not allow customers the natural benefits of face-to-face interaction (Gefen, 2003; Gefen, Karahanna, & Straub, 2003; Yousafzai, et al., 2003), and are characterized by uncertainty, anonymity, spatial and temporal separation, lack of control, and potential opportunistic behaviours. Worries about Internet-related technology and infrastructures' robustness, privacy and security, and possibility of fraud play a key role in adoption of e-banking.

All these characteristics have made risk perception and trust crucial elements for users (Gefen, 2000). Trust is an important factor in many social interactions involving uncertainty and dependency. Trust in e-banking is defined as willingness of customers to perform online banking transactions, expecting that the bank will fulfill its obligations irrespective of ability to monitor or control the banks' actions (Citera, Beauregard, & Mitsuya, 2005). This definition underlines the two dimensions of trust proposed by McKnight, Cummings, and Chervany (1998), institutional trust and trust beliefs. They defined trust beliefs as the customers' perception of the capability, benevolence, and integrity of the web service. The bank's reputation is considered to be part of the trust beliefs domain. Institutional trust, instead, refers to systems factors and elements, such as security and privacy policies and website quality. The bank can influence customers' trust beliefs (perception of trustworthiness of the bank) through institutional trust (trust of the internet control mechanisms).

According to Laberge and Caird (2001) usability and accessibility are two crucial factors in adoption of a service. Usability is the extent to which a product can be used by specific people to achieve specified with effectiveness, efficiency, and satisfaction. Accessibility refers to understanding, navigation, and interaction on the web by anyone at anytime from anywhere. Institutional trust can be improved by optimizing the usability and the accessibility of the e-banking systems (Dayal, Landesbeg, & Zeisser, 1999; Yousafzai, Pallister, & Foxall, 2005). In fact, website design, quality, and usability may drive perceptions of trustworthiness, giving customers a safe and comfortable feeling during the website navigation (Kim & Moon, 1998). According to McKnight, et al. (McKnight, et al., 1998; McKnight, Choudhury, & Kacmer, 2002) these website characteristics drive customers' trustworthiness giving rise to so-called Situational Normality.

The present study aimed to analyse the interaction between personal, institutional, and technological factors in structuring users' trust in e-banking services. Two hypotheses were tested. It was expected that expert computer users, those scoring high on the European Computer Driving License, would rate themselves as having higher trust of e-banking than would nonexperts. E-bank users would report usability as being more important than would people who did not use e-banking (Laberge & Caird, 2001).

METHOD

Subjects

One hundred and eighty-five undergraduate working students attending evening classes of the University of Milan took part as volunteers in the experiments. One hundred and seven were men, and 78 were women (M age= 31 yr., SD=3.3).

Measures

The European Computer Driving License.-This test of practical skills and competencies consists of separate modules covering computer theory and practice. The questionnaire has 60 items grouped into six areas (document management, word processing, spreadsheets, database, presentation, Internet, and electronic mail). The scores may range from 0: No competence at all to 360: Highest competence. There were 81 subjects in the Nonexpert group, and 104 subjects in the Expert group.

E-banking use.-One hundred and eighty-five participants (M age =30.5 yr., SD=3.1) were asked to answer two questions concerning their e-banking services use. The two questions were: "Have you got an e-banking account?" and "If yes, how many times do you use e-banking services (collect account information, transaction, and so on) per month?"

Trust and usability.-An ad hoc questionnaire developed by authors and previously tested was administered. Items were grouped into three sections, each having a final score between 0 to 80: Technology trust, Institutional trust, and Usability Importance. The first section of the questionnaire had 20 items exploring trust about the stability and reliability of the e-banking system, e.g., "How much do you believe that the connection will be lost during the transaction?" and "How much do you believe that the system will not allow you to complete the transaction?" This scale had a Cronbach coefficient alpha of .78 and a test-retest correlation (Pearson coefficient) of 20. The second section (20 items) investigated the major concerns about customers' feelings of safety, assuredness, and comfort during the transaction, e.g., "To what extent do you expect to become a victim of fraud?" and "How much do you fear that your personal information will be made accessible to others?" Cronbach coefficient alpha of this scale was .80, and the test-retest correlation (Pearson coefficient) was .79. The third section included 20 items exploring the perceived importance of the usability of an e-banking Website, e.g., "How important is it that the website is intuitive?" and "How important is the ease-of-use of the Website?" Cronbach coefficient alpha of this scale was .8I, and the eight-week test-retest correlation (Pearson coefficient) was .83 for each scale.

The questionnaire was presented in a paper-and-pencil format. Nonusers were instructed to answer the questions based on their expectations of an e-banking experience. For each item the participants were asked to respond on a Likert-type >-point scale (0: Nothing to 4: Very much). The sum of the first and the second scale scores was the global Trust score.

Procedure

To evaluate computer expertise, the participants were first asked to complete the European Computer Driving License questionnaire (ECDL, which is known as the International Computer Driving License outside Europe), a standard and recognized tool used to certify computer skills. On the basis of the outcomes, 185 participants were selected for the experiment (107 men, 78 women). For experimental purposes, participants who obtained a score lower than 80 on the European Computer Driving License questionnaire were included in the Nonexpert group, while those with a score higher than 260 were assigned to the Expert group. According to how participants answered the two questions on use of e-banking, the were assigned to one of two independent groups: Users of e-banking services, subjects with a frequency of use higher than five operations per month (n = 93; 57 Experts and 36 Nonexperts) and Nonusers of e-banking services (n = 92; 47 Experts and 45 Nonexperts).

Statistical Analysis

Descriptive statistics were used to examine the distribution of responses between groups. Pearson correlation coefficient was used to evaluate correlation between scales.

RESULTS

Users reported higher scores on Technology Trust than Nonusers (see Table I).' Both Expert and Nonexpert Users had lower scores on the Usability Importance (t -5.89, p = .02 and t = 6.21, p = .01, respectively). Finally, both Expert and Nonexpert Users reported a lower mean score on Institutional Trust (t = 7.92, p = .003 and t = 6.82, p = .06, respectively). The correlation between Technology Trust and Iristitutional Trust was significant. Usability Importance had only a moderate correlation with Technology Trust and Institutional Trust.

Table 1: means and standard deviations for four measures with pearson correlation matrix

			Measure			
			1	2	3	4
Users						
Experts	*M*		35.6	29.2	37.6	295
	SD		5.8	5.1	5.0	9
	r	1. Technology Trust				
		2. Institutional Trust	.6†			
		3. Usability Importance	.2	.2		
		4. European Computer Driving License	.4	.3	.2	
Nonexperts	*M*		24.5	23.5	30.1	65
	SD		6.6	4.1	4.2	8
	r	1. Technology Trust				
		2. Institutional Trust	.5†			
		3. Usability Importance	.2	.2		
		4. European Computer Driving License	.3*	.2	.2	
Nonusers						
Experts	*M*		24.3	48.3	54.0	289
	SD		5.3	5.0	3.1	6
	r	1. Technology Trust				
		2. Institutional Trust	.5†			
		3. Usability Importance	.1	.2		
		4. European Computer Driving License	.4*	.3*	.2	
Nonexperts	*M*		20.3	46.0	61.4	68
	SD		5.5	6.0	2.8	5

r			
1. Technology Trust			
2. Institutional Trust	.3*		
3. Usability Importance	.2	.1	
4. European Computer Driving License	.3*	.3*	.2

*$p < .05$. †$p < .001$.

DISCUSSION

These results suggest that for Expert Users the use of e-banking depends on the trust attributed to the bank. Usability did not seem to play a significant role either in the actual use of e-banking or in trust. Among Nonusers there is widespread psychological resistance to e-banking use: fears about security, personal data fraud, and lack of reliable customer care (Kim & Moon, 1998).

The questionnaire successfully differentiated groups according to computer abilities and e-banking use. In fact, while usability is an envisioned rather than directly perceived obstacle for the Nonexpert group, they reported the main usability issues previously noticed by Laberge and Caird (2001). For Expert Users, internet technology was not a problem for interaction; the problems seem to be related to "trusting the system."

The study suggests that low use of e-banking may have a twofold explanation. Expert Users may not make much use of it simply because they do not trust banks (lack of institutional trust) or internet banking technology, regardless of interface usability and the economic convenience of e-banking. Thus, overall trust in the bank seemed to play a crucial role in determining actual use of e-banking. Naturally, generalization is limited by the constraints of the study. The use of nonstandardized measures and the small sample did not permit further analysis which might better explain the differences between groups. The cross-sectional design does not allow assessment of causal links. Usability may not always play a crucial role in determining use of e-banking, since other factors, such as trust in a specific bank, may be more important. However, the usability factor could influence customer e-banking behaviour at a second stage, when the customer actually uses e-banking services and has the option of choosing between traditional banking and e-banking, or between different e-banking providers. Other aspects that may explain the interaction between perceived importance of usability and ebanking use are the frequency with which e-banking is utilized and the typical e-services used. A professional user may prefer a reliable transaction than an easy interface, while an occasional user may be attracted by ease of procedures or graphic aspects. Researchers could address these issues to understand better individual motivations in e-banking adoption and to improve customers' satisfaction.

REFERENCES

1. ALADWANI, A. M. (2001) Online banking: a field study of drivers, development challenges, and expectations. international Journal of Information Management, 21, 213-225.

2. ALBA, L., LYNCH, J., WEITZ, B., JANISZEWSKI, C., LUTZ, R., SAWYER, A, &WOOD, S. (1997) Interactive home shopping: consumer, retailer, and

manufacturer incentives to participate in electronic marketplace. Journal of Marketing, 61, 38-53.

3. CITERA, M., BEAUREGARD, R., &MITSUYA, T. (2005) An experimental study of credibility in enegotiations. Psychology & Marketing, 22, 202-231.
4. CUSAMANO, M. A., & YOFPIE, D. B. (1998) Competing on Internet time: les~ons from Netscape and its battle with Microsoft. New York: Free Press.
5. DAYAL, S., LANDESBEG, H., &ZEISSER, M. (1999) How to build trust online. Marketing Management, 8(3), 64-69.
6. DEUTSCHE BANK RESEARCII. (2006) Onlzne banking: what we learn from the dt#ttrences in Europe? Frankfurt am Main: Author.
7. GEFEN, D. (2000) E-commerce: the rate of familiarity and trust. Omega: The International lournal of Management Science, 28, 725-737.
8. GEFEN, D. (2003) TAM or just plain habit: a look at experienced online shoppers. Journal of End User Computing, 15, 1-13.
9. GEFEN, D., KARAHANNA, E., &STRAUB, D. (2003) Trust and TAM in online shopping: an integrated model. MIS Quarterly, 27, 51-90.
10. GUNASEKARAN,,, &LOVE, P. D. (1999) Current and future applications of multimedia technology in business. International Journal of Information Management, 19, 105-120
11. KIM, J., &MOON, J. Y. (1998) Designing towards the emotional usability in customer interfaces: trustworthiness of qberbanking system interfaces. Interacting with Computers, 10, 1-29.
12. LABERGE, J., & CAIRD, J. K. (2001) Trusting the online banking interface: development of a conceptual model relevant to e-commerce transactions. l'roceedings of the CHI 2000 Workshop: designing interactive systems for 1-10-1 E-commerce.
13. MCKNIGHT, D., CHOUDHURY, V., &KACMER, C. (2002) The impact of initial trust on intentions to transact with a Web site: a trust building model. journal of Strategic Information Systems, 11, 297-323.
14. MCKNIGHT, D., CUMMINGS, L.,&CHERVANY, N.(1998) Initial trust formation in new organizational relationships. Academy of Management Review, 23, 472-490.
15. MISHRA, S., &OLSHAVSKY, R. (2005) Rationality unbounded: the Internet and its effect on con- sumer decision making. In C. P. Haugtvedt, K. A. Machleit, & R. F. Yalch (Eds.), Online conrumer psychology: understanding and influencing consumer behaviour zn the virtual world. Hove, UK: Erlbaum. Pp. 361-378.
16. PAGE-THOMAS, K. L., &UNCLES, hf. D. (2004) Consumer knowledge of the World Wide Web: conceptualisation and measurement. P.sychology C Marketing, 21, 575-593.
17. SILLENCE, E., BRIGGSA, P., HARRIS, P., & FISHWICK, L. (2006) A framework for understanding trust factors in web-based health advice. journal of Human-Computer Studies, 64, 697-713.

18. YOUSAFZAI, S. Y., PALLISTER, J. G., &FOXALL, G. R. (2003) A proposed model of e-trust for electronic banking. Technovation, 23, 847-860.

19. YOUSAFZAI, 5. Y., PALLISTER, J. G., &FOXALL, G. K. (2005) Strategies for building and communication trust in electronic banking: a field experiment. Psychology & Marketing, 22, 181- 201.

2
CHAPTER

THE ADOPTION OF THE E-BANKING

Regaieg Essafi Raida and Bouslama Néji

Keywords: Bank on Internet; Perceived Usefulness; Perceived Ease; Intent to Use

INTRODUCTION

The Technology Acceptance Model is a model of general acceptance for several types of technology. It explains the adoption of information technologies, the adoption of the microcomputer [1] and the adoption of the Internet [2]. In this research, we will inspire to this model [3], which has benefited from a good validation in several empirical studies [4,5], and it explains the behavior of information technology adoption [6]. Thus the proven relevance of Technology Acceptance Model justifies its application to this research. Indeed, given the number of research that supported the Technology Acceptance Model, this model will provide a reference for the identification of the determinants of Internet use in the relationships between bank and firm. So how the Technology Acceptance Model is able to explain determinants of the use of the Internet by the leaders of companies in Tunisia?

THE TECHNOLOGY ACCEPTANCE MODEL (DAVIS 1989)

The theory of reasoned action was developed by Ajzen and Fishbein [7]. In their model from the research in social psychology, they define the links between beliefs, attitudes, norms and intention. The behavior of the individual is determined by its intention of adoption or rejection, this intention is influenced by subjective standards of the individual

Citation: R. Raida and B. Néji, "The Adoption of the E-Banking," Technology and Investment, Vol. 4 No. 3, 2013, pp. 197-203. doi: 10.4236/ti.2013.43023.

and his attitude toward the behavior. This principle was supported by technology acceptance model [3] which has been adopted by several previous researches. However this is able to be supported by our research to explain determinants of acceptance of Internet technology in the relationship between bank and firm. The Technology Acceptance Model (TAM) is a specific model to explain the acceptance and use of new information technologies in organizations [8]. It was developed by Davis in 1989 to explain the behavior of use of the computer [6]. It is based on the fact that the adoption is based on the influence of the perceived ease and the perceived usefulness of the user [9]. The Technology Acceptance Model can predict the determinants of acceptance of a system and guide the experience with the system [5]. The Technology Acceptance Model may explain the success or failure of the adoption of new technologies. It has been supported by the analysis of the determinants of acceptance of e-mail by administrative staff [10]. In this model, Davis makes the relation between the perceived usefulness, perceived ease of use, attitudes and actual behavior for the use of the computer-based technologies. Indeed, Davis identified a number of fundamental variables suggested by previous studies on the determinants of cognitive and emotional of the computer-based technology. The model is based on the assumption that the acceptance of the information system is determined by the intentions of using the system. That the intentions are influenced by the attitude of the individual to the use of the information system and that this attitude is influenced by the perceived usefulness and ease of use. It is a model that explains how the characteristics of technology affect perception and later its use [11]. This model has been tested empirically by several studies [11-13]. Technology Acceptance Model was cited 425 times in research between 1989 and 2000 [11]. It has been tested on different groups and organizations and was analyzed by various statistical tools [14]. This model was applied to several modes of uses of technologies such as the use of the e-mail [3,15], the use of the Word processors [15,16], the use of groupware [5], and the use of the world wide web [17].

The original TAM was supported by several researchers such as in presentation of the factors of acceptance of the web site [18], in implementation of the ERP system [19], in the study of the determinants of acceptance of telemedicine [20]. This model was also supported in the context of the use of computers at work [21] and the use of the web [22,23] to test the e-learning. Referring to a Meta-analysis realized between 1980 and 2001 [24], on the work using TAM, all research shows the existence of significant relations between the perceived usefulness, perceived usability, the attitude and intention. Based on the acceptance of the technology model developed by Davis and the attitudinal model [25-27], we will consider that the usefulness and ease of use are therefore the key variables in the model of Davis given the importance of their impact on behavior. Therefore, we consider that the intention of Internet use is influenced by the attitude to the use of the Internet which is determined by the perception of the ease and the usefulness of Internet use.

CONCEPTUAL FRAMEWORK

The Perception of the Use of Internet

According to De Vito [28] the perception is the process of awareness of many stimuli affecting our senses; it affects the stimuli or messages received. In marketing, "is the process by which a consumer becomes aware of its marketing environment and the interpreter in such a way as it is in agreement with its reference scheme [29]". The theory of the adoption and diffusion of innovation postulate that use of innovation tend to influence the behavior of the adoption of this innovation [30].

Ease Perceived of Internet Use

It's a concept used by the work of the acceptance of the technology. Ease of use means non-complexity and the use of a system without mental effort [3].

It includes the judgments of the efforts required to use technology [3] and expresses the degree to which innovation is difficult to understand or use [30,31]. The perceived usability refers to the effort expected by the individual. This built also refers to the complexity of Rogers [30] which expresses the degree to which the innovation is difficult to understand or use. In 1989, Davis defined the ease perceived by the degree to which the user of the system does not require a great effort. He believes that the facility is: "the degree with which a person grows that the use of a specific system is free of any effort". Indeed, the user can be to focus on his work and therefore improves its performance. The definitions of the ease of use and the personal efficiency are identical [11,32]. This definition is a criterion to be considered in the design of a tool of ease of use. The concept of usability is widely used in the literature on the acceptance of a technology by users and on the behavior of users. This concept determines the adoption [33]. The ease of use is regarded as an important determinant of the use of the technology [34]. It determines the intent of its use [11]. Katz showed that the complexity of technology and discomfort with the use of the computer, represent obstacles to the adoption of the Internet [35]. Indeed, ease of use affects the intent for the use of the Web [36]. Similarly, in a study conducted in Singapore on a comparison between the adopters of the e-banking and non-adopters of this new financial distribution channel, Gerrard and Cunningham noted that among the factors that influence the adoption of the Bank on the Internet is the fact that they found that the use of Internet offers less complexity [37]. This was also approved by Qureshi and khagan [38]. Thus, at the level of this research and based on the work of Davis [3], ease of use of Internet bank will be seen as a determinant of Internet use.

Perceived Usefulness of Internet Use

The perceived usefulness of use is a determinant of satisfaction related to the use of self-service technologies [39]. It is considered as being the perception of the positive consequences of the use; it refers to the perceived benefit [40]. This is the concept of comparative advantage developed in the theory of the adoption [41], which is considered to be the degree to which innovation is seen as offering a greater benefit [42]. The concept of usefulness of information technology is derived from the work of Davis on the acceptance of information technology. This author defined usefulness by the additional contribution that can improve the performance and efficiency of the work. It suggests that if users see that they have an advantage by the use of a technology, then the likelihood of its use increases [3]. Where he believes that the usefulness of use refers to the degree with which the use of the technology improves the performance of the user in the organization [30], and assimilate the concept of usefulness to benefit, "defined as the degree to which an innovation is seen as being better than its formulated precursors". The perceived utility refers to the benefits that the organization think derive from the use of the Internet in terms of gain of time, gain money, convenience and access to additional information [6,30]. It equates utility and functionality [43]. Perceived usefulness is one of the determinants of use. It is an important determinant of the intent of the use of the technology [44] as the use of the Internet [45] and the acceptance of the use of the online bank [38]. Bendana and Rowe show that the utility of use influences consumption on the Internet and based on the fact that the benefit of innovation is positively correlated with the rate of adoption [46]. We will consider in this research that usefulness perceived of the use is one of the factors supporting the use of Internet.

Attitude of the Use of Internet

The concept of attitude occupies a central place in the analysis of the behavior of the consumer. Traditionally, attitudes are considered sustainable mental predisposations, speaking in a manner favorable or unfavorable to the object and that lead the individual to respond in a determined sense. The attitude is the psychological tendency depending on a degree of favor or disfavor [47]. It may refer to one of the perceived benefits [40]. The attitude expressed positive or negative evaluation to make the behavior [3]. A first difficulty related to this concept is the abundance and variety of the definitions. Other authors have defined the attitude, by establishing a relationship between attitude and needs with which it is associated. Howard offers the following definition: "the attitude to a mark is defined as the degree of satisfaction of its requirements that the consumer considers that this brand can bring him." [48]. The attitude towards innovation explains the adoption decision and it is considered as an explanatory determinant of the acceptance of the use of technology [3,30]. Indeed, the attitude towards the merchant site is represented as the predisposition of Internet users to respond in a manner favorable or unfavorable to a web site [49].

The Intent of the Use of Internet

Ajzen and Fishbein define the intent as an intermediate factor between attitude and behavior. They demonstrated the existence of a relationship between the behavior and intent [7]. The theory of reasoned action and the theory planned behavior are theories explaining the intention. One of the key to the success of implementation of new technologies is the intention of their use [50]. The use of a system is a reflection of the acceptance of the technology by users [11]. The use of new technologies [24], or even their current adoptions are determined by the behavioral intention of their uses [42].

PERCEPTION AND ATTITUDE

The perception of the characteristics of the use of the Internet is the first factor that determines the formation of attitudes towards this new technology. In effect, the approach adopted for Internet is the result of processing the user of certain attributes and characteristics of the Internet tool [51].

- The ease of the perceived use and attitude to the use of the Internet: We consider that the adoption or not of trade depends on the attitude which is a function of the perceived ease of use of the Internet [26-52]. Perceived ease of use positively affects the attitude to the use of self-service technology and specifically the use of the Internet [52]. Indeed, very often the difficulties of navigation are cited as barriers to purchase online [53]. The ease of use influences consumption on the Internet [3,46]. The diffusion of innovations depends on the perception of the complexity of the product, so we can consider that the perception of the degree of difficulty of use of the Internet is one of the explanatory factors of its use which affects the degree of its dissemination [30-54].

The perceived usability is a determinant of the attitude towards the interactive shopping [55]. The ease of use and perceived usefulness are the determinants of attitudes toward the use of online stores [49], also Bangaly Kaba in an application to the case of Quebec concerning the study of the adoption of cell phones said the existence of a positive influence of the ease of use on attitudes. Thus, the difficulty of use can create a negative attitude towards the use of Internet. Indeed, many consumers use the new techniques of self service that traditional techniques of the fact that they perceived ease of use [39-56]. According to the theory of reasoned action, Ajzen and Fishbein require the existence of a causal relationship between the ease of use and the attitude to the use of technology. According to data collected from one hundred and four Canadian organizations, the usefulness of perceived use affects the purchase on the Internet [46]. The perceived difficulty therefore has a direct impact on the attitude to the use of the Internet [5]. Indeed, more the users will think that buying on the Internet is difficult, more their attitude to the use will be negative [8]. In the context of the adoption of Internet, Dulyalak, Settapong and Lederer supports the existence of a positive relationship between the ease of use and intend to use [6-17]. The ease of use of the Internet allows the adoption of the financial services in banking [57]. Some others authors found that the ease of use of the Internet affects the attitude to its use [27-58]. So we will consider that users who see ease of use to the Bank on the Internet will have a favorable attitude towards its use.

H1: The ease perceived the use of Internet in the relationship between banks and firm positively influences the attitude of its use.

- The usefulness of the perceived use and attitude to the use of the Internet.

Perceived use consequences influence behavior by an indirect effect via attitudes. Indeed, in information system [59], there is a causal relationship between the perceived usefulness of the use and the attitude to the use of the technology [1]. Nelson, Todd and Davis report that the acceptance of a system and therefore its use is due for much utility [3,15]. Other studies have also reported that the utility is positively related to the use of a system [60]. The usefulness of e-mail is considered a dimension that has a direct effect on the satisfaction of users and on the degree of use of the tool. On the use of the Internet, the perceived use of usefulness is source of a positive attitude [27,39,60]. The perceived utility is the first determinant of the use of online stores [41]. In the banking, perceived usefulness of Internet is a determinant of the attitude to its use [61]. So we will consider that the adoption depends on the attitude which is a function of the value perceived in the use of the Internet. Where we will lead to the following hypothesis:

H2: The value perceived in Internet use in the relationship between bank and firm positively influences the attitude of its use.

ATTITUDE AND INTENT TO USE

Several studies require the existence of a positive relationship between a positive attitude and intent of acquisition [62]. Thus psychologists developed the hypothesis that attitudes influence the behavior [63]. The attitude is a factor that influences the behavior [64]. It's directly correlated with intention [25]. So there is a large and significant link between attitude and intention of adoption [1]. According to Al Ali, the characteristics of innovation beliefs determine the intention of the behavior [65]. Thus, the attitude is considered as a determinant for the use of the technologies [3,24,26]. A favorable attitude to the use of the Internet can have a positive effect on the intention to use this new technology of self-service [25,26]. In this same context, Internet use is influenced by attitudes to the use of the Internet [66,67].

The behavior on the web is influenced by the attitude of the individual to this new technology [68]. This is also verified at the level of the Bank on the Internet [61]. Based on these theoretical developments, we will consider that:

H3: The attitude to the use of the Internet in the relationship between bank and firm influences positively the intention of use.

METHODOLOGY OF RESEARCH

The questionnaire was administered at 130 Tunisian business leaders by following the method of convenience. The questionnaire was administrated conducted according to the technique of face to face (118 questionnaires) and the technique of administration via Internet (12 questionnaires). Concerning the operationalization of variables, we are based on the adaptation of the existing measures scales in the literature to the context of Internet use at the relationship between bank and firm. Factor analysis was conducted under SPSS17, accordingly to determine the dimensionality of the scales of measurement. We conduct ACP analysis with varimax rotation. To ensure the purification and the reliability of the scales of measures adapted to the use of the Internet in the relationship between bank and firm, we assessed cronbach alpha (its value varies between 0.778 and 0.96). We have retained the factors having a value greater than 1 (the value varies between 1.812 and 4.324). The items with low factor contributions (less than 0.50 values) and those whose contributions were shared between several factorial axes have been eliminated. To test causal relationships, we will apply the methods of linear regressions.

Test of the Influence of Perceived Ease and Perceived Usefulness on the Attitude

To test the influence of ease and usefulness perceived on the attitude to the use of the Internet, we used the method of multiple regression and we verified the absence of high co linearity between the explanatory variables (perceived usefulness and perceived ease). Tolerances and VIF are close 1 and within the recommended limit (VIF = 1.152 is less than 3 and tolerance = 0.868 is greater than 0.3). Explanatory variables usefulness and perceived ease of use are not correlated, which is indicating a quality of the model index. So we can go to test the influence of the perceived usefulness and ease on the attitude to the use. The calculated F is equal to 79.756, which is greater than the critical value of F (2, 127) = 2.82 (at the level of confidence 0.05), so we can conclude that the regression model is of quality. R square = 0.557, it means that the model explains 55.7% of the variation of the intention of Internet.

- Impact of perceived ease on the attitude:

Ease T = 4.745, it's greater than 1.96, and the sign of Beta is positive (0.301), (Table 1) so we can conclude that ease perceived of Internet has a positive impact on the attitude to its use, so the H1 hypothesis is validated.

- Impact of the perceived usefulness on attitude:

T attitude = 9.179, it's greater than 1.96 and the sign of Beta is positive (0.582), (Table 1) therefore we conclude that usefulness perceived the use of Internet has a positive influence on the attitude to its use, so the H2 hypothesis is validated.

Table 1: Influence of the ease and usefulness on the attitude

Variable to explain	Explanatory variables	Regression coefficients	Student's T	p
Attitude	Perceived ease	0.301	4.745	0.00
	Perceived usefulness	0.582	9.179	0.00

Note: Prepared from the data collected by the researcher.

Test of the Influence of the Attitude on the Intention

The calculated F is equal to 108. 057, which is greater than the value critical (1, 128) f = 3.84 (at the level of confidence 0.05), so we can conclude that the regression model is of quality. R square = 0.458, which means that attitude explains 45.8% of the variation of intent.

T in absolute value is equal to 10.395, which is greater than 1.96 (significant) and the sign of Beta is positive (0.667) (Table 2). We can conclude that attitude influences positively the intention of Internet use in the relationship between banks and firm therefore the H3 hypothesis is validated. The results converge with the hypotheses assumed by TAM and other previous research which supported it by postulating that the ease of use positively influence the attitude to the use which influences positively to turn the intention of using the Internet in the relationship between bank and firm. Finding that this technology is clear and understandable and easy to operate motivates the behavior of the user who will experience an attitude conducive to the use, as a consequence the triggering of intent to positive use. The usefulness of the use is revealed through the positive contributions of the use such as the improvement of the performance of the work, the development of a positive appreciation of technology deemed as beneficial to the management of the company. This variable will in turn positively influence the attitude which will positively influence the intention of Internet use in the in the relationship between bank and firm (Figure 1).

There is the model tested in the Tunisian context to explain the determinant of the use of Internet banking by the leaders. This model tested in our study demonstrate that perceived ease and perceived usefulness determines the attitude and that attitude determine the intent if use of e-banking.

CONCLUSION

The majority of existing research explaining the determinants of the use of Internet technology is based on the factors of explanation of the adoption at the report the "Business to Consumer".

Table 2: Influence of the attitude on the intention

Variable to explain	Explanatory variable	Regression coefficient	Student's T	p
Intention	Attitude	0.677	10.395	p = 0.00

Note: Prepared from the data collected by the researcher.

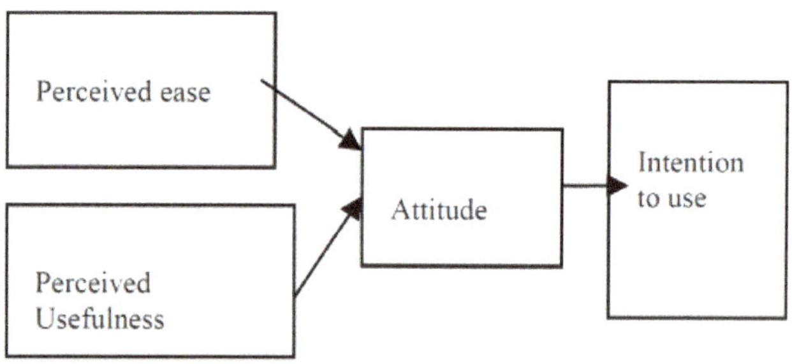

Note: Tested in Tunisian context in order to determine the use of e-banking by the leaders.

Figure 1: The model explained the determinants of the use of Internet banking.

But in the "Business to Business" report, it is important to understand the diffusion of technology among professional. The determination of explanatory factors of the intention of Internet use in the relationship between bank and firm became more necessary competitiveness. Thus, through explaining the factors that determine the intention of Internet used in the relationship between bank and firm, we are referred to the TAM model which has been widely supported by previous research [3,25,27] and we have tested the TAM model in the context of the use of technology among professionals.

REFERENCES

1. M. Igabria, G. B. Davis and T. Guimaras, "Testing the Determinants of Microcomputer Usage via Structural Equation," Journal of Management Information System, Vol. 11, No. 4, 1995, pp. 9-30.
2. M. C. Cheung and C. Chang, "Perceptual Factors Underlying User Preferences toward Product Form of Mobile Phones," Industrial Ergonomics, Vol. 27, No. 4, 2001, pp. 247-258.
3. F. D. Davis, R. P. Bagozzi and P. R. Warshaw, "User Acceptance a Computer Technology: A Comparison of Two Theoretical Models," Management Science, Vol. 35, No. 8, 1989, pp. 982-1003.
4. K. Mathieson, "Predicting User Intentions Comparing the Technology Acceptance Model with the Theory of Planned Behavior," Information Systems Research, Vol. 2, No. 3, 1991, pp. 173-191.
5. S. Taylor and P. A. Todd, "Understanding Information Technology Usage: A Test of Competing Models," Information System Research, Vol. 6, No. 2, 1995, pp. 144- 176.
6. D. Phuangthon and S. Malisawan, "A Study of Behavioral Intention for 3G Mobile Internet Technology: Preliminary Research on Mobile Learning," A Proceedings of the 2nd International Conference on E-Learning for Knowledge-Based Society, Bankok, 4-7 August 2005.
7. I. Ajzen and M. Fishbein, "Understanding Attitudes and Predicting Behavior," Prentice Hall Inc., Upper Saddle River, 1980.
8. I. Zaoui and A. E. Akremi, "L'intention D'achat du Consommateur sur Internet: Déterminants et Rôle Modérateur de la Confiance, cas du site Marchand du Magasin Géné- ral," The 8th AIM Conférence, Grenoble, May 2003.
9. D. Harker and Van Akkeren, "Mobile Data Technologies and SME Adoption and Diffusion: An Empirical Study on Barriers and Facilitators," The Australian Journal of Information Systems, Vol. 9, No. 2, 2002, pp. 3-16.
10. D. François and S. P. Antoin, "Une Analyse des Déterminants de L'acceptation de la Messagerie Electronique par des Personnels Administratifs à L'université," Systè- me d'Information et Management, Vol. 7, No. 4, 2002, p. 127.
11. V. Venkatesh and F. D. Davis, "A Theoretical Extension of the Technology Acceptance Model: Four Longitudinal Studies," Management Science, Vol. 46, No. 2, 2000, pp. 186-204.

12. G. C. Bruner and A. Kumar, "Explaining Consumer Acceptance of Handheld Internet Devices," Journal of Business Research, Vol. 58, No. 5, 2005, pp. 553-280.
13. Y. Foxalle and Pallister, "Technology Acceptance: A Meta Analysis of the TAM," Journal of Modeling in Management, Vol. 2, No. 3, 2007, pp. 251-280.
14. D. Gefen, "E-Commerce: The Role of Familiarity and Trust," Omega, Vol. 28, No. 6, 2000, pp. 725-737.
15. D. R. Adams, R. N. Peter and A. Tod, "Perceived Usefulness, Ease of Use and Usage of Information Technology: A Replication," Management Information System Quarterly, Vol. 16, No. 2, 1992, pp. 227-247.
16. R. P. Bagozzi and R. Warshaw, "User Acceptance of Computer Technology: A Comparison of Two Theoretical Models," Management Science, Vol. 35, No. 8, 1989, pp. 982-1003.
17. A. L. Ledrer, D. J. Maupin, M. P. Sena and Y. Zhuang, "The Role of Ease of Use, Usefulness and Attitude in the Prediction of World Wide Web Usage," CRP, 1998.
18. E. Huang, "The Acceptance of Women-Centric Websites," The Journal of Computer Information Systems, Vol. 45, No. 4, 2005, pp. 75-83.
19. A. K. Gyampah and F. Salam, "An Extension of Technology Acceptance Model in an ERP Implementation Environment, Information and Management, Vol. 41, No. 6, 2004, pp. 731-745.
20. P. Y. K. Chau and P. Hu, "Investigating Health Care Professionals Decisions to Accept Telemedicine Technology: An Empirical Test of Competing Theories," Information and Management, Vol. 39, No. 4, 2004, pp. 297-311.
21. S. S. Liaw and H. M. Huang, "An Investigation of User Attitudes toward Search Engines as an Information Retrieval Tool," Computers in Human Behavior, Vol. 19, No. 6, 2003, pp. 751-765.
22. F. Lin and J. Wu, "An Empirical Study of End-User Computing Acceptance Factors in Small and Medium Enterprises in Taiwan: Analyzed by Structural Equation Modeling," Journal of Computer Information Systems, Vol. 44, No. 3, 2004, pp. 98-108.
23. N. Ndubisi, R. Supinah and P. Gurting, "The Extend Technology Acceptance Model and Internet Banking Usage Intention," International Logistics Congress Proceeding, Turkey, December 2004.
24. P. J. Legris and P. C. Ingham, "Why Do People Use Information Technology, A Critical Review of the Technology Acceptance Model," Information and Management, Vol. 40, No. 3, 2003, pp. 191-204.
25. L. Moez and F. Selma, "Les Déterminants de L'achat sur Internet: Revue de la Littérature et Proposition de Modèle," 2004. www.iae.univ-nantes.fr/emarket/emarket
26. J. R. Leroy Robinson, W. Greg Marshall and M. B. Stamps, "Sales Force Use of Technology: Antecedents to Technology Acceptance," Journal of Business Research, Vol. 58, No. 12, 2005, pp. 1623-1631.

27. C. E. Porter and N. Donthu, "Using the Technology Acceptance Model to Explain How Attitudes Determine Internet Usage: The Role of Perceived Access Barriers and Demographics," Science Direct, Journal of Business Rerearch, Vol. 59, No. 9, 2006, pp. 999-1007.

28. J. A. DeVito, "Les Fondements de la Communication Humaine," Edition Gaétan Morin, 1993.

29. C. Dussart, "Comportement du Consommateur et Straté- gie de Marketing," McGraw Hill, New York, 1983, p. 77.

30. M. Rogers, "Diffusion of Innovations," 4th Edition, The Free Press, New York, 1995.

31. G. C. Moore and I. Benbasat, "Development of an Instrument to Measure the Perceptions of Adopting an Information Technology Innovation," Information Systems Research, Vol. 2, No. 3, 1991, pp. 192-222.

32. T. Hill, N. D. Smith and M. F. Mann, "Role of Efficacy Expectations in Predicting the Decision to Use Advanced Technologies: The Case of Computers," Journal of Applied Psychology, Vol. 72, No. 2, 1987, pp. 307-313.

33. E. Karahanna and D. W. Straub, "The Psychological Origins of Perceived Usefulness and Ease of Use," Information and Management, Vol. 35, No. 4, pp. 237-250.

34. I. Ajzen, "From Intentions to Actions: A Theory of Planned Behavior, Action Control: From Cognition to Behavior," New York, 1985.

35. J. Katz, "Motives, Hurdles and Droputs," Communications of the ACM, Vol. 40, No. 4, 1997, pp. 97-102.

36. P. Don and R. Martha, "Le One to One: Valoriser Votre Capital Client," Les Editions d'Organisation, 1998.

37. P. Gerrad and J. B. Cunningham, "The Diffusion of Internet Banking among Singapore Consumers," International Journal of Bank Marketing, Vol. 21, No. 1, 2003, pp. 16-28.doi:10.1108/02652320310457776

38. T. M. Qureshi, M. K. Zafar and M. B. Khan, "Customer Acceptance of Online Banking in Developing Economies," Journal of Internet Banking and Commerce, Vol. 13, No. 1, 2008, p. 1. www.arraydev.com/commerce/jibc/

39. M. L. Matthew, A. L. Ostrom, R. I. Roundtree and M. J. Bitner, "Self-Service Technologies: Understanding Customer Satisfaction with Technology-Based Service Encounters," Journal of Marketing, Vol. 64, No. 3, 2000, pp. 50-64. doi:10.1509/jmkg.64.3.50.18024

40. A. K. Au and P. Enderwick, "A Cognitive Model on Attitude toward Technology Adoption," Vol. 15, No. 4, 2000, pp. 266-282.

41. L. D. Chen, M. L. Gillenson and D. L. Sherrel, "Enticing Online Consumers: An Extended Technology Acceptance Perspective," Information Management, Vol. 39, No. 8, 2002, pp. 705-719. doi:10.1016/S0378-7206(01)00127-6

42. L. Moez, M. Khalifa and A. Frini "What Makes Consumers Buy from Internet? A Longitudinal Study of Online Shopping," IEEE Transaction on Systems, Man and Cybermetics, Vol. 30, No. 4, 2000, pp. 421-432. doi:10.1109/3468.852436

43. N. C. Goodwin, "Functionality and Usability," Communication of the ACM, Vol. 30, No. 3, 1987, pp. 229-233.

44. P. Y. K. Chau, "An Empirical Assessment of a Modified Technology Acceptance Model," Journal Management Information Systems, Vol. 13, No. 2, 1996, pp. 185-204.

45. A. L. Ledrer, D. J. Maupin, M. P. Sena and Y. Zhuang, "The Technology Acceptance Model and the World Wide Web," Decision Support Systems, Vol. 29, No. 3, 2000, pp. 269-282.doi:10.1016/S0167-9236(00)00076-2

46. M. Bendana and F. Rowe, "Du Minitel à l'Internet: Perception du Risque et Transition Chez les Internautes Utilisateurs des Services Bancaires," Annales des Télécommunications, Vol. 58, No. 1-2, 2003, pp. 197-211.

47. A. H. Eagly and S, Chaiken, "The Psychology of the Attitudes," Harcourt Brace College Publishers, New York, 1993.

48. J. A. Howard, "Consumer Behavior in Marketing Strategy," Prentice Hall, Englewood Cliffs, 1989.

49. Q. Chen and W. D. Wells, "Attitude toward the Site," Journal of Advertising Research, Vol. 39, No. 5, 1999, pp. 27-37.

50. C. Amel, "Implantation d'un ERP (Entreprise Ressource Planning): Antécédents et Conséquence," XVème Confé- rence Internationale de Management Stratégique, Annecy/ Genéve, 13-16 June 2006.

51. S. Debbabi, S. Baile and M. Daassi, "La Fidélité à un Site Marchand: Les Déterminants et le Rôle Médiateur de la Confiance et de la Satisfaction," Actes du Colloque Cyber-Gestion, Montpellier, 2003.

52. A. O'cass and T. Frenech, "Web Retailing Adoption: Exploring the Nature of Internet Users Web Retailing Behavior," Journal of Retailing and Consumer Services, Vol. 10, No. 2, 2003, pp. 81-94. doi:10.1016/S0969-6989(02)00004-8

53. C. Ranganathan and S. Garrapathy, "Key Dimensions of Business to Consumer Web Sites," Information and Management, Vol. 39, No. 6, 2002, pp. 457-465. doi:10.1016/S0378-7206(01)00112-4

54. G. Alexander, "La Notion de Confiance et le Droit du Commerce Electronique," LX Electronica, Vol. 12, No. 3, 2008, pp. 1-20.

55. T. L. Childers, J. Peck and S. Cason, "Hedonic and Utilitarian Motivations for Online Retail Shopping Behavior," Journal of Retailing, Vol. 77, No. 4, 2001, pp. 511-535.doi:10.1016/S0022-4359(01)00056-2

56. P. A. Dabholkar, "Consumer Evaluation of New Technology-Based Self Service Options: An Investigation of Alternative Models of Service Quality," International Journal of Research in Marketing, Vol. 13, No. 1, 1996, pp. 29-51. doi:10.1016/0167-8116(95)00027-5

57. M. Weiss, "Bricks to Clicks: What Drives Customer Use of the Internet in a Multi-Channel Environment," Working Papers, 2000.

58. M. S. Sohail and B. Shanmugham "E-Banking and Customer Preferences in Malaysia: An Empirical Investigation," Information Sciences, Vol. 150, No. 3-4, 2003, pp. 207-217.doi:10.1016/S0020-0255(02)00378-X

59. N. K. Malhotra and J. D. McCort, "A Cross-Cultural Comparison of Behavioral Intention Models: Theoretical Consideration and an Empirical Investigation," International Marketing Review, Vol. 18, No. 3, 2001, pp. 235-269. doi:10.1108/02651330110396505

60. R. L. Thompson, C. A. Higgins and J. M. Howell, "Personal Computing: Toward a Conceptual Model of Utilization," Management Information System, Vol. 15, No. 1, 1991, pp. 125-143. doi:10.2307/249443

61. J. M. Pearson and Md N. Khalil, "The Influence of Trust on Internet Banking Acceptance," Journal of Internet Banking and Commerce, Vol. 12, No. 2, 2007, 10 p. www.arraydev.com/commerce/jibc/

62. R. P. Bagozzi, "Attitudes, Intentions and Behavior: A Test of Some Key Hypotheses," Journal of Personality and Social Psychology, Vol. 41, No. 4, 1981, pp. 607- 627.doi:10.1037/0022-3514.41.4.607

63. C. Derbaix and J. Bree, "Comportement du Consommateur, Présentation des Textes Choisis," Edition Economica, Paris, 2000.

64. J. V. Petrof, "Comportement du Consommateur et Marketing," Les Presses de l'Université Laval, Quebec City, 1998.

65. Al A. Samer, "La Crédibilité Perçue Comme Facteur Explicatif du Comportement des Internautes," Journée du e-Marketing, Université de Nantes, Nantes, 2004.

66. J. H. Zhu and H. Zhou, "Diffusion, Use and Impact of the Internet in Hong Kong: A Chain Process Model," Journal of Computer Mediated Communication, Vol. 7, No. 2, 2002. www;Ascusc.org/jcmc/vol7/issue2/hongkong.html

67. D. J. Atkin, L. W. Jeffres and K. A. Neuendorf, "Understanding Internet Adoption as Telecommunications Behavior," Journal of Broadcasting and Electronic Media, Vol. 42, No. 4, 1998, pp. 475-409. doi:10.1080/08838159809364463

68. J. Moon and Y. Kim, "Extending the Tam for a Word Wide Web Context," Information and Management, Vol. 38, No. 4, 2001, pp. 217-230. doi:10.1016/S0378-7206(00)00061-6

3

CHAPTER

EXCELLENCY IN BANKING SERVICES - A NEW ROAD MAP FOR BANKS IN THE EMERGING NEW COMPETITION

R. K. Uppal and Bishnupriya Mishra

Keywords: Desirability and Availability of Service Quality, Gap between Desirability and Availability, Measures to Bridge the Gap

INTRODUCTION

Globalization, liberalization, deregulation have resulted in a sea change in the form of time and cost effective consumer banking services (Javalgi, 1992). These competitive innovations have made bank customers more concerned about their money value and surrounding environment that leads to high customer expectations from service providers. In fact the customer expectations rise with the use of latest technology, like on-line services or e-banking, inspiring them to explore the alternatives available to all from around the world and eventually arming them with an unprecedented amount of market knowledge (Parasuraman, 2000). Thus, with ever escalating customer expectations, companies have to offer additional values to make an ever-lasting impression in the minds of customers because merely delivery of satisfaction as the confirmation of expectations is considered as minimum threshold. Hence, it is important for business managers to understand the provisions, symbols, and tangible clues used by the customers in evaluating the service offered by business organizations. Quality is thus relative and subjective and depends on the perceptions and expectations of the customer with respect to the service offered. For service sector companies such as banking, insurance, and tourism, the issues and challenges of service quality are of the utmost significance. Poor service quality places such organizations at a competitive disadvantage. If customers perceive that service quality is unsatisfactory, they will not

Citation: R. K. Uppal, Bishnupriya Mishra, Excellency in banking services - A new road map for banks in the emerging new competition, ISSN: 2220-6140.

hesitate to switch over business elsewhere. In recent years, it has been witnessed that there is discontentment with regard to service quality, even when the quality of many manufactured goods appear to have improved significantly. The recent trend in many service organizations is to consider service quality as a critical factor enabling them to achieve a differential advantage over their competitors (Kotler, 2006). Increasingly, quality is becoming a key variable in strategic planning. Organizations which are becoming leaders in service quality are characterized by the commitment of the top management and a corporate culture that encourages a focus on customer and quality throughout the company (Albrecht and Zemke, 1985).

In India, public sector banks meet nearly 90 pc banking needs of the country and retail banking constitutes 80 pc of this total banking business (Ram Mohan, 2002). Many academicians and practitioners have highlighted the need for better service quality in banks. Several researchers have suggested the adoption of modern banking technology as a means to improve customer services (Sundaram, 1984; Nageswar, 1987; Nageshwar and Parmod, 1990; Brahmanand and Narayana, 1990; Seshasai, 1999; Gani and Bhat, 2003). These studies have made public sector banks aware that if the present trend of customer dissatisfaction continues, they will loose their valuable clients to their competitors especially to private and foreign banks. In fact this was realized much earlier when the Rangarajan Committee Report (1989) stressed the need for mechanization of the Indian banks. Many other researchers have suggested the adoption of modern banking technology as a means to improve customer services (Ammayya, 1996). Therefore, the banks have to provide quality service to their customers for survival, as well as to have competitive advantage. The present paper has been divided into six sections. After the introduction, section II reviews some related studies. Section III fixes some research objectives, hypothesis & highlights the research methodology and the data base. Section IV is devoted to the results and discussion. Section V gives some recommendations to enhance the service quality in banking industry, implications of the study, limitations of the study and future areas for comprehensive research and last section concludes the paper.

REVIEW OF LITERATURE

There are a number of studies that refer to the importance of clients/ customers' perceptions of quality (Takeuchi and Quelch, 1983). These result from comparisons by expectations of service with actual performance (Gronroos, 1982 and Berry, et al, 1985). Berry (1980) along with Booms and Bitner (1981) argued that due to intangible nature of services, customers use elements associated with the physical environment when evaluating service quality. Managing the evidence and using the environmental psychology are often seen as important marketing tools. Levitt (1981) proposed that customers use appearances to make judgments about realities. The less tangible a product is the more powerful shall be the effect of packaging while judging that product. Gronroos (1982) had identified two service quality dimensions, viz., functional quality and technical quality. Functional quality represents the perception of the manner in which the services are delivered. Technical quality or outcome quality on the other hand, represents the outcome of the service act or what the customer receives in the end (Brady and Cronin, 2001). Parasuraman, et al. (1985) suggested that the criteria used by consumers mould their expectations and perceptions of delivered service quality fit into ten dimensions: tangibility, reliability, responsiveness, communication, credibility, security, competence, courtesy, understanding/knowing the customer and access. Subsequent researches, by Parasuraman, et al. (1988) have condensed these into five dimensions of service quality. The Penta-dimentional model has now become the standard way of measuring service quality in banking sector.

1. `Tangibility includes physical facilities, equipment, and appearance of personnel
2. Reliability includes ability to perform the promised service accurately and with reliability.
3. Responsiveness includes willingness to help customers and provide prompt Service
4. Assurance includes knowledge and courtesy of employees and their ability to convey trust and confidence
5. Empathy includes caring and individualized attention the company provides to its customers.

Parasuraman, et al. (1988) developed a 22-item scale, referred to as SERVQUAL Scale, which is widely used as a generic instrument for measuring service quality. The basis for identifying the five components was factor analysis of the 22-item scale developed from focus groups and from the specific industry applications undertaken by the authors (Parasuraman, et al., 1985, 1988; and Zeithaml, et al., 1990). Though, the veracity of conceptualising the SERVQUAL scale has been questioned by Carman (1990), the validity of the 22 individual performance scale items that make up the SERVQUAL scale appears to be well supported both by the procedures used to develop the items and by their subsequent use as reported in the literature (Brown and Swartz, 1989; Zeithaml, et al., 1990; Lewis, 1991; Young, et al., 1994; Berry and Parasuraman, 1997).

There are some limitations with SERVQUAL, which have been highlighted by the authors themselves (Parasuraman, et al., 1991) and also by other researchers (Babakhus and Boiler, 1992; Lewis and Mitchell, 1990; Lewis, 1993; and Smith, 1992). These relate to respondents' difficulties with negativelyworded statements using two lists of statements for the same items. There is also a disagreement among various researchers regarding the number of dimensions of service to be assessed. Another problem relates to the time factor at which the service quality has to be measured, i.e., before, during or after a service encounter, while there is a healthy and productive debate regarding the dimensionality of SERVQUAL items to be included to service quality scale across different industries. Researchers, however, generally agree that the scale items are good predictors of overall service quality (Bolton and Drew, 1991; and Cronin and Taylor, 1992). A number of other empirical studies have been conducted using the SERVQUAL scale which include car retailing (Carman, 1990), travel and tourism (Fick and Ritchie, 1991), and hospitality (Saleh and Ryan, 1991), banks (Lewis, 1991), and medical services (Brown and Swartz, 1989). There have been a number of such studies that deal with service quality in banking industry in general and in particular the application of

SERVQUAL instrument in commercial banks (Blanched and Gallway, 1994; Angur, et al., 1999; Bahia and Nantel, 1998; Lassar, et al., 2000, Sureshchander and Rajendran, 2003; Kang and James, 2004; Jain, 2005; and Dogra, 2006).

The review of literature exhibits that no study has been conducted regarding the gap between desirability and availability of service quality parameters. The present study is directed to know the extent of gap between desirability and availability of service quality parameters and some recommendations are prepared to bridge this gap.

OBJECTIVES AND HYPOTHESES OF THE STUDY

Objectives

1. To explore the extent of gap between the desirability and availability of banking services.
2. Recommendations to bridge the gap between the desirability and availability of banking services.

Hypotheses

1. There is no difference in the opinion of respondents of three bank groups regarding the desirability of service quality parameters.
2. There is no difference in the opinion of respondents of three bank groups regarding the availability of service quality parameters.

METHODS

In the light of the aforesaid objectives and hypothesis an instrument (see annexure) was developed to collect information on desirability of bank customers regarding reliability, accuracy, confidentiality, flexibility, e-channels, high attention to customers, low service charges and overall satisfaction of customers. Similarly, information is collected regarding the availability of above said aspects. This instrument was pre-tested on a small sample of 50 respondents residing in Chandigarh. With the variability in responses from the sample drawn from the population of approximately 10 thousand households, sample size for the main study thus, came out to be 1200 customers. The survey was conducted in Chandigarh in the month of October, 2008. For data collection, the respondents were selected with the help of an abridged list of random numbers. The study was conducted in Chandigarh as it, being the capital of Punjab, witnessed the latest changes in the banking services and has almost all present day banking service dimensions which delight the customers. Moreover, Chandigarh is a representative of people belonging to various demographic profiles of urban life relevant to modern banking services.

Likert type five point scale was used to know the desirability and availability of the service quality parameters. The whole banking industry is divided into three bank groups namely, public sector banks, Indian private sector banks and foreign banks. Further, three bank branches one from each bank group has been selected for the survey purpose. The various statistical methods like percentage, average, standard deviation, coefficient of variation and weighted average score (WAS) were used to compare the results. To test the hypothesis, chi^ test is used. Field Survey conducted in the month of October, 2008 at Chandigarh

RESULTS AND DISCUSSION

Socio-Economic Profile of Customers

In the present study, the main focus of analysis is on service quality in banking industry. Opinions of three bank group customers have been calculated separately. The total sample survey of 1200 customers have been taken into consideration (Table1) & further these respondents are equally divided into three bank groups i.e. public sector banks (G-I), private sector banks (G-II) & foreign banks (G-III). Among these customers, 37 pc customers are post graduate & similarly 40 pc are the youngsters. Service class and business class dominates in the respondents. The Sampled respondents are divided as per the pattern mentioned in table 1.

Table 1: Socio-Economic Profile of Customers

Group	Number	%
Bank Type		
1. G-I	400	33.33
2. G-II	400	33.33
3. G-III	400	33.33
Present Age		
1. Upto 25	296	24.67
2. 26-35	476	39.67
3. 36-45	220	18.33
4. 45-55	168	14.00
5. Above 55	40	3.33
Occupation		
1. Service	380	31.67
2. Business	304	25.33
3. Industry	272	22.67
4. Agriculture	16	1.33
5. Professional	16	1.33
6. Others	212	17.67
Education		
1.Matriculate	116	9.67
2. Graduate	408	34.00
3. Post Grad.	444	37.00
4. Professional	232	19.33
Total	1200	100.00

Source: Field Survey
G-I: Public Sector Banks, G-II: Private Sector Banks
G-III: Foreign Banks

Desirability of Service Quality Parameters

For a bank it is necessary to gain the confidence of its customers and it is possible only when it is reliable. About 85 pc of respondents responded that reliability of a bank is highly desired and overall 94.33 pc customers feel that the reliability of a bank is desirable to attract customers (Table 2). Except 5 to 6 pc of respondents, all other desired that the bank services should be accurate because it directly affects their satisfaction. Similarly, majority of customers i.e. 93 pc and 97 pc desired confidentiality and flexibility in banking services. In today's e-age, e-channels like internet banking, mobile banking, tele-banking, ATM, smart cards, debit cards, etc. are very necessary and 66 pc of respondent's highly desired e-channels. Overall, 86 pc of customers have shown the desirability of echannels. About 89.3 pc of respondents think that the main duty of bank employees is to serve their customers because customer is the sole purpose of their work. Therefore, they should pay high attention to their customers rather than working with computers only. Nearly 94 pc of customers are of the opinion that banks should keep low service charges of their products and services. Similarly, 90 pc customers feel that overall satisfaction of bank customers is highly desirable.

Table 2: Desirability of Service Quality - (Percent)

Service Quality Parameters	Ab.Unneces.	Unnecessary	Somewhat	Desirable	Highly Desirable	WAS
Reliability	-	3.00	2.67	9.33	85.00	1.76
Accuracy	-	1.67	4.00	17.00	78.33	1.73
Confidentiality	0.33	2.33	4.33	19.67	73.33	1.63
Flexibility	-	3.00	10.00	22.67	64.33	1.48
E-Channels	2.00	1.67	10.33	20.00	66.00	1.46
High attention to customers	0.33	2.67	7.67	18.3	71.00	1.57
Low service charges	0.33	1.67	4.33	15.00	78.6	1.70
Overall Satisf.	2.00	1.33	7.00	21.67	68.00	1.52

Source: Source: Field Survey
Note: Ab. Unneces. - Absolutely Unnecessary

In case of all parameters under study WAS is greater than one which indicates that these quality parameters are highly desirable by bank customers.

Availability of Service Quality Parameters

Nearly 86 pc customers opined that the banks are reliable but still there are 14 pc customers who have less or no confidence in banks. Although, accuracy in bank procedures is highly desirable by customers but only 25.33 pc customers opined that banks accurately do their work. Only 66 pc and 66.33 pc of respondents respectively think that banks keep their identity and amount confidential and flexibility is available in banks. Although e-channels are highly desired by bank customers but only 61.34 pc customers responded that banks provide e-channels to their customers successfully.

Table 3: availability of service quality (per cent)

Service Quality Parameters	Not at all	Not Avail.	Somewhat	Available	Highly Avail.	WAS
Reliability	0.67	3.00	11.00	59.67	25.67	1.07
Accuracy	0.33	4.67	20.67	49.00	25.33	0.94
Confidentiality	4.00	5.67	24.33	31.67	34.33	0.87
Flexibility	0.33	11.67	21.67	44.33	22.00	0.76
E-Channels	0.33	10.33	28.00	40.67	20.67	0.71
High attention to customers	6.33	20.33	23.67	32.00	17.67	0.34
Low service charges	9.00	10.00	21.00	35.67	24.33	0.56
Overall satisfaction	-	7.33	31.33	43.67	17.67	0.72

Source: Field survey results

Note: Avail. - Available, satisf. - Satisfaction

Similarly a high majority of customers desired high attention of employees but only 49.67 pc of them are satisfied from the bank employees. About 40 pc of respondents think that banks charge high service charges from them. Only 61.34 pc of the customers are satisfied from the overall performance of banks. In case of all parameters under study WAS is less than one except reliability parameter which indicates that bank customers are dissatisfied by the availability of these parameters in a bank. It is one of the causes of dissatisfaction among customers of banking sector.

Gap between Desirability and Availability

The average gap in the desirability and availability is 0.697 & 0.787 for reliability and accuracy respectively which indicate that banks have less accuracy and reliability than desired. Therefore, they should work in this direction to gain the confidence of their customers. Similar is the case with confidentiality, flexibility, and e-channels parameters where average gap is 0.767, 0.723 and 0.753 respectively. In case of employees attention to customers and low service charges the average gap is very high i.e. 1.227 and 1.137 respectively which indicated the fact that bank employees pay less attention to their customers and also customers are less satisfied by the service charges charged by the banks.

Table 4: Gap between Desirability and Availability

Service Quality Parameters	Average	SD	CV
1. Reliability	0.697	0.937	134.499
2. Accuracy	0.787	1.033	131.359
3. Confidentiality	0.767	1.154	150.550
4. Flexibility	0.723	1.086	150.184
5. E-Channels	0.753	1.160	153.995
6. High attention to customers	1.227	1.479	120.603
7. Low service charges	1.137	1.467	129.039
8. Overall satisfaction	0.807	1.141	141.487

Source: Field survey results

Overall satisfaction of bank customers is not a different aspect and average gap in this case is 0.807. Coefficient of Variation indicates that there is instability in the opinion of bank customers on confidentiality, flexibility, e-channels, and overall satisfaction aspects of banks. While comparatively consistency is found in their opinions in case of other aspects under study. The present study clearly indicates that in the e-age, customers have become more concerned about their money & time and have become more demanding. They highly desire reliability, accuracy, confidentiality, flexibility, echannels, and employee's attention to customers. Moreover, they desire these services at low service charges. But responses of these customers regarding the availability of these parameters are not satisfactory which has created a wider gap between the desirability and availability of service quality parameters in banking industry.

CONCLUSION AND RECOMMENDATIONS

The paper concludes that desirability regarding reliability, accuracy, confidentiality, flexibility, echannels, high attention to customers, low service charges and overall satisfaction is much higher than the availability. This is the cause of dissatisfaction among the customers and to some extent the customers are shifting from one bank to another. Bridging this gap will increase the reputation of the bank and hence the customer base. The banking industry should be reliable, accurate and customers should be overall satisfied. E- Banking services are the need of hour. The present line well summarizes the paper "Zero plus zero will always remain zero no matter how many zeros you add to it". The same is for banking industry i.e. banks should add more and more qualitative services. The present paper attempts to give following recommendations for banks to bridge the gap between the desirability and availability of service quality parameters and to win the confidence of new customers and to retain their old and valuable customers:

Banks should reliable to win the confidence of potential customers and to retain the old ones. The various procedures of banks should be transparent and accurate e.g. working of bank employees with computers should also be displayed to customers sitting on front chair and money counting machines should be available for customers also. Banks should keep the identity, amount deposited, etc. of their customers should be confidential. The various procedures of banks should not be rigid. They should be flexible to facilitate the customers. Present age is a e-age. Therefore, it is necessary for all banks to provide more and more e-channels. Public sector banks need to give more attention in this regard. It is crystal clear from our study that the customers are less satisfied by the services provided by bank employees. Therefore, it is necessary that bank employees should pay high attention to their valuable customers. They should serve their customers with smiling face. Further, they should be polite and co-operative. Bank customers experienced that banks charge high service charges for their products and services offered. This impression is more for private sector banks. Therefore, all banks, particularly, the private sector banks should work in this direction and they should charge as low service charges as possible. Overall- satisfaction of a customer from his bank is very necessary because this is the only factor that helps any organization to increase its business because a delighted customer will give you one more customer but an unhappy customer will curtail your ten customers. Thus, it is expected that if all bank groups add quality to their work their business can further be multiplied because in the e-age, customers judge an organization not only by the number of products offered by it but by the quality of that products and services. Same is for banking industry because 'quality counts in services too'.

Implications

The analysis indicates a widening gap between the desirability and availability of the service quality parameters in banking industry. This gap between desirability and availability is an alarming bell for some banks, particularly, the public sector banks. The bridging of this gap is the need of the hour. The analysis of this study is very useful for the banking industry as well as for other organizations. Due to the problem of space, separate analysis of responses gender-wise, age-wise, occupation-wise and bank group wise has not been shown in the paper. Due to the same reason, chi^ test is not shown in the analysis. Only three banks working in Chandigarh are taken due to shortage of time. The analysis is based on the responses of customers.

REFERENCES

1. Albrecht, K., and R. Zemke (1985), "Service America: Doing Business in the New York in Lewis.
2. Ammayya, T. (1996), 'Developing Competitive Advantage through Absorption of Technology in Knowledge, Skills and Attitudes of People', IBA Bulletin, 18(12): 38-42.
3. Angur, M. G., Nataraajan J. R. and Jahera, S. J. (1999), "Service Quality in the Banking Industry: An Assessment in a Developing Economy", International journal of Bank Marketing, 17(3): 16- 123.
4. Babakus, E., and Boiler, W. G. (1992), "An Empirical Assessment of the SERVQUAL Scale", Journal of Business Research, 24: 253-268.
5. Bahia, K., and Nantel, J. (1998), "A Reliable and Valid Measurement Scale for the Perceived Service Quality of Banks", International Journal of Bank Management, 18(2): 84-91.
6. Berry, L. L., Zeithaml, A. V. and Parasuraman, A. (1985), "Quality Counts in Services Too", Business Horizons, May-June, 44-52.
7. Berry, L. L. (1980), "Services Marketing is Different", Business, May-June, 8-30.
8. Berry, L. L., and Parasuraman, A. (1997) "Listening To the Customer -The Concept of A ServjceQuality Information System", Sloan Management Review, Spring, 65- 76.
9. Bitran, G., and Lojo, H. (1993), 'A Framework for Analyzing Service Operations', European Management Journal, 2(3): 271-282.
10. Blanchard, R.F., and R.L. Galloway (1994), "Quality in Retail Banking", International Journal of Service Industry Management, 5: 5-23.

11. Bolton, R. N., and Drew, H. J. (1991), "A Multistage Model of Customer's Assessment of. Service Quality and Value", Journal of Consumer Research, 17(4): 375-384.

12. Booms, B. H., and Bitner, J. M. (1981), "Marketing Strategies and Organization Structures for Services Firms", in Zeithaml V.A., Parnasuraman, A. and Berry, L. L. (1985) "Problems and Strategies in Service Marketing", Journal of Marketing, 49(2): 33-46.

13. Brady, M. K., and Cronin, J. J. (2001), "Some New Thoughts on Conceptualizing Perceived Service Quality: A Hierarchical Approach", Journal of Marketing, July, 65-77.

14. Brahmanandam, G. N., and Narayana, S. M. (1990), "A Study on Customer Service in Commercial Banks", Indian Journal of Marketing, 20(5): 7-8 and 16.

15. Brown, S. W., and Swartz, A. T. (1989), "A Gap Analysis of Professional Service Quality" Journal of Marketing, 57: 92-100.

16. Carman, J. M. (1990), "Consumer Perceptions of Service Quality: An Assessment of the SERVQUAL Dimensions", Journal of Retailing, 66: 33-56.

17. Cronin, J. J., and Taylor, S. A. (1992), "Measuring Service Quality: A Re-examination and Extension", Journal of Marketing, 60: 55-68.

18. Dogra, B., and Awasthi A. K. (2005), "Measuring Service Quality in Banks: An Assessment of Service Quality Dimensions", in Conference Proceeding on 'Global Competitiveness' at the Indian Institute of Management Kozhikode, October.

19. Elias, A. H. (1982), "Indian Banking Service", Journal of Indian Institute of Bankers, 35(3): 119-124

20. Fick, G. R., and Ritchie, J. R. B. (1991), "Measuring Service Quality in the Travel and Tourism Industry", Journal of Travel Research, 30(3): 2-9.

21. Gani, A., and Bhat, A. M. (2003), "Service Quality in Commercial Banks: A Comparative Study", Paradigm, 7(l): 24-36.

22. Gronroos, C. (1982), "Strategies Management and Marketing in the Services Sector" in Parasuraman A., Zeitilaml, V. A. and Berry, L. L. (1985) "A Conceptual Model of Service Quality and its Implications for Future Research", Journal of Marketing, 50(4): 41-50.

23. Jain, S. K. (2005), "Searching for Critical Success Factors: A Dimension-Specific Assessment of Service quality and its relationship with Customer Satisfaction and Behavioral Intentions in Fast Food Restaurants', Paper from the International Conference on Service Management (pp. 111- 125), Institute for International Management and Technology, Gurgaon, India.

24. Javalgi, G. R. (1992) "Marketing Financial Services to Affluent Consumers", Journal of Services Marketing, 6(2): 33 – 44.

25. Kang, G. D. and James, J. (2004), "Service Quality Dimensions: An Examination of Gronroos' Service Quality Model", Managing Service Quality, 14(4): 267-277.

26. Kotler, P. (2006), Marketing Management, 12th ed. (Delhi: Pearson Education (Singapore) Pvt. Ltd.).

27. Kwan, W., and Lee, T. J. (1994), "Measuring Service Quality in Singapore Retail Banking", Singapore Management Review, 6(4): 7-11.

28. Lassar, W. M., Manolis, C. and Winsor, R. D. (2000), "Service Quality Perspectives and Satisfaction in Private Banking", Journal of Services Marketing, 14(2, 3): 244-272.

29. Levitt, T. (1981), "Marketing Intangible Products and Product Intangibles", Harvard Business Review, May-June, 94-102.

30. Lewis, B. R. (1991), "Service Quality: An International Comparison of Bank Customers Expectations and Perceptions", Journal of Marketing Management, 7: 47-62.

31. Lewis, B. R. (1993), "Service Quality Measurement", Marketing Intelligence and Planning, 11(4): 4-12.

32. Lewis, B. R., and Mitchell, W. V. (1990), "Defining and Measuring the Quality of Customer Service", Marketing Intelligence and Planning, 8(6): 11-18.

33. Nageswar, R. (1987), "Customer Service in Banks Must Improve", Yojana, 31(13): 20-31.

34. Nageswar, R., and Pramod, P. (1990) "Customer Services and Banks", Yojana, 34(13): 15- 22.

35. Parasuraman, A. (2000). Overall Satisfaction with a Relational, Multichannel Service Provider. Journal of the Academy of Marketing Science, 31: 448-458.

36. Panasuraman, A., Zeithaml, V. A. and Berry, L. L. (1988), "SERVQUAL: A Multiple Scale for Measuring Consumer Perceptions of Service Quality", Journal of Retailing, 64(1): 12-40.

37. Parasuraman, A., Berry, L. L. and Zeithaml, V. A. (1985), "A Conceptual Model of SQ and its Implications for Future Research", Journal of Marketing, 49: 41-50.

38. Parasuraman, A., Berry, L. L. and Zeithaml, V. A. (1993), "Research Note: More on Improving SQ Measurement", Journal of Retailing, 69(3): 140-147.

39. Parasuraman, A., Berry, L. L. and Zeithaml, V. A. (1991), "Undertaking Customer Expectations of Service", Sloan Management Review, 32(3): 44.

40. Mohan, R. (2002), "Deregulation and Performance of Public Sector Banks", Economic and Political Weekly, 7(5).

41. Saleh, F, and Ryan, C. (1991), "Analyzing Service Quality in the Hospitality Industry Using the SERVQUAL Model", Service Industries Journal, 11(3): 324-343.

42. Seshasai, P. V. (1999), "Customer Service - Some HRD Interventions", IBA Bulletin, 21(2): 11-16.

43. Smith, A. M. (1992), "The Consumer's Evaluation of Service Quality: Some Methodological Issues" in Glynn, W. J., and Barnes, J. G. (1995) Understanding Services Management, New York, John Willey & Sons, 57-88.

44. Sundararn, S. (1984), 'Customer Service in Banks at Crossroads', The Journal of the Indian Institute of Bankers, 55(4): 217-223.

45. Sureshchandar, G. S., and Rajendran C. (2003), 'Customer Perceptions of Service Quality in Banking Sector of a Developing Economy: A Critical Analysis, International Journal of Bank Marketing, 21(5): 233-242.

46. Takeuchi, H. and Quelch, J. A. (1983), "Quality is more than Making a Good Product", Harvard Business Review, July-Aug, 139-145.

47. Young, C, Cunningham, L. and Lee, M. (1994), "Accessing Service Quality as an Effective Management Tool: The Case of Airdne Industry", Journal of Marketing, 63: 76-95.

4
CHAPTER

SERVICES ORIENTED TECHNOLOGIES IN FINANCIAL SERVICES SECTOR

Mazanai Musara

INTRODUCTION

Over the years, business and our daily lives have been bombarded with various forms on inventions and technology. The public adopted technology at an exceedingly fast rate and the world was transformed. In the 21st century, technology rules our daily lives. We assemble documents and reports on computers, use them for PowerPoint presentations, take laptops on the road and communicate via email and social networks, complete our banking transaction using cell phones and do online banking to mention just a few. The 21st century worker has the freedom to work from any place at any time, with always available access to information. Laptops, notebooks, wireless broadband, Smartphones and social networking have transformed the world into a global market. The shape of the business landscape took a different course because of the proliferation of technology.

The financial services sector in South Africa is one of the sectors, where the impact of the information and connection era is highly felt and ever changing. There is a growing recognition across financial service providers in South Africa that technology and innovation is the cornerstone for surviving in the 21st century economy. This is evident in almost all corporate messages in the banking sector. Therefore, the chapter focuses on technological innovations in the financial services sector. The chapter presents a theoretical review as well as the results of the empirical research that was conducted in South Africa. It is paramount as the starting point to shed light on the concept of technology and innovation in detail. Understanding the concept of technology in detail is paramount as a basis from which innovation can clearly be articulated. Innovation can be in the form of product innovation (that results in new products or services) or process innovation (that involves the introduction of new ways of performing tasks in an organisation).The following section begins with an explanation of the concept of technology and technological innovations.

Citation: Musara, Services Oriented Technologies in Financial Services Sector, DOI: 10.5772/36362.

LITERATURE REVIEW AND CONCEPTS

The section will provide a concise discussion of the key concepts, key events and literature related to technological innovations with a particular focus on financial services sector. This is intended to shed light on the key issues related to technological innovations and their impact in the 21st century economy.

Technology and technological innovation

The term technology can be defined in many different ways depending on the context in which it is applied. For the purpose of this chapter, technology can be defined as, material objects or tools that are used by human beings such machines, hardware and utensils, in performing different activities (Bain, 1937). Technology furthermore, includes systems, methods of organisation and techniques used by the business. The term technology can be applied generally or to specific area, for example information technology (technologies use in obtaining, storing, retrieval and dissemination of information), medical technology (tools, machinery, utensils, etc, used by medical practitioners), state-of-art technology, etc.

In the financial sector, technologies which are mainly going to be focused on in this chapter includes Automated Tellers Machines (ATMs), computer hardware and software, telephones and mobile phones, the internet, among others. Technological innovations have been attributed to contribute to the distribution channels in the financial services sector. Electronic Banking (E-Banking) is one of the most notable channels. E-Banking merges several different technologies such electronic fund transfer point of sale technologies, internet banking, cell phone banking, etc. Each of these evolved in different ways, but in recent years different groups and industries have recognized the importance of working together. Several technologies were invented with a particular aim to improving service delivery in the business sector. Of particular influence in the financial services sector is the information technology, the following section discuses information technology.

Information Technology

Information technology (IT) refers to hardware and software that are used to store, retrieve and manipulate information. IT comprises computer hardware and software as well as other telecommunication equipment such as telephones, fax machines and mobile communication devices to mention just a few (Jürgen, 2002). The introduction of telecommunications into bank markets dates back to 1846 when the telegraph reduced stock price differentials between New York and regional stock markets (Garbade and Silber, 1978). According to Leslie (2000), the most important IT applications had their origins in US governmentsponsored research in the first half of the twentieth century. Interactive IT applications would never have existed without a long and expensive gestation period in which computer power and telecommunication applications were devoted to help the US gain the initiative in science and technology. Indeed, the British experience with computer hardware development would tend to confirm the view of a defence-based technology push. The first stored-program computer in the world was developed in 1948 by academics (Freddie Williams and Tom Kilburn) at Manchester University (Anonymous, 1998).

In brief, early adoptions of telecommunications and computer applications had greatest impact in organised high value wholesale bank markets, that is, those activities that had traditionally been further away from volume transactions through retail bank branches (Anonymous, 1998). Banks absorbed the new technology on the back of a growing market for retail bank services, which expanded as middle income individuals became a growing proportion of the population. Information technology has enormous effects on the functioning of each and every enterprise operating in the 21st century economy. Jürgen (2002) argued that IT facilitates complementary innovation, enabling firms to increase output via the introduction of new processes and altering the competitive environment, thereby creating pressure for firms to adjust. Meeting these challenges require changes in the organisation of firms, for instance in the form of vertical disintegration, streamlining of managerial levels and more decentralised production, and a well-educated labour force able and motivated to exploit the opportunities offered by new technology.

Knowledge on the existence and importance of IT to an enterprise alone is not sufficient for the successful running and competitiveness of the enterprise in the market. The ability to develop new and unique ways of doing things is the key to success in the 21st century economy, which is characterised by rapid changes in technology. Hence, to be competitive in the market the enterprise should be innovative. The financial services sector in South Africa is bombarded with information technologies, a differentiation strategy by several banks.

Technological innovation

Innovation involves using new knowledge to transform organizational processes or create commercially viable products and services. The sources of new knowledge may include the latest technology, the results of experiments, creative insights or competitive information. Innovation can be broadly defined as the process of creating new ideas and putting them into practice. It is the means by which creative ideas find their way into everyday practice in the form of new goods or services that satisfy consumers or as new systems or practices that help organisations to improve the produce of goods or services (Wood, Wallace, Zeffane, Schermerhorn, Hunt and Osborn, 2001:611).

Rogers (1998:2) defined innovation as a process of introducing new ideas to the firm which result in improved performance of the firm. He identified five types of innovation which are:

- Introduction of new products/services or a qualitative change in the existing product,
- Process innovation new to the industry,
- Opening of a new market,
- Development of new sources for raw materials and other inputs, and
- Changes in industrial organisation.

Innovation can be thought of in two contexts: product innovation and process innovation.

a. Product Innovation

Product innovation results in the creation of new or improved goods or services. Product innovation encompasses development of new products, changes in design of established products, or use of new materials or components in manufacture of established products (Wood et al., 2001). Product innovation can take one of the following ways:

- a modified version of an existing product range,
- a new model in the existing product range,
- a new product outside the existing range but in a similar field of technology,
- a totally new product in a new field of technology

b. Process Innovation

Innovation that results in better ways of doing things, which is new efficient and effective processes and structures, is called process innovation (Wood et al., 2001). Process innovation is aimed at improving the operations of the organisations. This includes increasing productivity, efficiency, safety at work and waste reduction to mention just but a few. Process innovation culminates in the production of high quality products at lower costs, thus process innovation can be viewed as instrumental to product innovation.

Both product and process innovation are important in creating, communicating and delivering superior value to consumers. Technological innovations, which encompass both product innovation and process innovation, should be part of the organisation's culture to survive the competitive pressures of the 21st century economy. Technological innovation comprise of product or process, continuous or discontinuous, radical or incremental innovations in the financial services sector leading to improved or new products. 'Radical' innovations refer to new products that result from advances in knowledge/technology. 'Incremental' innovations include improvement of process or product designs, with or without up gradation of machinery/acquisition of new machinery. Two main aspects form the core of innovation namely invention and application. Invention is the process of discovery, while application is the act of use (Wood et al, 2001). Thus;

Innovation = Invention + Application

Innovation should be viewed as a continuous process in an organisation if the organisation is to continue operating successfully. Having laid out the major aspect of technology and innovation, the meaning of technological innovations becomes apparent. In this case technological innovations can be viewed in terms of the creation of new tools, machines and processes that are used by human beings in the quest to develop better goods or services, and better ways of doing things. According to Subrahmanya (2005) technological innovation is the transformation of an idea into a new or improved saleable product or operational process in industry or commerce. It is therefore important to examined technological innovations in relation to their deferential impact on the business landscape. The following section provides an overview of a few selected services oriented technologies that impact the financial services sector and business in South Africa.

An overview of services oriented technologies in the financial services sector

Technological innovations in the financial services sector appeared in the form of the introductions of automated tellers machines, the rise of internet banking, electronic cards, cell phone banking and various other customers tracking and accounts management software to mention just a few. In the financial services industry at large, the banking sector was one of the first to embrace rapid globalization and benefit significantly from Information Technology (IT) developments. Technological developments in the banking sector started in the 1950s with the installation of the first automated bookkeeping machine at banks. Automation in the banking sector became widespread over the next few decades as bankers quickly realized that much of the labour intensive information handling processes could be automated with the use of computers. The first Automated Tellers Machine (ATM) is purported to have been introduced in the USA in 1968 and it was only a cash dispenser (Jayamaha, 2008). The emergence of the ATM marked the beginning of self service banking as services provided by the bank teller could be performed on a 24-hour schedule and at the customers' convenience rather than during banking hours. The following case study illustrates the way technology is shaping the financial services sector, in particular banking.

Partnering around technology to tackle poverty

The mobile money transfer service M-Pesa (M stands for "mobile", Pesa means "money" in Swahili) is one of the best examples of transformative power of partnerships. With the initial support of the UK Department for International Development (DfID) through matching a fund, the Kenyan mobile phone service provider Safaricom has created a service which allows users to make and receive payments, transfer money to other users and non-users, and deposit and withdraw money without needing to visit a bank.

By relying solely on the ubiquitous mobile phone, M-Pesa has significantly expanded financial access among Kenya's poor. By bringing the unbanked into the market, it has also created new markets for goods and services tailored to mobile banking. Already serving more than 14 million users in Kenya, this service is being replicated in other African countries including Rwanda, South Africa, Tanzania and Uganda.

These new technologies in the financial services sector introduced new ways of doing financial transactions and also, had made possible the introduction of other financial products or services. For example, in South Africa, technological innovations made it possible for Standard Bank to introduce the E-Plan (Electronic Plan – a card based transaction product that was introduced in 1994). Also a result of technological innovation is FNB's Smartsave suite of products – card-only account access, often with some savings or other features (such as funeral insurance) built in (Porteous and Hazelhurst 2004). ABSA also offers a Business Essentials package that includes QuickBooks Pro Bookkeeping which also assists in financial management. Various transformations took place in the banking sector which resulted in new banking products, services and processes. Of notable importance is the introduction of online banking, card based banking and ATMs which played a significant role in increasing convenience to banking services by customers. A number of ATMs can be found in most of rural towns and townships as well as in major towns in South Africa.

Also notable in the South African banking sector is the increasing use of electronic commerce (e-commerce). E-commerce is the sharing of business information, maintaining business relationships and conducting business transactions by means of telecommunication networks (Chaffey 2002). The increasing use of the internet and mobile phones has made possible the implementation of e-commerce. The arrival and wide use of credit cards in the South African economy is also a notable consequence of technological innovations in the South African Banking Sector. Credit card alliances with non financial institutions have been common practices in South Africa. For example credit card alliances were noted in 2006 between Edgars and Standard Bank, Metropolitan and Mercantile Bank, Kulula and FNB and Virgin and ABSA and Voyager and Nedbank among others (Hawkins 2006). These alliances allow customers to do their trading transactions with these companies anywhere without having to go to the bank or the bank's ATM to make withdrawals, thus increasing easy access to funds for customer whenever on demand.

Apart from consumer intended technologies, technologies such as smart phones, notebooks, broadband access and social networking sites and applications among others, found a place in the day to day operations of businesses. For example, smart phones have increased productivity by enabling employees to work outside the confines of their offices by creating a new phenomenon in business that I would like to term, 'the mobile workforce". Besides being an integral part of our daily lives, smart phones play a critical role in businesses and smart phones are fast becoming a replacement for laptops and notebooks.

Furthermore, the use of social networking sites as marketing tools as well as connecting with customers is fast becoming common practice among several businesses in South Africa and elsewhere around the world. According to Intergr8 co-founder, Rob Sussman, an estimate of about 10% of the world population is on Facebook, with 50% active every second day. From a business perspective, Facebook allows you to build a substantially larger social network than one can build in an isolated non-networked geographically restricted environment. "I use Facebook to connect to the Intergr8 employees and customers for more direct personal communication" said Rob. The majority of companies in South Africa have Facebook pages where they can connect with customers anytime. Almost all banks in South Africa have Facebook pages where customers can "like" and express their views, raise their concerns and ask questions. Furthermore, banks also use this platform to communicate their corporate messages to their customers and potential customers. The introduction and use of different technologies in the banking sector is mainly to create, communicate and deliver superior value to consumers with the major objective of being competitive in the market. A question will arise as to how consumers are viewing such a technology wave and whether it is beneficial to them. The next section will account for consumers' use of technology and their reactions to technological changes.

The use of technology in the services sector

Technological innovations play an important role in increasing the competitiveness of the firm, particularly in the 21st century economy where advances in technology are a common phenomenon. Simple technologies in the financial services sector came in terms of the widespread issuing of magnetic stripe ATM cards and the phasing out of high cost manual methods of banking such as transacting at counters with savings books (Porteous and Hazelhurst 2004). A study by the research company, Gartner (2011), estimated that by 2014 more than three billion of the world's adult population will be able to transact electronically via mobile and internet technology. Gartner (2011) revealed that two trends are emerging that will drastically change the future of the world's trading economy, viz; (i) the rapid rise of the adoption of mobile and internet technology in emerging economies; and (ii) advance in mobile payment, commerce and banking. These trends exhibit the shape of our technological era. Also contributory to the banking sector is the increasing use of cell phones. World Bank analysts have suggested that mobile commerce, (the use cell phone in doing trading transactions) and electronic finance are apparent in developing countries as connectivity levels and reliability increases. They predicted that this trend will allow developing countries to leapfrog in the development of their financial systems. For South Africa, 2006 was projected as the take off year for online banking (Porteous and Hazelhurst, 2004).

Herferman (2001) asserted that the retail banking sector has witnessed rapid process technology, where new technology has altered the way key tasks are performed. In his study in the UK, the number of ATMs in services has risen from 568 in 1975 to 15208 in 1995, a trend he said was also observed in all industrialized countries. In another study, Berger (2003:143) identified the changes in the use of selected banking technologies, indicating a significant growth in the use of new information technologies (IT) and financial technology. To this extent, the role of technology in the banking sector and financial services sector at large need to be examined critically, as the information and communication technologies (ICT) is changing the banking sector operations and efficiency The benefits accruing from the introduction of new technologies in the banking sector determines greatly the reactions of consumers to these technologies. In that light this chapter highlight some of the perceptions about new technologies by both consumers and the corporate.

RESEARCH METHODOLOGY AND DESIGN

The empirical study was approached from the perspective of a formal research design through the definition of the study population, the incorporation of suitable measuring instrument and reliable techniques for data analysis as stipulated in Cooper and Schindler (2008). The empirical research for the study was conducted in two ways; a pilot study and the main survey. The measuring instrument was designed to measure the influence to technological innovations in the financial services sector. Following the design of the initial questionnaire, a pilot study on 20 respondents was conducted. The result of the pilot study and a discussion with a panel of experts led to the initial questionnaire being revised accordingly taking into consideration all the flaws identified in the process. The questionnaire was later administered to 613 respondents which consisted of financial services sector customers as well as members of the general public in the Eastern Cape province of South Africa. Following rigorous follow-ups on respondent a response rate of 65.7% was achieved. Figure 3.1 below illustrated the percentage respondents by age who participated in the survey. The majority of the respondents (27%) were between the ages 26-35 and the least number of respondents was from the ages of more 65.

Furthermore, to supplement the results of the questionnaire survey, interviews were conducted with banking sector officials. Fifteen employees from banks were interviewed and they were from Standard Bank, First National Bank, ABSA, NedBank and Capitec Bank.

RESULTS AND DISCUSSIONS

This section presents the results of the study that was conducted in the Eastern Cape Province of South Africa. A discussion of the results, linking them to previous studies was also incorporated in this section.

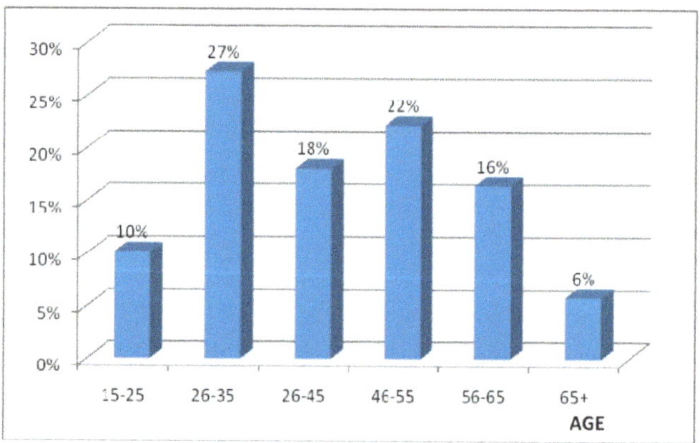

Figure 3.1: Percentage respondents by Age.

Perceptions about services oriented technology

Customer perceptions

There is a mixed reaction by consumers about the ever changing technological advances. In a study conducted in South Africa, the results reviewed that adult population is not so pleased by rapid changing technological advances. 86% of the adult population (65 or more years old) interviewed argued that technological advances are becoming a burden on their part and in several cases they need a technological savvy or well up individual to assist them in making certain transactions using technology. The reaction was markedly different from that of the younger population with more than 73% viewing technology as a must have necessity to function effectively. Arguments raised include the fact that the use of technology, particularly for business purposes is funny and more convenient.

While the introduction of new technology into the banking sector come with several benefits to the organisation and consumers, the reactions of different groups of people to such changes are different. Some consumers see technological changes as a threat to their old ways of doing things (they have inertia), while other groups of consumers see it as opening doors to learning new things and ways of doing things.

The results of the study further suggested that many people perceive new technologies as a "push" by banks. In this study, 63% of SA adults agreed that banks force them to use new technology due to circumstantial reasons. However a closer analysis of the results suggested that it is not technology per se that is a problem but rather how it is applied. Two thirds of people, rich as well as poor, prefer face to face service to an ATM, a third of the elderly claim to avoid banking machines as much as possible. However 75% of poorer and 83% of the richer people say they are prepared to learn new technology. The rapid acceptance of cell phones across the population is an indication of an ability to learn new technology if the benefit are substantially enough. These results corroborates with findings presented by Porteous and Hazelhurst (2004). The fact that businesses exist to serve consumers any action should have a customer focus in mind. Business must ensure that their new technologies are received positively by consumers or ensure a thorough market assessment before investing in some sophisticated technologies which may make the consumer worse off.

Corporate perceptions

The impression that we get from the business sector is that technology is a 'necessary evil', something that every enterprise operating in the 21st century economy must embrace in order to improve and maintain its competitiveness. An analysis of the banking sector in South Africa revealed that every bank is striving to stand out with a unique technological innovation that distinguishes it from competitors. In every corporate message, every bank is trying to convey the message that, 'We are leaders in technology and we give you the best value for money'. This message is evident in the adverts by FNB, ABSA, NedBank, Capitec and standard Bank among others.

Furthermore, too often businesses use technology as motivating tools for their employees. Social networking sites like Facebook, Twitter, Myspace and Skype are viewed as tools to boast the employees' moral during their spare times. However, the overuse of such will reduce productivity if employees use company time and resources to pursue their social needs. Using social media can be overwhelming but employees need not be carried away. However, employees can use sites that best fit their goals, market and personality for personal branding purposes. Spending time on social networking promoting yourself online can yield powerful positive results, however you need to be consistent in both promoting your image and your efforts. If employees approach the social media with a plan and a specific focus of providing and sharing useful information while interacting with fans, friends, family and followers, it can be an effective and even fun part of your marketing mix. Overall, businesses view technological innovations as a tool that must be embraced and be kept improving to remain competitive in the ever-changing market.

Costs and benefits of technological innovations in the financial services sector

Technological innovations have had major contributions in improving the efficiency of the financial services sector. Of particular note is the fact that technological innovations have reduced significantly the cost of transacting and this will benefit both the bank and the consumer. The use of ATMs, Credit cards, internet banking, among other recent advances in technology in the South African Banking Sector, has seen substantially decreases in the cost of doing banking transactions. The new channels for delivery of banking products and services, such as through the internet, ATMs and cell phone banking, have the advantage for customers of longer hours of service and more efficient and cheaper means of delivering the products (Reixach 2001).

Changes in ways of transacting from the recent advance of information and communications technology are not limited to improving the efficiency of traditional businesses but are also enabling the development of new instruments in specific fields. A good example is the development of a new supply channel for financial services, namely the internet, which has made it possible to establish extensive and low-cost financial networking (Hayami, 2000). To this end, information and communications technology has enabled the more diversified and convenient provision of financial services, including via the internet and ATM networks. These will significantly reduce costs compared to old ways of doing banking transactions, which require face to face-over the counter transactions associated with huge travelling costs for customers to bank branches. Furthermore, IT innovation affects the competitive position of firms both through production efficiency and changes in the goods markets. Firms that are competitive in the modern market are those that are able to create, develop and implement new and better ways of carrying out tasks. This calls for all the firms to be innovative in order for them to be competitive in the marketplace. Technological innovations enable firms to increase output via the introduction of new processes and altering the competitive environment, thereby creating pressure for firms to adjust (Jürgen et al 2002).

Technological innovations have undoubtedly introduced enormous benefits to banks, particularly in terms of productivity increases, cost reduction through labour saving and increased profitability. The use of new technology has increased outputs and reduced costs as both technological capital investments and technology human resources have a positive relationship to productivity (Jayamaha 2008). Consumers should be awarded the chance to enjoy the full benefits derived from the use of latest technological advances. This would increase banks' competitiveness through differentiation and customer service improvement, reduced transaction costs, better risk avoidance, and maintaining a stable customer base and market share (Jayamaha 2008). Despite the wide spectrum of benefits identified from the introduction and use of technological innovations in the banking sector, there are some social and economic problems associated with technological innovations some of which have enormous consequences to the society and the nation at large if left unattended.

One of the problems brought in by technological innovations is their strain on the budgets of the banks. Most of the banks' resources are being channelled towards advancing and coping with rapid changes in technology. Apart from personal costs, technology is the biggest item in the budget of the bank, and is the fastest growing one (Reixach 2001). If not managed with caution, emphasis may be put on pursuing technological advancement while compromising other activities which are important to the success of the enterprise. Technological innovations, particularly in information and communication technology (ICT) have resulted in globalisation of businesses and business operations. Under such conditions, competitive pressures are likely to intensify in many parts of the economy and increasingly affect previously sheltered sectors such as energy, transport, communication and distribution. The result is an increased pressure to adjust and could lead to transition problems in economies which are insufficiently able to change, a common problem of most African economies (Reixach 2001). To the society, technological innovations, if not managed properly may result in such problems as pollution and unethical behaviours. For example the use of short message services (SMS) had been an instrument in conveying malicious information and images among teenagers which lead to moral decay.

Furthermore, the advances in technology also mean that consumers must learn how to use such technologies. Such learning should furthermore be fast to be up to date with the fast changing technologies. Slow learners and the elders who have inertia may be frustrated with such demands leading to psychological problems on consumers. More importantly, technological innovations have significant effects on service quality, efficiency and profitability.

Technological innovations vs services quality

Studies have shown that among consumers, service quality and experience is the most spoken about topic, followed by a great product or service which is closely related to something "astonishing". Customer service should focus on understanding and meeting the needs of customers effectively. According to Accenture (2007) the customer service levels in South Africa leaves a lot to be desired. South Africa is rated as one of the worst countries globally in terms of customer service, with a service maturity rating of 6%. Compared to the leader, Singapore with a rating of 89%, there is a need for improvement in customer service in South Africa. This outstandingly poor customer service in the country, however provide a fantastic opportunity for all business owners who want to gain a competitive advantage by tapping into exceptional customer service offering. Providing the best customer service is the best, if not the only solution to gain customer satisfaction, customer retention and creating customer value. Technological innovations plays a significant role is delivering quality customer service. Effective and prompt modes of communication, instant feedback and customer tracking solutions are all ingredients of an excellent customer service package. This has been enabled by the advent of the latest information and communication technologies.

A study into on the banking sector in South Africa revealed that consumers (88.5%) are satisfied with the level of communication they get from banks about their accounts information and in terms of how quick their complaints are addressed due to advanced technologies. Consumer however indicated their displeasure with some bad systems in a few banks. The study revealed that an estimated 80% of the aggrieved customers' problems with technology are caused by bad systems. It became apparent that most of the service problems customers' encounter in trying to do business occurs as a result bad delivery systems, which are out of date, too complex or just customer unfriendly. Taking for instance, most dysfunctional systems include telephone technology that are characterised by features like call director or voice-mail systems with frustratingly lengthy menu options, or caller holder features that attempt to entertain customers with sometimes annoying music. In several cases some businesses even interrupt the entertainment with an occasional commercial message. Imagine an aggrieved customer on the other end of the line. To aggravate the problem, imagine when a customer finally reaches a real person, too often to find that the person is a company's newly appointed secretary with little knowledge of the company's product and no authority to solve the customer's problem. Such technologies cost companies millions in lost customers due to poor management of technology. It is therefore paramount to ensure that a smooth and efficient management system of technology is embraced in every aspects involving direct contact with customers and elsewhere in the services chain.

Technological innovations vs efficiency

Efficiency is a general term in economics that describes how well a system is performing in generating the maximum output for given inputs with the available technology. Efficiency is improved if more output is generated without changing the level of inputs, or in other words, the amount of "friction" or "waste" is reduced. The idea of efficiency broadly refers to the fact of using limited resources in the best possible way (Caruana, 2003). Qayyum and Khan (2007) defined efficiency as the ratio output per unit input in which case they suggested that efficiency is decomposed into two components namely, allocative (economic) efficiency and technical efficiency.

Efficiency relates the cost incurred compared to the product obtained. In general terms, the idea of efficiency broadly refers to the fact of using limited resources in the best possible way. In other words, an economic system is efficient if it does not waste its resources, in such a way that it minimises individuals' well-being (Caruana, 2003). A system can be called economically efficient if no one can be made better off without making someone else worse off. The most output is obtained from a given amount of inputs and when production proceeds at the lowest possible per unit cost. Efficiency introduces an additional factor to an enterprise, namely risk. Thus in every effort to improve efficiency, the risk factor should be taken into account. This idea factors in significant constraints and makes it necessary to focus on improved efficiency as a balanced process in which attention must be paid to a series of management elements that should not be taken for granted in cost-cutting drives. For example, no clear efficiency gain is achieved if it is done at the expense of increasing operational risk (Caruana, 2003). Operational risk refers to the risk of loss resulting from inadequate or failed internal processes, people and systems, or from external events. The definition includes legal risk, which is the risk of loss resulting from failure to comply with laws as well as prudent ethical standards and contractual obligations (Anon 2003).

These definitions of efficiency are not exactly equivalent. However, they all encompass the idea that nothing more can be achieved given the resources available. Thus efficiency is achieved through making the best use of the available resources. Measures of technical output efficiency include estimates of banks' scale efficiency. Scale efficiency refers to banks or branches achieving an optimum size for producing financial services and thereby, ensuring operation at the minimum point of the average cost curve.

There is a negative relationship between bank branch size and branch efficiency (Oster and Antioch 1995). Some of the strategies adopted by banks includes re-engineering its processes (through identifying key business activities that can either be streamlined or eliminated), improving the skills of its labour force through training and increasing the use of technology. Over time, the net effect of these initiatives will result in significant improvements in branch efficiency and elimination of the negative relationship between branch size and efficiency (Oster and Antioch 1995). Furthermore, the increased competition resulting from financial deregulation may provide impetus for the achievement of further technical output efficiencies through scale economies. Economies of scale are achieved when a bank recognises that the cost of producing a range of outputs is less than the cost of producing them independently (Oster and Antioch 1995). To measure the efficiencies of the banks the major interest is in Xefficiency, which shows whether banks use their inputs efficiently or not (Schure and Wagenvoort, 1999). To customers efficiency is perceived in the sense of the bank completing transactions in the shortest possible time thus minimising the amount spent by customers to complete transactions.

In the financial services sector at large, the concept of efficiency can be thought of in terms of how well a bank employs its resources relative to the existing production possibilities frontier (or, in other words, relative to the current 'best practice') – how an institution simultaneously minimises costs and maximises revenue, based on an existing level of production technology (Oster and Antioch 1995). Investment in technology is an important mechanism for attaining greater efficiency. This is because technological development allows processes to be undertaken more easily, simultaneously eliminating certain time and labour-intensive tasks so that operating cost cuts are achieved. In addition the capacity to process massive amounts of data efficiently in real time allows for better risk management and also for services better tailored to client needs. However, efforts to improve efficiency must be compatible with the challenges posed by new technologies (Caruana, 2003). In that light, the costs of new technologies should not outweigh the benefits associated with these technologies. Thus a thorough cost-benefit analysis is important in making decisions regarding new technologies. In other words it is imperative that when employing a new technology that the anticipated benefits should outweigh the anticipated costs. Technical efficiency correlates directly to overall company efficiency, this means if a business spends wisely on information technology it will reap the rewards in sales and customer service improvements and ultimately improved profitability.

A detailed account on the determined measurement of efficiency in the South African banking sector is the one provided by Mboweni (2004). According to him, the efficiency of the banking sector can be determined by expressing operating expenses as a percentage of total income. "Currently, the international benchmark for efficiency is 60 per cent. In the past, South African banks were able to keep this ratio below or close to the international benchmark. The ratio, however, has increased from 60.2 per cent in 1999 to 67 per cent in 2002. The high volatility in efficiency in 2002 indicates that the South African banking sector was indeed experiencing problems with profitability in the first six months of 2002. This deterioration was confirmed by the return on equity of 5.4 per cent (smoothed over 12-months) and the return on assets of 0.4 per cent (smoothed over 12- months) as at the end of June 2002. Since 2002, however, the efficiency ratio has improved and, as at the end of October 2004, the efficiency of the banking sector was 65.2 per cent. By the end of October 2004, the return on equity and the return on assets of the banking sector had similarly improved" (Mboweni 2004).

The historical account of the efficiency of the South African Banking sector above shows a growing trend. This is an indication of various new approaches to service delivery which improve efficiency, most notably advance in new technologies. Looking at the efficiency trend in the South African banking sector, a possibility for further improvements is there if new approaches to improving efficiency are sought. In a study of the banking sector in South Africa on the view of consumers regarding the improvement of efficiency of the banking sector in the past ten years, 92% of the respondents agreed that the efficiency of the banking sector has improved in the past ten years due to improvement in technology. Only 2% disagree of the fact that the efficiency of the banking sector has improved while 6% neither agree nor disagree. The perceived improvement was attributed to continued improvements in technologies used in banks. The perceptions of respondents on ATMs, online banking and cell phone banking on their contributions to efficiency and cost reductions were also sought. These also receive a positive response with 53% of the respondents indicating that ATMs are cost effective, 77% of the respondents agreeing that online banking and cell phone banking are cost effective.

Technological innovations vs profitability

Approaches to increasing efficiency in every venture are aimed at ultimately increasing profitability. This objective is tantamount to that of the firm namely wealth creation for the owners. Thus it is critical to address the link between technological innovations, efficiency improvement and ultimately profitability.

Several studies revealed a positive relationship between efficiency and profitability, that is, the higher the efficiency, the greater the profitability. However in a study carried out by Abbaso˘glu, Aysan and Gunes, (2007) it appears that there is no clear relationship between efficiency and profitability. In their study of the Turkish banking sector, the results indicated that there is no significant evidence from the data that efficiency affects profitability. In the study which took the return on assets into account, foreign banks were found to be significantly more profitable than domestic banks. While the least efficient banks turned out to be foreign with the exception of a few, being foreign increases banks' profitability. This result shows us that foreign banks are less efficient but more profitable compared to the domestic banks. Hence, there is no clear evidence that there is a positive relationship between efficiency and profitability (Abbaso˘glu, Aysan and Gunes, 2007). Increasing profitability is one of the fundamental objectives of any business operating as a going concern. To achieve increased profitability, the business should aim at reducing costs in the best way possible. The use of advanced and up to date technological innovations is instrumental in this regard. The major focus on improving efficiency is to reduce the costs of producing a desired level of output. Strategies and actions to minimise costs are paramount in the bid to reduce the firm's expenses and this leads to increased profitability of the venture. In the banking sector it is important that the bank be able to employ the most cost effective approaches to complete every transaction. A study on the banking sector in South Africa revealed that 75% of the respondents agree that technological innovations resulted in cost savings. Sixty five percent (65%) of the respondents agreed that cell phone banking is helping in reducing costs of banking. Among the reasons cited included cheapness of cell phone banking, no costs of travelling to the bank and the convenience of cell phone banking (customers can do their transaction anywhere, anytime). 35% of the respondents were of the opinion that cell phone banking does not help in reducing banking costs for customers. The reason for their argument ranged from the need for airtime, the need for cell phones with access to internet (that is, a phone with GPRS) which are expensive and the fact that some transaction are simply not feasible using cell phone banking.

Linking efficiency to profitability

Approaches to increasing efficiency in every venture are aimed at ultimately increasing profitability. This objective is tantamount to that of the firm namely wealth creation for the owners. Thus it is critical to address the link between efficiency improvement and profitability. Soteriou and Zenios, (1997) suggested a joint analysis of operational efficiency and profitability as shown in Fig 1. In the analysis bank branches were categorised into four categories similar to the (Boston Consultants Group (BCG) matrix, namely stars, dogs, sleepers and cows.

Sleepers are those branches that are highly profitable, while they are inefficient. Hence, their profitability can be further increased if they are awakened and improve their operational efficiency. Stars are the branches that match their superior operational efficiency with profitability, while cows are lagging in profits and a major reason for this is their operational inefficiency. Finally, for the dogs it was concluded from the analysis that enhancement of their profitability can not come from improvements in operations, since they are already efficient on the operational side (Soteriou and Zenios, 1999). The analysis revealed a positive relationship between efficiency and profitability, that is, the higher the efficiency of a bank branch the greater the profitability. However in a study carried out by Abbaso˘glu, Aysan and Gunes, (2007) it appears that there is no clear relationship between efficiency and profitability. In their study of the Turkish banking sector, the results indicated that there is no significant evidence from the data that efficiency affects profitability.

In the study which took the return on assets into account, foreign banks were found to be significantly more profitable than domestic banks. While the least efficient banks turned out to be foreign with the exception of a few, being foreign increases banks' profitability. This result shows us that foreign banks are less efficient but more profitable compared to the domestic banks. Hence, there is no clear evidence that there is a positive relationship between efficiency and profitability (Abbaso˘glu, Aysan and Gunes, 2007).

Increasing profitability is one of the fundamental objectives of any business operating as a going concern. To achieve increased profitability, the business should aim at reducing costs in the best way possible. Thus the use of advanced technologies to improve efficiency and cut costs should the focal strategy to remain competitive in the 21st century economy.

CONCLUSION

Overall, the analysis leads to the conclusion that technological innovations have changed the business landscape of the 21st century. The majority of the respondents interviewed showed positive responses with respect to the improvement of efficiency and cost reductions as a result of the use of advanced technological innovations in the financial services sector. From the above discussion, it can be noted that the importance of technological innovations in the financial services sector reign supreme for the success of banks operating in the 21st century economy. It is important to lay a foundation to understanding the concept of technology and technological innovations. Understanding the concept of technology in detail is paramount as a basis for which innovation (the creation, introduction and use of new ideas and tools) can take root. Innovation can be in the form of product innovation (that results in new products or services) or process innovation (that involves the introduction of new ways of performing tasks in an organisation).

More contributory to the new developments in the banking sector is the innovation in information technology (hardware and software that are used to store, retrieve, and process and communicate information). This has been discussed in this chapter. Furthermore the acceptance, use and reactions of consumers to new technologies in the financial services sector had been discussed. Finally, the contributions of technological innovations to the banking sector as well as to consumer had been alluded to in this chapter. It can be deduced from the contributions of new technology that, technological innovations has resulted in reduced transaction costs for both the customers and banks, as well as improved efficiency in the banking sector.

REFERENCES

1. Abbaso˘glu, O. F., Aysan, A. F and Gunes, A., (2007). Concentration, Competition, Efficiency and Profitability of the Turkish Banking Sector in the Post-Crises Period [Online: available http://mpra.ub.uni-muenchen.de/5494/ MPRA Paper No. 5494, posted 07. November 2007 / 04:45, Accessed April 17, 2008.

2. Abhiman, D., Subhash, C. R. and Ashok, N., (2007). Labour-use efficiency in Indian banking: A branch-level analysis, Omega 37 (2009) pp 411 – 425 [Online: available at www.sciencedirect.com accessed April 17, 2008)]

3. Anon (2003). Supervisory Guidance on Operational Risk Advanced Measurement Approaches for Regulatory Capital.

4. Bain, R. (1937). Technology and State Government. American Sociological review Vol. 2 No. 6 p. 860-865.

5. Caruana, J. (2003). Savings banks - Efficiency and an ongoing commitment to society. Efficiency of financial institutions [Online: available at www.bis.org, Accessed April 17, 2008].

6. Chaffey, D., (2004). E-Business and E-commerce Management 2nd Edition, Essex: Pearson Education Limited.

7. Halkos, G. E. and Salamouris, D. S., (1999). Efficiency measures of the Greek Banking Sector: A non-parametric approach for the period 1997-1999. University of Thessaly, Department of Economics, Discussion paper series 01/04

8. Hawkins, P., (2006). South African banking landscape: Introduction & Background, Greenside: FEAsibility Pty Ltd

9. Hayami, M., (2000). The impact of innovation in information and communications technology on financial systems [On-line]. Available: www.bis.org [accessed April 3, 2008].

10. Jayamaha, R, (2008). Impact of IT in the Banking Sector [On-line]. Available: www.bis.org [accessed February 7, 2008].

11. Jürgen, S., (2002). IT innovations and financing patterns: implications for the financial system [On-line]. Available: www.bis.org [accessed April 3, 2008].

12. Mboweni, T. T, (2004). The South African banking sector - an overview of the past 10 years [Online: available at www.bis.org, Accessed April 17, 2008].

13. Oster, A. and Antioch, L., (1995). Measuring Productivity in the Australian Banking Sector [online: available at http://www.rba.gov.au/PublicationsandResearch/Conferences/1995/OsterAntio ch.pdf Accessed (May 26, 2008).

14. Porteous, D. and Hazelhurst, E. (2004). Banking on Change: Democratizing Finance in South Africa, 1994-2004 and beyond, Cape Town: Double Story Books

15. Qayyum, A. And Khan, S., (2007). X-efficiency, Scale Economies, Technological Progress and Competition: A Case of Banking Sector in Pakistan. Islamabad Pakistan Institute of Development

16. Reixach, A., (2001). The effect of information and Communication technologies on the Banking Sector and Payment System, University de Girona

17. Rogers, M., (1998). The Definition and Measurement of Innovation, Melbourne Institute Working Paper No. 10/98

18. Schatzberg, E. (2006). Technik Comes to America: Changing meanings of Technology before 1930. Technology and Culture, Vol. 47, No, 3 pp. 486-512.

19. Schure, P. and Wagenvoort, R.(1999). Economies of Scale and Efficiency in European Banking: New Evidence, European Investment Bank Economics and Financial Report, 1999.

20. Soteriou, A. and Zenios, S. A. (1999). Operations, Quality, and Profitability in the Provision of Banking Services. Management Science, Vol. 45, No. 9, Performance of Financial Institutions, (Sep., 1999), pp. 1221-1238

21. Subrahmanya, M. H., (2005). Pattern of technological innovations in small enterprises: a comparative perspective of Bangalore (India) and Northeast England (UK). Technovation 25, pp 269-280 [online]

22. Wallace J., Zeffane R. M., Schermerhorn, J. R., Hunt J. G., and Osborn R. N., (2001). Organisational Behaviour: A global Perspective 2nd Edition, Milton: John Wiley & Sons Inc.

5
CHAPTER

A BEHAVIOURAL MODEL OF E-BANKING USAGE

Guendalina Capece and Domenico Campisi

Keywords E-Banking Usage, Behavioural Model,Satisfaction

INTRODUCTION

The financial and economic crisis, which began in 2008, permeating throughout the production and service sectors, influencing business performances (e.g. [1,2]), pushed companies to develop new and innovative customer-oriented services in order to maintain competitiveness against competitors. In this paper we analyse the available pure and hybrid e-banking services in Italy and examine the role of passive and proactive users. Recent research efforts have continuously suggested that efficiency increases with the level of e- banking usage. With reference to different countries in Europe, efficiency augments the overall capacity of users to adapt to new technologies or ways of doing business by improving personal ability to draw new results from traditional channels [3-7]. Even though e-banking is a predominantly goal-directed service, the computer- mediated channel provides wider possibilities for hedonic perceptions and behaviours [8,9].

The interactive nature of online channels opens new possibilities for exploratory behaviour, traditionally linked to intrinsic motivation [10-14]. The literature refers to the Internet as a channel that simultaneously provides recreational and utilitarian features [15-18]. However, despite the evidence that online banking provides many advantages, such as faster transaction speed and lower handling fees [19], there are still a large group of customers who are reluctant to adopt such services [20,21]. Understanding the reasons for this resistance would be useful for bank managers in formulating strategies aimed at increasing online banking usage.

Citation: Guendalina Capece, and Domenico Campisi, A Behavioural Model of E-Banking Usage, DOI: 10.5772/56606.

The challenge of this work is therefore to prove the existence of the flow construct (also called cognitive absorption or playfulness) as representative of the hedonic component at a typical goal-directed service such as internet banking. In our study the basic assumption is that banking consumers have to be proactive in detecting relevant trends and early signals provided by the environment within which the organization operates. We measure the potential e-banking usage by means its effective usage. Then, we investigate the behaviour of users, identifying the major causes influencing real adopters' satisfaction and usage and the impact of these causes on the intensity of use. The analysis is based on a panel of 495 real online clients, allowing the profiling of the Italian adopter to discover the causes of factual usage and outline strategies for the growth of e-banking services in this country.

Although several research projects have focused on the factors that impact on the adoption of Information and Communication Technologies (ICTs) or Internet over the past decade [22-29], there is limited empirical work which captures the success factors or positive factors of online banking to help form a strategic agenda. In this study, we explore and integrate the advantages of online banking to develop a predictor named "satisfaction" to explain and predict customer intention to adopt online banking. Our research may give practitioners an increased understanding of customers' risk perceptions which can then be used to develop strategies and trust-building mechanisms [30-34] to encourage online trading adoption. Indeed, in order to gain and maintain the long lasting trust of their customers, companies have to adopt a socially responsible behaviour aligning their conduct to consumer values and beliefs [35,36]. In particular, in the banking sector customers are more sensible to trust issues [37].

The main purposes of this study are twofold:

The first aim is to investigate whether satisfaction significantly impacts customers' behavioural intention to use online banking. The second aim is to clarify which factors are more influential in affecting the decision to use online banking.

The paper is organized into six sections. In the next section we discuss the advantages of online banking. In Section 3 we provide the preliminaries and the background material for our study. Then, we focus the objective of our study, outlining a model of the e-banking usage, and propose the related measurement framework. Reliability measures and construct validity measures are carried out. Finally, we present a short discussion of the implications of the research and consider possible future directions for research in the concluding section.

THE ADVANTAGES OF ONLINE BANKING

Online banking has recently come to be considered as one of the most effective banking transaction methods [38] because it possesses many advantages which offline banking channels cannot offer. Online banking managers aim to utilize these advantages to increase the online banking adoption rate.

Based to a certain extent on reasons offered by Lee [39], there are two main types of perceived benefits, which can be categorized as direct and indirect advantages. Direct advantages refer to immediate and tangible benefits that customers would enjoy by using online banking. For example, customers can benefit from series of services [40], as a wider range of financial benefits, faster transaction speed, and increased information transparency. First, this wider range of financial benefits includes the lower transaction handling fees, higher deposit rates, opportunities to win prizes and extra credit card bonus points. Second, the faster transaction speed obviously means that time can be saved since online banking does not need paper documents, the processing of which can give rise to errors and delays, and which also requires more personnel. Online banking automates this process by mediating transactions through websites and electronic data interchange, and can also reduce the need for customers to communicate with bank staff regarding transaction details because these can be obtained from a website. Third, during the transaction, online banking allows customers to monitor contractual performance at any time, or to confirm delivery automatically. In other words, more relevant information is immediately available and transparent to customers.

Indirect advantages are those benefits that are more intangible and difficult to measure [41,42]. For example, online banking allows customer to perform banking transactions anywhere in the world and enjoy 24-hour service, as well as offering customers more investment opportunities and services, such as stock quotations and news updates. The factors outlined above are the perceived benefits that will be considered in the preliminary model of online banking adoption [43].

A MODEL OF E-BANKING USAGE

In this section we investigate the factors influencing the usage of e–banking services and measure both the satisfaction level of consumers and their level of usage. The starting point is based on recent studies on intrinsic motivation in online banking [44,45]. In particular, starting from a recent paper dealing with the role of intrinsic motivation in Portuguese Internet banking [46,47], we focus our interest on the satisfaction levels modelled both as constituent elements of the service (perceived quality and usage facility) and elements related to behavioural elements (intrinsic motivation) [48- 50]. The Theory of Planned Behaviour (TPB) has been proven successful in predicting and explaining human behaviour across various information technologies [49, 51-53]. According to the TPB, a person's actual behaviour in performing certain actions is directly influenced by his or her behavioural intention and, in turn, is jointly determined by his or her attitude, subjective norms and perceived behavioural controls towards the behaviour. Behavioural intention is a measure of the strength of one's willingness to exert effort in certain behaviours. Attitude explains a person's favourable or unfavourable assessment regarding the behaviour in question. A favourable or unfavourable attitude directly influences the strength of the behaviour and beliefs regarding the likely outcome.

Notice that the three elements satisfaction, perceived quality and intrinsic motivation are strongly linked by the intrinsic interactive nature of the service. The perceived quality can be revealed through a number of components such as quality of services and information, comfort and trust in the instrument. In accordance with these aims, we formulate a series of research hypotheses (H) to be tested by means of our online technology acceptance model:

- H1: The quality level of the banking service and information service has a positive impact on the satisfaction level.
- H2: The perceived comfort perception has a positive impact on the satisfaction level.
- H3: Trust in the e-banking instruments positively influences the satisfaction level. Furthermore, if we believe that ease of use (user friendliness) has a positive impact on the level of service and client satisfaction, we can assume:
- H4: The easier the e-banking instruments usage is, the higher the satisfaction level.
- H5: The easier the e-banking utilization is perceived to be, the higher the quality of services and information.
- H6: There exists a positive trade-off between quality of services and information gathering.

The net, thanks to its interactive nature, induces explorative behaviour in the e-banking services. This intrinsic motivation [54] easily induces the flow-state (a pleasant activity produces a "friendly" usage of the web instrument and increases the user's inclination to repeat the experience). Then, we can hypothesize the following:

- H7: The intrinsic motivation to use e-banking services is related to the flow [55,56].
- H8: The flow perception is positively related to the level of interest. Furthermore, we wish to establish whether the satisfaction level is positively related to the flow and that the latter is influenced by the quality of service and information [56-59]. Therefore, we presume that:
- H9: A higher flow perception leads to a higher level of satisfaction.
- H10: A higher quality of service and information has a positive impact on the flow state.

The proposed ten research hypotheses are linked by causality relationships modelled as illustrated in the flow chart design in Fig. 1.

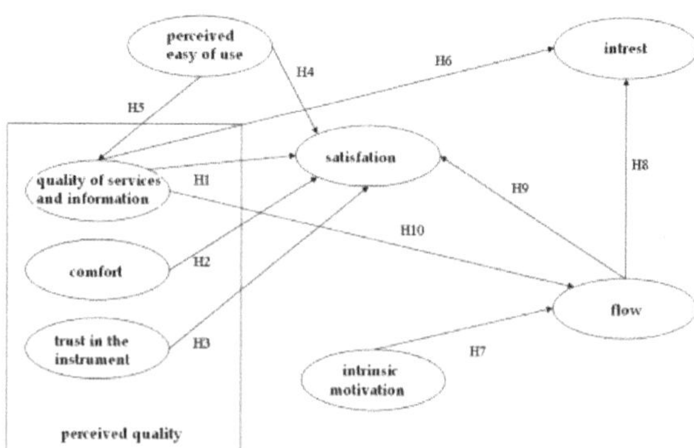

Figure 1: Flow chart: the acceptance model and research hypotheses.

Our research hypotheses aim to answer the following research questions: Does the perceived quality lead to client satisfaction (H1, H2, and H3)? Does the ease of use have a positive impact on the satisfaction level (H4) and on the quality of services and information (H5)? Does the quality of services and information have a positive impact on the level of attention (H6)? Does the intrinsic motivation, proper of users with explorative behaviours, lead to a higher level of involvement measured by the flow state (H7)? Does the flow perception have a positive impact on the level of attention (H8)? Are high flow levels positively related to the level of satisfaction in the use of the service (H9)? Does the quality of services and information have a positive impact on the flow state (H10)?

AN APPLICATION TO THE ITALIAN CASE

The model depicted in Figure 1 was tested on a panel of 495 e-banking users. The private bank helped to email invitation letters to its users with a message explaining the need to understand their (the users') experience in their initial adoption of online banking services. The invitation letter also linked to a website where users could fill out an online questionnaire.

To encourage participation, incentives of the latest models of mobile phones and MP3 players were offered as lucky draw prizes. To reduce the possibility of a respondent participating in the survey more than once, each respondent was required to provide his/her mobile phone number in the survey. Later, duplicate mobile phone numbers were used to filter out multiple responses from the same respondent. Users were free to participate at their own discretion and the survey was in anonymous form. This online survey, which yielded 564 responses, was conducted over three months, with incomplete responses and missing values deleted, resulting in a sample size of 495 users with an overall response rate of 87%. The first part of the survey concerns basic information about respondents' characteristics, including gender, age, education, occupation, and experience in using online banking.

Sample demographics are depicted in Table 1. 65.5% percent of the respondents were male and the remaining 35.5% were female. The majority of respondents (77.3%) were over 30 years old. 21.8% of the respondents were pure online users, while 78.2% used a conventional bank with e-banking services. Finally, 46.4% of respondents had graduated from high school and 53.6% had a university degree. The second part of the questionnaire was developed based on the constructs of our model.

Each respondent was asked to provide answers to each question in the form of a response on a multi-dimensional Likert scale from one to six. Likert scaling is a bipolar scaling method, measuring either positive or negative response to a statement. Level of agreement or disagreement is then measured. A pair-point scale is used. This is a forced-choice method since the middle option of "neither agree nor disagree" is not available. We wanted people to think before answering the questions and therefore we eliminated the "middle" response equivalent to "I don't know". The following interpretation of the numerical values was provided to the respondents:

- Strongly disagree
- Disagree
- Slightly disagree
- Slightly agree
- Agree
- Strongly agree.

Before conducting the main survey, we performed a pre- test to validate the instrument. The pre-test involved 15 respondents with more than three years' experience using online banking. Respondents were asked to comment on the length of the instrument, the format, and the wording of the scales. Therefore, the instrument has confirmed content validity.

Data set

The main indicators of the date on the socioeconomic nature of our marker sample are reported in Table 1.

Table 1: Univariate analysis of the sample

Variable	Category	Frequency	% of the sample
Sex	Male	324	65.5
	Female	171	34.5
Age	21-30	112	22.7
	31-40	171	34.5
	41-50	135	27.3
	51-63	77	15.5
Job	Student, Retired	41	8.2
Job	Employee	306	61.8
	Autonomous	54	10.9
	Other	94	19.1
Studies	University Degree	265	53.6
	Graduated	230	46.4
Bank	Online	108	21.8
	Conventional with e-banking services	387	78.2
Experience	High	326	65.8
	Normal	169	34.2

The sample is composed of skilled users with experience of several years and with a frequency of use of more than once a week. We further distinguish heavy users (daily frequency usage) and normal users (weekly frequency). With reference to our sample, the main results on the frequency of usage and the relative banking operations are respectively reported in Table 2 and Figure 2 below.

Table 2: Usage frequencies

Usage	Frequency	Percentage
1 day	85	17.3
2 days	68	13.6
3 days	68	13.6
1 week	148	30.0
2 weeks	126	25.5
Total	495	100.0

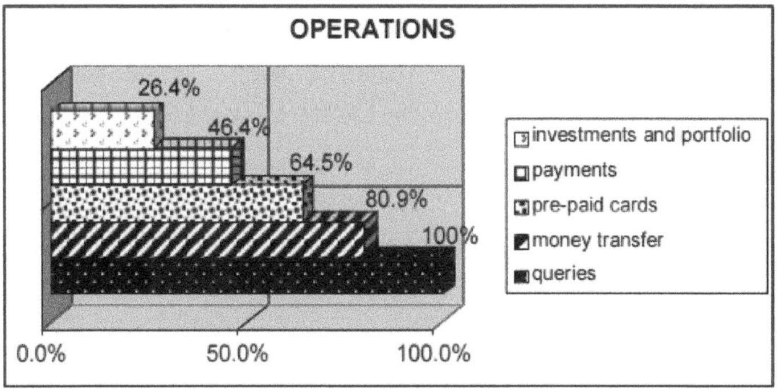

Figure 2: Lines of usage.

Measurement

The statistical analysis was conducted using standard SPSS software. The questionnaire contained multiple measurement items related to each construct explained in the previous section. The results of the reliability tests are reported below. In an attempt to avoid causal ambiguity, various statistical instruments have been used.

It should be noted that the concept of causal ambiguity here refers to the poor understanding of the idiosyncratic features of the new environment in which the new technology will be used. Reliability is of great importance when summed scales are used as predictor components. Since summed scales are an assembly of interrelated items designed to measure underlying constructs, it is important to understand whether the same set of items would elicit the same responses if the same questions were recast and re-administered to the same respondents. The internal reliability of each construct was analysed by means of Cronbach's alpha index, which indicates the reliability of factors extracted from the multi-point scale; the higher the score (between 0 and 1), the more reliable the item. The next step is to perform an exploratory factor analysis, in order to test the validity of the five constructs outlined above. Finally, armed with the background knowledge provided by the reliability measure and the exploratory factor analysis, the statistical hypotheses are then tested by means of a standard regression analysis.

Reliability assessment

As stated above, the internal reliability [54] of each construct is analysed by means of the Cronbach's alpha index. The Cronbach's alpha increases when the correlation between the items increases.

The complete set of results can be seen in Table 3 below. Three of the items were dropped as they were found not to be significant. The remaining Cronbach's alpha coefficients had significant values with scores of greater than or equal to 0.7, the recommended lower bound reported in the scientific literature (see [60] for details). Average values were achieved by Trust (0.77), Flow (0.76), and Perceived ease of use (0.75). Lower, but acceptable, values were achieved by Quality in products and information (0.71) and Comfort (0.70).

Table 3: Assessment: summary of measurement scales

Variables	Number of items	Cronbach's Alpha	Mean	Standard Deviation	Sample
Service	6	0.711	4.97	1.02	495
Comfort	2	0.707	5.79	0.44	495
Trust	2	0.775	5.25	0.77	495
Perceived ease of use	2	0.754	5.14	0.98	495
Satisfaction	2	0.810	5.25	0.85	495
Intrinsic motivation	2	0.891	3.02	1.84	495
Flow	4	0.766	3.2	1.76	495
Interest	3	0.833	4.13	0.98	495

Mean values well depict our reference model. High values are reached by the perceived Quality of service and Comfort (5.79). We can deduce that time-saving and comfort predominates over the other factors and that security factors are also appreciated. The relatively high scores in the remaining factors show that the encountered difficulties are considered non-heavy by users, and that sufficient satisfaction levels in the use of the e-banking instruments are reached. We can therefore conclude that users do not limit themselves to a passive use of the web services, but assume an explorative behaviour with respect to the online banking offer.

Validity of the constructs

In order to assess whether our constructs are distinct and well-posed, a factorial validity analysis was performed. In particular, a principal component analysis using Varimax Oblique Rotation with Kaiser Normalization was performed on the 14 items. Rotation converged in seven iterations. Data were pooled across the items for a total of 500 observations. It may be observed in the results shown in Table 3 that each item loads on a distinct factor. This is why only the first eight factorial components are fully reported in Table 4.

To complete the study, the two components connected with Eigen values smaller than one (which explain more than then 72.5% of the total data) were considered. Overall, the factorial analysis supports the model structure and the hypothesized constructs. Therefore, a one-to-one correspondence map between statistical factors and research hypotheses can be constructed. The factors, shown in Table 5, are ranked in order of significance, thus demonstrating the accuracy of the conjectures. The number of principal components exactly coincides with the number of constructs. With reference to Table 5, it can be observed that the second component corresponds to items 21, 22 and 23 whereas the fourth component relates to items 5 and 9. Furthermore, items 8 and 20 are clustered around the sixth component; 7 and 12 around the seventh, and 10 and 11 around the eighth. In addition, in the first component we can observe variables associated to items 2, 4, 19.

As far as the third component is concerned, we can observe that the variables associated to items 14, 15, 16, and 17 are highly correlated, whereas the factor related to item 13 does not allow a net separation from the fifth component (loads of 0.348 and 0.400 respectively).

Table 4: Components and explained variance

Item	Initial Eigenvalues			Rotation Sums of Squared Loadings		
	Total	% of Variance	Cumulative %	Total	% of Variance	Cumulative %
1	5.053	21.971	21.971	2.585	11.241	11.241
2	3.424	14.885	36.856	2.397	10.423	21.663
3	1.922	8.355	45.210	2.251	9.785	31.448
4	1.509	6.561	51.772	2.026	8.810	40.259
5	1.377	5.989	57.760	2.024	8.799	49.058
6	1.278	5.558	63.319	1.921	8.353	57.410
7	1.141	4.959	68.278	1.872	8.138	65.548
8	1.004	4.365	72.643	1.632	7.095	72.643
9	.892	3.880	76.523			
10	.739	3.215	79.738			
11	.709	3.084	82.822			
12	.633	2.753	85.575			
13	.547	2.379	87.954			
14	.518	2.254	90.208			
15	.388	1.685	91.893			
16	.335	1.455	93.348			
17	.316	1.374	94.722			
18	.296	1.287	96.010			
19	.240	1.044	97.054			
20	.210	.912	97.965			
21	.182	.793	98.758			
22	.149	.648	99.406			
23	.137	.594	100.000			

Validity of the constructs

The model presented in Section 2 considered as major factors influencing the e-banking usage the ease of use and the perceived quality. The quality of service has been evaluated exploring three parameters: quality of service and information, comfort and trust. We further investigated the existence of explorative behaviours generally characterized by flow. Finally, we assumed that people heavily involved in e-banking usage believe that this instrument is interesting.

We are now ready to confirm our assumptions by means of a regression analysis. Assuming a linear relationship between each couple of constructs, we presume as independent the variable associated to the exiting arrow and as dependent the variable associated to the entering arrow. Notice in Table 6 that almost all of the coefficients are significant, which therefore confirms the research hypotheses, even though in some cases we arrive at the lower bound of acceptability. This is particularly striking for the H9 hypothesis (the incidence of flow on the level of satisfaction) where the corrected R^2 is close to zero (0.015) and there is a p-value larger than 0.001. We can therefore conclude that the satisfaction level is caused by the intrinsic quality of the service, whereas the interactive experience given by the flow does not make any relevant contribution.

Table 5: Rotated Component Matrix

	Components							
	1	2	3	4	5	6	7	8
1) satisfaction1	-.065	.109	,146	,206	.821	.127	.021	.055
2) flow1	.833	-.023	.057	-.130	-.103	.039	.127	-.044
3) satisfaction 2	-.065	.117	.166	.079	.852	.141	.016	.139
4) flow2	.798	.137	.164	-.031	.028	-.110	.219	.035
5) ease 1	-.226	-.003	.089	.815	.169	.070	.008	.127
6) flow3	.496	.217	-.183	-.185	.247	-.067	-.224	.067
7) motivation 1	.222	.063	-.012	-.006	.095	-.094	.899	-.028
8) comfort1	.050	-.002	.010	.169	.003	.798	-.082	.182
9) ease 2	-.039	.023	-.063	.872	.081	.079	.097	.167
10) trust 1	.132	.110	.153	.343	.190	.069	-.033	.716
11) trust 2	-.089	.157	.163	.154	.114	.302	-.024	.803
12) motivation 2	.174	.118	-.002	.125	-.061	.007	.913	.007
13) quality 1	-.172	.192	.348	-.024	.400	.337	.019	.217
14) quality 2	.058	.184	.699	-.102	.082	.170	-.039	.042
15) quality 3	.132	.167	.536	.468	.057	.293	.099	.052
16) quality 4	.265	.056	.712	.173	.287	-.164	-.048	-.071
17) quality 5	-.227	.204	.302	.223	.268	.247	-.073	-.364
18) quality 6	-.090	.144	.711	-.004	.070	.017	.059	.374
19) flow4	.781	.100	.054	.030	-.203	.017	.217	.035
20) comfort2	-.075	.054	.074	.029	.211	.834	-.004	.010
21) interest 1	.115	.816	.213	.059	.105	.024	.053	.160
22) interest 2	.173	.830	.109	-.010	.167	.014	.153	.094
23) interest 3	.013	.848	.102	.029	.019	.080	.005	-.026

Extraction Method: Principal Component Analysis;
Rotation Method: Varimax with Kaiser Normalization;
Rotation converged in 7 iterations

Table 6: Rotated Component Matrix

Hypothesis	Coefficient	p-value	Adjusted R^2
H_1	0.477	0.22	< 0.001
H_2	0.339	0.107	< 0.001
H_3	0.362	0.123	< 0.001
H_4	0.350	0.114	< 0.001
H_5	0,372	0.131	< 0.001
H_6	0.378	0.135	< 0.001
H_7	0.355	0.118	< 0.001
H_8	0.332	0.102	< 0.001
H_9	-0.156	0.015	0.103
H_{10}	0.373	0.131	< 0.001

IMPLICATIONS OF THE STUDY

The results of this study highlight some important issues related to customer attitudes towards online banking. First, although both perceived quality and ease of use have a significant influence on satisfaction, this study reveals that the first is a more influential factor, implying that controlling the quality of online banking is more important than providing benefits through ease of use. This finding is particularly important for managers as they decide how to allocate resources to retain and expand their current customer base. However, building an online transaction environment perceived as good quality is much more difficult than providing one that is perceived as easy to use, because the latter characteristic can heavily depend on the confidence users have with ICT instruments and the Internet. Therefore, online banking companies need to search for quality improvement strategies that might assist in inspiring high confidence and satisfaction in customers. This approach is likely to ensure a stable theory development. Hence, the proposed model makes an important contribution to the emerging literature on e-commerce, especially with regard to online banking.

In terms of theory building, this study attempts to develop a new theory by establishing a new significant and important variable for online banking: satisfaction. The empirical results show that quality of service and perceived ease of use have significant effects on satisfaction in using online banking. Therefore, both these factors have significant effects on the intention to use the online banking as a daily instrument for banking operations. According to the risk theory of consumer behaviour [61], Bauer indicated that benefits deriving from satisfaction are often accompanied by risks; in terms of future research, it would be interesting to investigate the casual relationship between these two elements.

RESULTS AND CONCLUSIONS

This paper aims to develop a behavioural model to predict and explain customers' intentions with regard to adopting online banking.

In order to reach our goal we analysed the available e- banking services in Italy and examined the complex relationships among the different market players (pure and hybrid online banks, passive and proactive users). We considered a panel of active users, defined as those accessing on–line services at least once every two weeks. We further distinguished heavy users (with an access of at least once every 1-3 days) and normal users (with an access of at least once every 1-2 weeks). Heavy users turned out to be younger (21-30 years old) than normal users (50-63 years old). Heavy users utilize Internet services more intensively and are more accustomed to the virtual bank. Older people use online services less intensively, seeing them as a complementary channel of conventional usage. We investigated the quality of the available services in the fundamental three dimensions: intrinsic quality of services and information, comfort and trust in the instrument.

On this basis we formulated ten different research hypotheses. For each construct we made use of 2-6 items whose correctness was verified through a Reliability Assessment (computation of Cronbach's alpha coefficients applied to the replies). The validity of the constructs had been further confirmed by a factorial analysis. Finally, the interdependence relations have been investigated by means of a linear regression analysis. Our aim was to provide a more comprehensive investigation covering both the positive and negative aspects of online banking. The results show that the proposed model has good explanatory power and confirms its robustness in predicting customers' intentions to use such services.

From a practical point of view we can state that the e- banking service is in an affirmative phase. In particular, the passage from an informative, monitoring use of such instruments towards a transaction operative use has been evidenced. Italian users have a high level of satisfaction and trust in online banking; they also declare themselves confident with the instrument.

REFERENCES

1. Capece G, Cricelli L, Di Pillo F, Levialdi N (2008) A productivity analysis of the Italian gas retail market. Environmental Economics and Investment Assessment II, Aravossis, Brebbia e Gomez eds, WIT Press, UK, pp. 43-52.
2. Capece G, Bazzica P (2013) A practical proposal for a "Competence Plan Fulfillment" Key Performance Indicator. Knowledge and Process Management 20(1): 40–49.
3. Barroso C, Martín E (1999) Nivel de servicio y retención de clientes: el caso de la banca en España. Revista Española de Investigación de Marketing- ESIC 3: 9-36.
4. Bracchi G, Francalanci C, Giorgino M (2000) Internet banking. Tecnologia, organizzazione e valutazioni economiche. Italy: Egea. 232p.
5. Bauer H, Hammerschmidt M (2002) Financial portals in the internet. WSEAS Conference on E-Commerce, Athens, Greece.
6. Bauer H, Hammerschmidt M, Falk T (2005) Measuring the quality of e-banking portals. International Journal of Bank Marketing 23: 153–175.

7. Deutsche Bank Research (2006) Online banking – What we learn from the differences in Europe. Available: http://www.dbresearch.com/PROD/DBR_INTERNET_EN-PROD/PROD0000000000196129.pdf

8. Webster J, Trevino L, Ryan L (1993) The Dimensionality and Correlates of Flow in Human Computer Interactions. Computers in Human Behavior 9: 411–426.

9. Shang R-A, Chen Y-C, Lysander S (2004) Extrinsic versus intrinsic motivations for consumers to shop on line. Information & Management 42: 401–413.

10. Davis F, Bagozzi R, Warshaw P (1989) User acceptance of computer technology: a comparison of the two theoretical models. Management Science 35: 982–1003.

11. Ghani JA, Supnick R, Rooney P (1991) The Experience of Flow in Computer-Mediated and in Face-to-Face Groups. Proceedings of the Twelfth International Conference on Information Systems, New York, NY, 229-237.

12. Ghani JA, Deshpande SP (1994) Task Characteristics and the Experience of Optimal Flow in Human- Computer Interaction. Journal of Psychology 128: 381-391.

13. Ghani JA (1995) Flow in Human Computer Interactions: Test of a Model. In: Carey J, editor. Human Factors in Information Systems: Emerging Theoretical Bases. New Jersey: Ablex Publishing Corp. pp. 291-311.

14. Agarwal R, Karahanna E (2000) Time Flies When You're Having Fun: Cognitive Absorption and Beliefs About Information Technology Usage. MIS Quarterly 24: 665–694.

15. Sun H, Zhang P (2006a) The role of moderating factors in user technology acceptance. Journal of Human–Computer Studies 64: 53–78.

16. Sun H, Zhang P (2006b) Causal relationships between perceived enjoyment and perceived ease of use: An alternative approach. Journal of the Association for Information Systems 7: 618–645.

17. Sun H, Zhang P (2008) An exploration of affect factors and their role in user technology acceptance: Mediation and causality. Journal of the American Society for Information Science and Technology 59: 1252–1263.

18. Eurostat News Releases (2012) Internet access and use in 2012 More than half of internet users post messages to social media... ...and over 60% read news online, STAT/12/185. Available: http: //europa.eu/rapid/press-release_STAT-12 185_en.htm

19. Kalakota R, Whinston AB (1997), Electronic Commerce: A Manager's Guide. New York: John Wiley and Sons..

20. Kuisma T, Laukkanen T, Hiltunen M (2007) Mapping the reasons for resistance to internet banking: a means-end approach. Int J Inform Manage 27(2):75– 85.

21. Littler D, Melanthiou D (2006) Consumer perceptions of risk and uncertainty and the implications for behaviour towards innovative retail services: the case of internet banking. J Retailing Consum Serv 13(6): 431–43.

22. Campisi D, Tesauro C (1992) The diffusion and spatial distribution of new telecommunication technologies in the Italian region of Campania. Technovation. 12 (6): 355-368.
23. Capece G, Costa R (2009) Measuring knowledge creation in Virtual Teams through the Social Network Analysis. Knowledge Management Research and Practice 7 (4): 329-338.
24. Di Pillo F , Cricelli L, Gastaldi M, Levialdi N (2010) Asymmetry in mobile access charges: is it an effective regulatory measure? NETNOMICS: Economic Research and Electronic Networking 11 (3): 291-314.
25. Capece G, Campisi D (2011) Technological change and innovation behaviour in high level education: An international comparison between Italian and Portuguese samples. Knowledge and Process Management 18(1): 67–74.
26. Capece G, Campisi D (2013) User satisfaction affecting the acceptance of an e-learning platform as a mean for the development of the human capital. Behaviour & Information Technology 32(4): 335-343.
27. Capece G, Costa R (2013) The new neighbourhood in the internet era: network communities serving local communities. Behaviour & Information Technology 32(5): 438-448.
28. Heijden Hvd (2003) Factors influencing the usage of websites: the case of a generic portal in the Netherlands. Inform Manage 40:541–9.
29. Taylor S, Todd P (1995) Assessing IT usage the role of prior experience. MIS Quart 19(4):561–70.
30. Lee MKO, Turban E (2001) A Trust Model for Consumer Internet Shopping. International Journal of Electronic Commerce 6(1): 75-91.
31. McKnight DH, Chervany NL (2001) What Trust Means in E-Commerce Customer Relationships: An Interdisciplinary Conceptual Typology. International Journal of Electronic Commerce 6(2): 35–59.
32. Papadopoulou P, Andreou A, Kanellis P, Martakos D (2001) Trust and relationship building in electronic commerce. Internet Research: Electronic Networking Applications and Policy 11(4): 322–332.
33. Ratnasingham P (1998) The Importance of Trust in Electronic Commerce. Information Research. Electronic Networking Applications and Policy 8(4): 313–321.
34. Schoder D, YinP-L (2000) Building Firm Trust Online. Communications of the ACM 43(12): 73–79.
35. Calabrese A, Costa R, Menichini T, Rosati F (2013) Does Corporate Social Responsibility Hit the Mark? A Stakeholder Oriented Methodology for CSR Assessment. Knowledge and Process Management 20 (2): DOI: 10.1002/kpm.1406.
36. Costa R, Menichini T (2013) A multidimensional approach for CSR assessment: the importance of the stakeholder perception. Expert Systems With Applications. 40 (1): 150-161.

37. Calabrese A, Costa R, Menichini T, Rosati F, Sanfelice G (2013) Turning CSR-Driven Opportunities in Competitive Advantages: a Two-Dimensional Model. Knowledge and Process Management. 20 (1): 50-58.
38. Huang S-M, Hung Y-C, Yen DC (2005) A study on decision factors in adopting an online stock trading system by brokers in Taiwan. Decis Support Syst 40(2): 315–28.
39. Lee M-C (2008) Predicting behavioral intention to use online banking. In: Proceedings of the 19th International Conference on Information Management, Taiwan.
40. Calabrese A, Scoglio F (2012) Reframing the past: A new approach in service quality assessment. Total Quality Management & Business Excellence. 23 (11-12): 1329-1343.
41. Costa, R (2012) Assessing Intellectual Capital efficiency and productivity: an application to the Italian yacht manufacturing sector. Expert Systems With Applications. 39 (8): 7255-7261.
42. Calabrese A, Costa R, Menichini, T (2013) Using Fuzzy AHP to manage Intellectual Capital assets: an application to the ICT service industry. Expert Systems With Applications 40 (9): 3747-3755.
43. 43.Lee M-C (2009) Factors influencing the adoption of internet banking: An integration of TAM and TPB with perceived risk and perceived benefit. Electronic Commerce Research and Applications 8(3): 130–141.
44. Fagan M, Neill S, Wooldridge B (2008) Exploring the intention to use computers: an empirical investigation of the role of intrinsic motivation, extrinsic motivation and perceived ease of use. Journal of Computer Information Systems 48: 31–37.
45. Liao Z, Cheung M (2002) Internet-based e-banking and consumer attitudes: an empirical study. Information and Management 39: 283–295.
46. Cruz P, Munoz P (2004) Flow in e-bank satisfaction measure. In: Proceedings of the 33th EMAC Conference, Murcia, Spain.
47. Cruz P, Munoz P (2007). Are Heavy Users Having Fun? The Role of Intrinsic Motivation: Portuguese Internet Banking Evidences. In: Proceedings of the 10th IBIMA Conference on Innovation and Knowledge Management in Business Globalization, Kuala Lumpur, Malaysia.
48. Rust RT, Oliver RL (1994) Service Quality: new directions in theory and practice. Thousand Oaks, California: Sage Publications, Inc. 300p.
49. Szymansky D, Hise R (2000) E-satisfaction: an initial examination. Journal of Retailing 76: 309–322.
50. Calabrese A (2012) Service productivity and service quality: A necessary trade-off? International Journal of Production Economics. 135 (2): 800-812.
51. Ajzen I (2002) Perceived behavioral control, self- efficacy, locus of control, and the theory of planned behavior. Journal of Applied Social Psychology 32: 665–683.

52. Ajzen I (1991) The theory of planned behavior. Organ Behav Hum Dec Proc 50(2): 121–79.
53. Mathieson K (1991) Predicting User Intentions: Comparing the Technology Acceptance Model with the Theory of Planned Behavior. Information Systems Research 2(3): 173–191.
54. Cruz P, Salo J, Munoz-Gallego P, Laukkanen T (2010) Heavy users of e-banking and Customer Experience Management: evidences on intrinsic motivation. Int. J. of Electronic Business 8(2): 187–209.
55. Day HI, Berlyne DE (1971) Intrinsic motivation. In: Lesser GS, editor. Psychology and educational practice. Glenview, Illinois: Scott Foresman, 294– 335pp.
56. Sandelands L, Glynn MA, Larson JR Jr. (1991) Control Theory and Social Behavior in the Workplace. Human Relations 44: 1107–1130.
57. Ghani JA, Supnick R, Rooney P (1991) The Experience of Flow in Computer-Mediated and in Face-to-Face Groups, In: Proceedings of the Twelfth International Conference on Information Systems, New York, 229–237pp.
58. Koufaris M (2002) Applying the Technology Acceptance Model and Flow Theory to Online Consumer Behavior. Information Systems Research 13(2): 205–223.
59. Koufaris M, Kambil A, LaBarbera (2001) PA Consumer Behavior in Web-Based Commerce: An Empirical Study. International Journal of Electronic Commerce 6(2): 115–138.
60. Stewart T (1986) Task fit, ease-of-use and computer facilities. Managing computer impact: An international study of management and organizations, In: Bjørn-Andersen N, Eason K, Robey D, editors, Managing computer impact. Norwood, NJ: Ablex, 63–76pp.
61. Bauer RA (1960) Consumer behavior as risk-taking. In: Hancock RS, editor. Dynamic marketing for a changing world. Chicago: American Marketing Association, 389–398pp.

6

CHAPTER

DEVELOPMENT OF A SECURED UNIFIED E-PAYMENT SYSTEM

Charles K. Ayo and Wilfred Isioma Ukpere

INTRODUCTION

E-Payment systems refer to the automated processes of exchanging monetary value among parties in business transactions and transmitting this value over the ICT networks. The common e-Payment channels include the payment cards (debit or credit), Online Web Portals, Point of Sales (POS) terminals, Automated Teller Machines (ATM), Mobile Phones, Automated Clearing House (ACH), direct debit/deposit and Real Time Gross Settlement (RTGS) system (Nnaka, 2009).

The wider patronage of e-Commerce is dependent on the availability of a secured and trusted e-Payment System (Baddeley, 2004). The various categories of e-Commerce include Business-to-Business (B2B): business transactions between organizations that involve companies buying and selling to each other; Business-to-Consumer (B2C): business transactions between organizations and consumers where goods and services are sold directly to the consumer; Consumer-to-Business (C2B): business transactions between consumers and organizations, where consumers can fix prices for both goods and services offered; and Consumer-to-Consumer (C2C): business transaction between consumers among others (Ayo, 2009). Therefore, appropriate considerations must be given to these categories so that the most suitable e-Payment system can be adopted.

According to Anderson (cited in Sumanjeet, 2009), e-Payment system was classified into:

- Online Credit Card Payment System
- Electronic Cheque System
- Electronic Cash System, and
- Smart Card-based Electronic Payment System.

Citation: K. Ayo and Wilfred Isioma Ukpere, Development of a Secured Unified E-Payment System, ISBN 978-953-51-0081-2.

Regardless of the adopted system, the problems militating against e-Payment as listed by Sumanjeet (2009), generally revolve around:

- Integrity: to ascertain that transmitted financial information is unchanged in • transit.
- Non-repudiation: to ascertain that all parties have non-deniable proof of receipt.
- Confidentiality: to ascertain that transactions are protected from possible eavesdroppers.
- Reliability: to ascertain that there is reduced possibility of failure.
- Authentication: to ascertain that there are reliable proofs of identities of all parties involved.
- Authorization: to ascertain that individuals are recognized and granted the desired rights and privileges.

Therefore, any reliable e-Payment System should guarantee privacy, integrity, compatibility, efficiency, acceptability, convenience, mobility, anonymity and low financial risk. The smart card-based e-Payment system is essentially a credit card sized plastic card with memory chips and probably an embedded microprocessor that offers greater storage capacity than the ordinary credit card. While the credit card stores a single charge account number in the magnetic stripe, the smart card can hold hundreds of such data, and can serve multiple identification purposes such as personal identification, bank account identification and transactions, health insurance identification among others (Sumanjeet, 2009). Therefore, the objectives of this paper is to design a unified (single) smart card-based e-Payment system that can be used for banking transactions in all the banks in Nigeria as well as serving other forms of identification.

Zulu (2006) identified the challenges of e-Payment in Africa as inadequate telecommunication infrastructure which include: connectivity failure in telephone lines; low Internet bandwidth; high Internet cost, unavailability of dedicated data service networks; and close financial networks as well as frequent power interruption. Similarly, he identified lack of proper legal and regulatory framework and low level of credit access as the other challenges. The threats notwithstanding, there are standard security features already developed to handle them. Some of the available solutions include public-key cryptography, digital signature and certificate, secure socket layer (SSL), and secure electronic transaction (SET) as well as the introduction of biometrics authentication among others (Pesonen, 1998; Zulu, 2006 and Ayo, 2009).

One of the greatest threats to e-Banking is the increasing trends of identity theft, which is a major challenge to the Internet age (Helmbrecht, 2008). Therefore, there is need for a technology that is safe, convenient and not too demanding on the part of the user because of the level of literacy in the developing nations of the world, particularly Nigeria. The other part of the paper is arranged as follows: section 2 presents the state of e-Payment in Nigeria; section 3 presents the research design; section 4 presents the system design; while section 5 presented the economic consideration of the design and; the conclusion of the work is presented in section 6.

THE STATE OF E-PAYMENT IN NIGERIA

Nigeria is predominantly a cash-based economy with a lot of cash in circulation. Analysts opined that the cash-based nature of payments in the country is responsible for the abysmally low level of participation in e-Commerce where the acceptable medium of settling transactions is e-Payment (Ojo, 2004; Ayo, 2007; & Ovia, 2002).

The Governor of the Central Bank of Nigeria embarked on bank recapitalization exercise as a strategic move to save the Nigerian banking sector from incessant failure and collapse (Nwachuku, 2005 and Gbolahan, 2005). The result of the exercise brought about a reduction of the 89 banks to 25 solid and strong banks through mergers, acquisition and recapitalization of asset base. As reported by Ayo et al. (2007), virtually all the 25 banks in Nigeria that survived the recapitalization exercise engaged the use of ICT for efficient service delivery. All the banks have one form of e-Payment system or the other.

Alao (2009) reported the colossal amount of money lost in Nigeria to ATM fraud through ATM card cloning, PIN theft among others and government had resorted to removing ATM from public places as well as installing security cameras at the ATM locations to track the activities of fraudsters. However, the level of ICT usage notwithstanding, the level of adoption of e-Banking by the citizen is still very low. Table 1 shows the distribution of the amount of currency in circulation from 2004 to 2008 in Nigeria.

Table 1: Distribution of the amount of Currency in Circulation

Year	Amount (₦billion)
2004	545.7
2005	642.4
2006	770.1
2007	960.5
2008	1,155.1
2009	1,184.3

Source: CBN Annual Reports: 2006, 2007, 2008, 2009

The table raised a lot of issues about the influence of ICT on e-Banking and the banking habit of Nigerians, particularly the volume of cash in circulation. The amount of currency in circulation has continued to increase in view of the various efforts of government. Tables 3 and 4 will help to shed more light on the inhibiting factors which probably revolve around lack of safety, trust and security.

It is evident from table 2 that the most prominent form of e-Payment system in Nigeria is the ATM card. It remained dominant over the years both in volume and value. The other media such as the Internet payment, POS and Mobile payments are still at their infancies. The level of involvement of these instruments of payment presents a clearer picture of the low level of involvement of Nigerians in e-Commerce, knowing fully well that ATM cards are not suitable for international settlement of transactions.

Table 2: Level of adoption of e-Payment system

Payment Instruments	Volume %			Value %		
	2006	2007	2008	2006	2007	2008
ATM	93.16	88.7	91.0	73.35	88.5	90.5
Web (Internet)	1.71	5.1	2.4	3.51	7.1	5.7
POS	4.83	2.4	1.8	23.04	4.3	3.7
Mobile	0.31	3.8	4.8	0.11	0.1	0.2

Source: CBN Annual Reports: 2006, 2007, 2008

Table 2: Level of adoption of e-Payment system

Payment Instruments	Value (₦' Billion) ($1 = ₦155)		
	2007	2008	2009
ATM	131.5	399.7	548.6
Web (Internet)	10.6	25.05	84.5
POS	6.4	16.12	11.04
Mobile	0.09	0.07	1.26

Source: CBN Annual Reports: 2007, 2008 and 2009

RESEARCH DESIGN

The research design is two-fold. On one hand, a set of questionnaire was designed and administered randomly to 300 respondents out which 239 were returned representing about 80%. Cronbach's reliability value of 0.782 was obtained, which attests to the reliability of the instrument. Pertinent questions about the demographic profile of respondents as well as the state and operations of ATM Card were asked and the data collected was analysed based on descriptive statistics using the SPSS and the results were presented in tables 3, 4 and 5. On the other hand, a design of the proposed unified Smart Card-based ATM was presented as well as its activity diagram.

Table 3: Demographic profile of Respondents

Gender of Respondents		
	Frequency	Percent
Male	140	58.6
Female	99	41.4
Total	239	100%
Age of Respondents		
	Frequency	Percent
<20	25	10.4
21 - 30	77	32.2
31 - 40	95	39.7
41 - 50	28	11.7
51+	14	5.9
Total	239	100%
Educational Level of Respondents		
	Frequency	Percent
Valid NONE	26	10.9
Primary School	4	1.7
High School	11	4.6
OND/NCE	24	10
BSc/HND degree	58	24.3
Post Graduate	102	42.7
Others	14	5.9
Total	239	100%
Sector where Respondents Work		
	Frequency	Percent
Valid Others	36	15.1
Finance	47	19.7
Manufacturing	33	13.8
Oil & Gas	13	5.4
Aviation	4	1.7
Education	21	8.8
IT & Telecom	85	35.6
Total	239	100%

Discussion

Out of the 239 respondents, about 59% of them are male while about 41% of them are female. From the age distribution, over 90% of the respondents are at least 20 years old. Keeping in mind that persons below the age of 18 years are not permitted to operate a bank accounts in Nigeria because that is seen as the age of apprenticeship. Furthermore, about 90% of the respondents have at least the first school leaving certificate (primary school), while only 10% of them (26 out of 239) did not indicate to have had any formal education at any level. Majority of the respondents (35.6%) work in the IT and Telecoms sector, followed by the finance sector (19.7%), the manufacturing sector

(13.8%), the education sector (8.8%) and those outside the finance, manufacturing, oil and gas, aviation, education and IT and Telecoms account for 15.1% of the respondents.

Table 4: Distribution of the respondents and banking transactions

Have Bank Accounts		
	Frequency	Percent
Valid None	2	8
No	3	1.3
Yes	234	97.9
Total	239	100
Number of ATM Cards Possessed		
	Frequency	Percent
Valid None	4	1.7
One	24	10
Two or More	211	88.3
Total	239	100

It is interesting to note that majority (about 98%) of the respondents operate a bank account. Also, about 88% of the respondents have two ATM cards or more. This gives validity to the proposed unified e-Payment system. Most of the respondents attested to the convenience of the ATM services (59%) as well as its simplicity (69%). However, its reliability (25%), safety (16.3%) and privacy (31.8%) are in doubt. Therefore, a greater percentage of the respondents disagreed with its reliability, safety and privacy features. However, most of the respondents favour the desirability of having a unified (single) ATM card for all banking transactions (36.8%) as well as the inclusion of a fingerprint reader on the teller machine (66.9%).

Table 5: Distribution of the respondents experience with ATM cards

	Agree	Disagree	Neutral	Do not Know	Total
Reliability of ATM Services	60 (25.1%)	97 (40.6%)	64 (26.8%)	18 (7.5%)	239 (100.0%)
Covenience of ATM Services	141 (59.0%)	56 (23.4%)	27 (11.3%)	15 (6.3%)	239 (100.0%)
Simplicity of ATM Services	165 (69.0%)	26 (10.9%)	31 (13.0%)	17 (7.1%)	239 (100.0%)
Safety of ATM Services	39 (16.3%)	123 (51.5%)	59 (24.7%)	18 (7.5%)	239 (100.0%)
Privacy of ATM Services	76 (31.8%)	90 (37.7%)	50 (20.9%)	23 (9.6%)	239 (100.0%)
Desirability of One ATM Card	88 (36.8%)	76 (31.8%)	36 (15.1%)	39 (16.3%)	239 (100.0%)
Include Fingerprint on ATM Machines	160 (66.9%)	19 (7.9%)	23 (9.6%)	37 (15.5%)	239 (100.0%)

SYSTEM DESIGN

A typical ATM has a keypad that is composed of:

1. Numeric Keys (0-9)
2. Character Keys (A – Z)
3. Operational buttons (Accept, Correction, Cancel)

The screen has eight (8) buttons arranged at the two sides (4 at each side). The features of the ATM are presented in table 6 and a typical picture shown in figure 1.

Table 6: Features of ATM Cards

Bank	Features		
	Numeric Keys • (0-9)	**Character Keys** • (A-Z, *, #, -, +)	**Operation buttons** • OK/Enter/Accept • Cancel • Correction/Change/Clear/Blank
UBA	Yes	Yes	OK, Change, Cancel and Blank
Oceanic	Yes	Yes	Accept, Correction, Cancel and Blank
InterContinental	Yes	Yes	Accept, Correction, Cancel and Blank
CMFB	Yes	No	Enter, Clear, Cancel and Blank

Table 6 shows the features of the ATM of four banks (UBA, Oceanic, Intercontinental and CMFB) in Nigeria. It is obvious that no special design is required. A common choice for the design is one that has numeric keys (0-9), character keys (A-Z, *, #, -, +), and operation buttons (OK, Change, Cancel), while the blank button can be replaced with the biometric fingerprint reader.

The structure in figure 2 represents the unified Smart Card-based ATM Card that has the possibility of being used for multiple identifications. Four (4) different ATM Cards for the four banks were considered and their features incorporated to arrive at this design. Furthermore, considering the spate of identity fraud, the law enforcement agencies should be able to check at random the various ATM locations to verify the identity of the carrier, though less frequently, hence the inclusion of the holder's passport, gender and or signature. Similarly, in case of accident the blood group is included. All other details are contained on the National Bank's Databank which is a repository of the identities of all banks' customers in Nigeria.

Figure 1: A typical ATM.

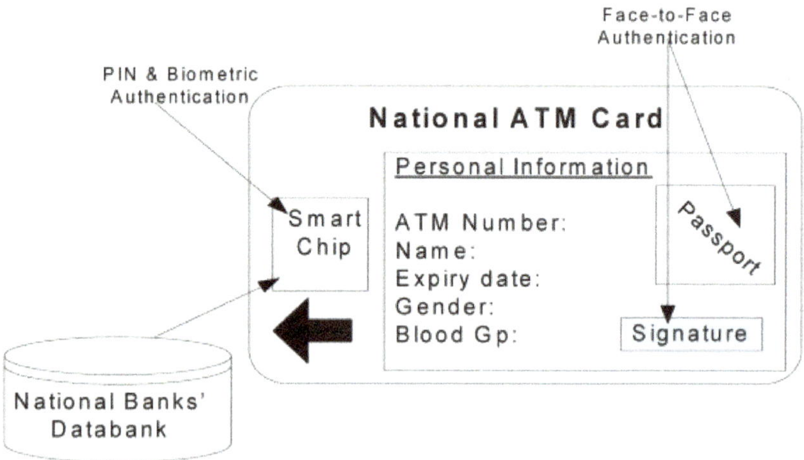

Figure 2: Smart Card-based ATM Card.

The activity diagram is shown in figure 3. It shows an additional layer of information, which is the selection of bank to transact business with since a single card is being used for several banks, after which the usual (old) display follows: User identification (PIN) but now with fingerprint capture; Selection of Operation (Enquiry, Withdrawal etc); Selection of amount of money; Request for receipts and Exit.

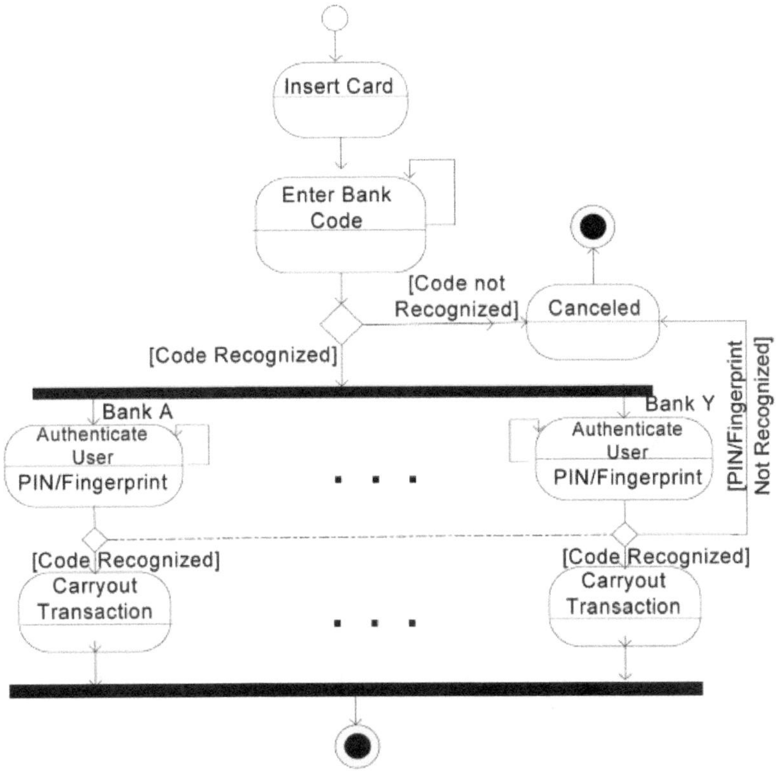

Figure 3: Activity diagram of the proposed system.

Furthermore, all other changes are software based. The ATM monitor has 8 operational buttons distributed at both sides of the screen. There are 25 banks in Nigeria, modeled banks A to Y, therefore 7 banks can be listed per screen while the 8th key reads "More" for the next screen of 7 banks and the "More" Key, more and more until all the banks are displayed.

COST IMPLICATION OF THE DESIGN

The cost implication of this design is very minimal on the part of the operators (banks). All the Keypads have a blank button which can be replaced with fingerprint reader through the USB Connection to the CPU. Similarly, the cost of card redesign is not considered a major challenge since each card has expiry date. Therefore, the cost of a new card is borne by the card holder. Similarly, all other changes are software based: the selection of banks and fingerprint authentication which can be taken for regular software update and the cost borne by the operator. However, the major task is the integration of the various banks accounts into the National Banks' Databank. This design approach will most likely be a cheaper alternative than installing security cameras at each location in addition to the cost of relocating the machines to more secure premises.

LIMITATIONS OF THE STUDY

From available statistics, 80% of the Nigerian populace are unbanked and 70% of the populace are illiterate (Ayo, 2009 and Okoegwale, 2011). Therefore, the limitations of the system include: high illiteracy level and lack of banking culture arising from lack of confidence and trust in the banking system.

SCOPE FOR FUTURE RESEARCH

Future research should investigate the Usability of the system as it is likely to impart positively on the banking habit if it is user friendly, reliable and efficient. Furthermore, since the Voting and Banking age is 18years, with increased percentage of the banking populace the card could be further developed for use as the voter's card with a reliable databank formed from the combined databases of the switching companies. Also, the incorporation of voice processing can help persons with disability, particularly the visually impaired to transact banking businesses.

CONCLUSION

The level of adoption of ICT in the banking sector in Nigeria is on the increase, yet the amount of cash in circulation is equally increasing, a situation which is attributable to lack of safety, security, privacy and reliability in the e-Payment instruments. Therefore, the introduction of a smart card-based ATM with biometric authentication will ameliorate these challenges. More than that, the design of a unified smart card-based ATM with biometric authentication is cost-effective and secured. No special design is required as the current system can accommodate the proposed features at minimal cost.

The fingerprint scanner can be accommodated on the keypad while a slight software redesign is required to accommodate a layer of service that will enable the user select a bank of choice. Most importantly, the number of ATM required is drastically reduced, which reduces the cost of production and renewal, and there is enhanced safety, security, and privacy. Furthermore, the fingerprint authentication will be a cheaper alternative than to relocate all ATMs in Nigeria (several thousands of them), to safer premises and the inclusion of security camera at each location.

REFERENCES

1. Alao Salimon (2009): Need to guard against ATM frauds, Financial Standard, Vol. 9, No. 479, pp17-18.
2. Ayo C. K. (2009): "Information Systems and Technologies". McKay Educational Series, 649p.
3. Ayo Charles K., Uyinomen O. Ekong, Fatudimu Ibukun Tolulope, and Adebiyi Ayodele A, (2007): M-Commerce Implementation in Nigeria: Trends and Issues, Journal of Internet Banking and Commerce, August 2007, Vol. 12, No.2, Available at: http://www.arraydev.com/commerce/JIBC/2007- 08/Ayo_final_PDF%20 Ready.pdf

4. Ayo Charles. K and Babajide Daniel O (2006): Designing a Reliable E-payment System: Nigeria a Case Study, Journal of Internet Banking and Commerce, August 2006, Vol. 11, No.2, Available at: http://www.arraydev.com/commerce/JIBC/2006-08/AYO.asp

5. Baddeley M. (2004): Using e-Cash in the new Economy: An Economic Analysis of Micropayment Systems, Journal of Electronic Research, Vol. 5, No. 7, pp239-253

6. CBN Report (2006): "CBN Annual Report for the Year 2006", Access date: June 2009, Available at: http://www.cenbank.org/documents/annualreports.asp

7. CBN Report (2007): "CBN Annual Report for the Year 2007", Access date: June 2009, Available at: http://www.cenbank.org/documents/annualreports.asp

8. CBN Report (2008): "CBN Annual Report for the Year 2008", Access date: June 2009, Available at: http://www.cenbank.org/documents/annualreports.asp

9. CBN Report (2009): "CBN Annual Report for the Year 2009", Access date: June 2009, Available at: http://www.cenbank.org/documents/annualreports.asp

10. Okoegwale Emmanuel (2011): "Nigeria Mobile Payment & Agency Banking Risk", accessed date: May, 2011, available at: http://mobilemoneyafrica.com/?p=3422

11. Gbolahan Dada (2005): Banking Sector Consolidation – Integration of IT applications is key, Finacial Standard, Vol. 6, No. 11, pg 24.

12. Helmbrecht U. (2008): The electronic identity card – A safe tool for unambiguous identification on the Internet, Acess date: Sept. 2009, Available at: https://www.bsi.bund.de/cae/servlet/contentblob/486520/publicationFile/3115 2/231008ANTS_VOE_pdf.pdf

13. Pesonen Lauri (1998): Electronic money, electronic identity impact on telecommunications Smart Card based solutions, Access date: June 2009, Available at: http://www.netlab.tkk.fi/opetus/s38001/s98/Session7_1.pdf

14. Nnaka Priscilia (2009): The Nigeria e-Payment System, Nigeria Monthly, Vol. 4, No. 8. pp25- 27

15. Nwachukwo Chris (2005): Recapitalization: Bank Workers endorse categorization, access date: 2005, Available at: http://allafrica.com/stories/200504010318.htm

16. Ojo A. T. (2004): "Enhancing the efficiency of the payment system: Conceptual Framework", A paper presented at the 9th CBN Monetary Policy Forum, Abuja, May 2004.

17. Ovia Jim (2002): "Payment System and Financial Innovations", A paper presented at the Annual Policy Conference, Nov. 2002.

18. Sumanjeet S. (2009): Emergence of Payment Systems in the age of Electronic Commerce: The State of Art, Global Journal of Business Research, vol. 2, no. 2, pp17-36.

19. Zulu Brenda (2006): E- payment a challenge for Africa, Access date: Sept. 2009, Available at: http://brendait.blogspot.com/2006/03/e-payment-challenge-for-africa.html

7
CHAPTER

STRENGTHENING RISK MANAGEMENT IN THE MIDST OF DOWNTURN TIMES

Amparo Marin de la Barcena

INTRODUCTION

Increasing Interest towards Risk Management improvement and timely identification of firms' failure are driving demand for the set-up of risk management principles, particularly within the financial and banking industries. Although there is no-one accepted definition for appropriate and infallible risk management principles, research in this field has led to identify best practices that have proven successful results at a variety of industries. Zooming into the Financial Sector, this case study is aimed to present six tips which have strengthened resilience to bankruptcy and economic losses at a leading European Bank which has depicted positive growth in the midst of the Downturn and world-wide economic recession.

THE BANKING BUSINESS AND THE IMPORTANCE OF RISK MANAGEMENT POLICIES

Financial Institutions' turnover is influenced by their risk management policies and the target risk profile they want to achieve in the market. For instance aiming towards a low-medium predictable risk profile, jointly with geographical diversification can be key elements of differentiation for a firm to achieve a leading position ahead of other industry players. [1]

The effectiveness of Risk management policies enacts as a firm's identity card, specifically in downturn times. This largely explains why seeking continuous improvement of risk management policies has stayed as a top priority for key industry players which have shown positive growth in the last years of financial turmoil.

"Risk Management means looking into the future" [2]

Citation: Marin de la Barcena, Strengthening Risk Management in the Midst of Downturn Times, http://dx.doi.org/10.5772/51008.

Fuelled by increasing competition, more stringent regulations and higher levels of interconnection amongst different players, the marketplace is becoming more and more complex. Concerned with such trend, financial institutions have realized that if they want to survive, they need to rely on a robust risk management framework, given by corporate organizational policies and supported by sophisticated IT systems and technology.

Since 2008, financial markets have experienced sharp declines. [3-5]. Analyzing several consumer surveys allows us to conclude that consumers, particularly those who have been severely affected by the crisis, would rather have opted for higher levels of prevention and anticipation, supported by management schemes with enough level of risk management considerations. The aforementioned risk management considerations are playing a greater role in companies' overall strategy and strategic choices. Indeed, companies are increasingly realizing the need of relying on strong risk governance and a sophisticated hedging program. This trend is largely explained due to the fact that these are seen as essential elements of a robust financial risk management program that will help them secure resilience to the economic problems affecting the marketplace.

To What Extent is ERM a "New" Concept?

In the last years ERM has been gaining momentum as a new concept, a new trend, a MUST HAVE. But perhaps in the midst of everyone rushing-up to implement it, it is worth stopping for a second in order to understand its meaning and ask ourselves ... is it really something new?

ERM stands for Enterprise Risk Management but its real origin is unclear. Some associate the birth of this concept to the definition of the Integrated Risk Framework by the Committee of Sponsoring Organizations (COSO) back in September 2004. Others believe that the starting point was in the 1970s when most of the Management theories arised. Being factual it would even be valid the mindset that it is a concept that has been in place since the beginning of times, when the Romans traded goods with the Carthagians. So if we agree that companies have managed risk forever the question here is what can Enterprises do better to manage Risk? Or what have been the best practices in risk management that companies have pursued to achieve recognized success?

Anyone involved in line management makes risk based decisions on a daily basis. The desire of such decision makers would be to count on a reliable crystal ball that would allow them to opt for the choices that would derive profit maximization.

Far from being the aforementioned magic tool, going down the road of ERM involves setting a structured approach or a reference framework to manage risk at companies. As of today, many companies have already understood the value proposition and experienced its benefits – which mainly tackle improved controls, better communications and decision-making, and a common language for risks. [7]. Nevertheless, for other companies the concern is still there: is there significant justification for an ERM program? Would the company really make different decisions if it did have an ERM program? According to some literature, a good ERM program has proven to enhance the company value through reduced costs, decreased variability in financial results, enhanced market reputation, and improved business decision-making. Such dimensions can even be measured and what is more, the Credit Rating Agencies have started considering these factors as part of their company assessment process. [8]

ELEMENTS OF A ROBUST RISK MANAGEMENT FRAMEWORK

Generally speaking, a robust risk management framework tackles five dimensions [9]:

1. Organizational culture
2. Processes
3. Technology
4. Risk measurement
5. Monitoring

Corporate Governance = Positive Risk Culture

Relying on strong corporate governance that diffuses a positive risk culture from the top to the bottom of the organization is an imperative to set up a robust risk management framework. Unless the employees of a firm are aligned and somehow willing to contribute towards improving risk management at their workplace, the organization will not be able to manage risk appropriately. The whole organization, from the last employee to the most powerful member of the Board of Directors should see some benefits in managing risk, and as long as this happens, a positive risk culture can be promoted across the overall organization.

From another angle, a positive risk culture can also be understood as that which is characterized by individual accountability, creativity, transparency and honesty. As long as employees understand the importance of accomplishing the organization's risk management approach, have a clear view of what such policies mean and believe they are transparent and honest, they will feel more creative and a healthy attitude of constant challenging of decisions and ideas will arise from them towards improvement the management of risk at their workplace.

Policies = Procedures

The second key element of a sound risk management framework is to have in place a set of policies and procedures, which are consistent with the organizational culture and clearly defined, with enough level of detail.

In a simplified view, the output of a firm's risk management strategy is determined by the balance between the firm's commercial objectives (appetite for risk) vs. its risk contention goals (risk control). In other words, organizations look for profit maximization at the lowest risk possible. (Figure 1)

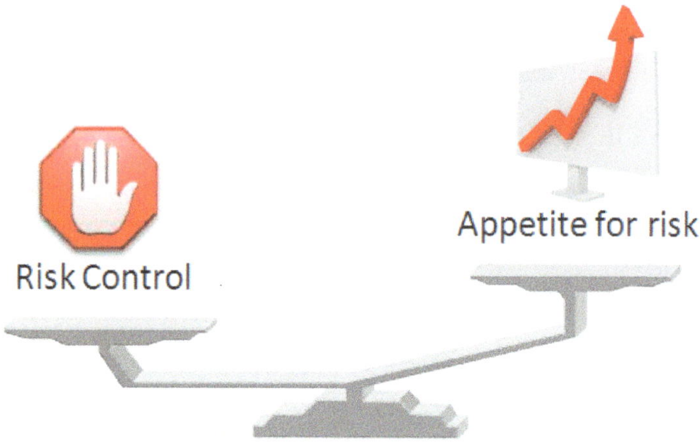

Figure 1: A company's Risk Management strategy should balance its appetite for risk over its measures for risk control.

Organizational processes are the means that a firm has to achieve its strategic goals. Therefore, firms' corporate policies should be well assembled, known by all and periodically updated not only with industry best practices, but also with the new regulation.

Data Utilization = Efficient Technology

Technology is changing the way people access and exchange information [10]. Information related to a firm's performance is a key success factor [11] and thus technological capability to extract such data can drive competitive advantage. [12].

Data collection and its enrichment are often tedious tasks but critical in any risk analysis phase. Such tasks have often a high manual processing component, which can be an inherent source of errors and productivity constraint. However, through technology and process automation, efficiency levels can significantly improve.

Timely and accurate information ease decision making, and therefore, counting on a well structured information management flow that incorporates advanced technology developments contributes extensively towards minimizing lead times whilst increasing a firm's level of pragmatism and effectiveness to meet its strategic objectives.

Additionally, it is worth referring, not only to the information gathering and processing dimensions, but also to how and when the information is communicated. Only when the information reaches the target recipient it can be utilized and in this context it is relatively obvious that automation can play a key role – let's assume that a piece of information is identified, checked, enriched and worked through; the outcome will only be useful if it reaches the right people at the right time which is achievable if there is for instance an automated process that can instantly distribute the information.

Risk Measurement = Value-At-Risk

The environment in which a firm operates is always subject to an uncertain level of risk, and it has to deal with it. A firm's know-how to measure risk levels is one of its main assets to understand to what extent it is worth to incur a certain risk and can even pre-empt a corporation from bankruptcy.

There are several risk measurement techniques which have been used for long. Some of the most common ones in the banking industry are:

- Size of open positions
- Degree of maturity mismatch in the net position
- Assets' exposures

The calculation of such measures often needs of many complex mathematical models. Furthermore, in some cases, their implementation at organizations is not easy. Therefore, since the late 1990s, companies have alternatively opted for another method: "Value-at-Risk" (VaR).

VaR calculates the risk of loss on a specific portfolio of financial assets. For a given portfolio, probability and time horizon, VaR is defined as a threshold value such that the probability that the mark-to-market loss on the portfolio over the given time horizon exceeds this value (assuming normal markets and no trading in the portfolio) is the given probability level [13]. See example in Figure 2.

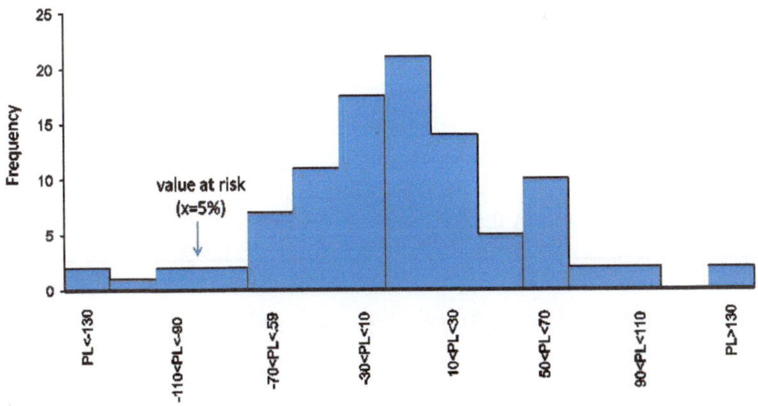

Figure 2: Histogram of daily hypothetic profits and losses over a long-term contract [14].

At this point it is worth highlighting that whilst VaR provides the quantitative perspective, it needs to be complemented by a more qualitative dimension resembling the market changes ("what-if scenarios" or "stress tests").

It is also worth pointing out that despite VaR is used in front of other methods which are perceived less powerful and more complex and difficult to understand, it is also constrained and only valid within a set of assumptions. This is one of the reasons why it is adviced that every VaR model is backtested, validating that the actual results are aligned to the forecasts.

Supervision = Ongoing Monitoring

The level of risk undertaken by a firm derives from its ability to monitor it. High capability to monitor risk helps to optimize the risk taking process. Risk monitoring should not only rely on the automated output of the VaR calculation, but should also be supported by a risk management function that is able to do a correct interpretation of the results. Risk monitoring aids in risk assessment and can result invaluable to senior management when they need to take a decision and they look for advice.

At this point it is worth pointing out that although risk monitoring has mainly focused on risk avoidance, there is another dimension: "the upside" or opportunity aspects for risk. This dimension is scarcely looked at, but on the other hand it can, if appropriately managed, derive significant level of profits.

Most frequent means to monitor risk consist on processes, reports, and discussion venues. However to ensure their reliability, these must be backed by a solid function of data management and a usable model.

All in all, monitoring implies tracking and thus, the more effort and time consuming this task requires, the later the relevant information will pop up and the lower the level of responsiveness to potential problems.

APPROACHING THE ECONOMIC CRISIS: 2008 – TODAY...

Although Risk Management has been for over a decade a central part of many organizations' strategic management [15], the trend towards adoption of more sophisticated techniques and technology, together with the bet for new models that can improve firms' Risk Management has been gaining pace. In general, the last years have seen rapid growth as concerns to the development and improvement of Risk Management tools which facilitate the evaluation of customers' credit worthiness, prediction of customer behavior and propensity of default [16-21]. Until 2008, a significant amount of investigation efforts within the financial environment had been towards providing assistance to banking agents on their daily decisions [22], but with the emergence of the economic crisis, researchers and practitioners began to strive even further to excel at their developments and come up with innovative and more diversified portfolios of Risk Management tools.

The economic downturn is seen as a worldwide phenomenon started in the US in 2008 and still ongoing. It is widely thought to be the result of a complex conglomerate of factors [23-26]. (Figure 3)

Such factors have been triggered by mistakes or defaults in Regulation and monitoring, as well as in the market behavior. Low interest rates jointly with financial innovation and globalization trends have evolved towards leverage and underestimation of liquidity and credit risk. The outcome of this mix has been excess indebtedness and excess asset valuation which has derived into a context characterized by: bankruptcy, recession, inflation, collapse in the Stock Markets, currency exchange volatility, dramatic decreases of monetary policy rates, slowdown of demand and consumption, boost of unemployment rates and shortages in profits.

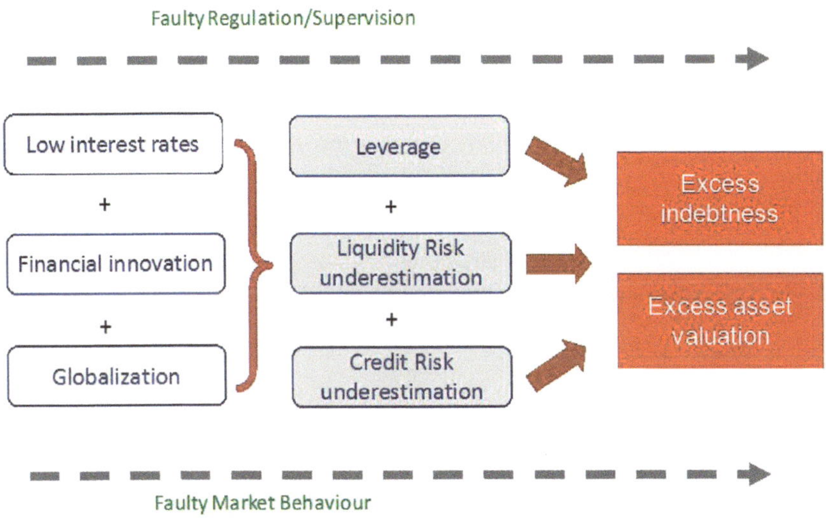

Figure 3: Possible root causes of the crisis.

In order to recover from the crisis, regulators and country heads worldwide have convened on the need of regulatory changes to reform the market risk – Basel III. But restructuring the financial sector jointly with strengthening international regulation policies are necessary but not sufficient conditions to reverse the economic situation. These need to be supported by financial institutions' risk management models.

Consequently, awareness of the fact that a risk culture can constitute a very important safeguard against financial losses and collapse has risen amongst industry players. In particular, Banks and most financial entities have demonstrated particular high interest in the last years on the implementation of appropriate operational and control models aimed at an adequate management of risk.

SEVEN DREADFUL MISTAKES IN RISK MANAGEMENT

Beyond looking at the economic crisis from a pessimistic angle, it is undeniable the existence of a brink of light considering the whole context – indeed the financial turmoil of the last years can be seen as an opportunity for change and learning from own or peer mistakes [27].

- So, what are the lessons learned?
- What have been the main mistakes that have led even former leading industry players to failure? (Figure 4)

Excess = Aggressive Policies in Risk Lending

"... lend, lend, lend ... we'll first get hold of the customers and afterwards make a fortune out of the interest rates ..."

Figure 4: Seven Dreadful Mistakes in Risk Management.

Excessive risk lending to others results in a sudden drought in available credit with catastrophic effects on business. Individuals are often more driven by their own interests, short-term impressive increases in market share and revenue, but under the assumption that this will continue for an indefinite period of time. Unfortunately, this attitude has a cost – forgetting the collective good of the whole group.

Inefficiency = Inefficient Risk Scoring Techniques

" ... - This risk scoring model does not seem very accurate - ... - Don't worry, just apply the thumb rule - ... "

There is a high number of companies that use outdated, static or inflexible assumptions to elaborate their risk scoring models. It is key that such models are funded on the bases of a balanced combination of quantitative and qualitative data. On the one hand, quantitative data can be considered "*the facts*", but complementarily, the use of qualitative data can contribute to a more flexible and dynamic risk assessment processes.

Apart from that it is also a poor practice over-reliance on credit agency risk scoring. The right approach should be for companies to look for consistent and independent risk measurement methods, validating and challenging constantly their obtained results against those provided by others, for instance credit agencies.

Faulty Management = Illiquidity Derived From Faulty Management of Assets And Passive

" ... – ups, it seems the firm is losing liquidity – ... well but competitors are going for it and as long as ASSETS = PASSIVE ... it's fine ... "

Wheras risk should be aligned to capital or liquidity positions, one of the mistakes incurred by companies is the failure to access cross-information. Such lack of information flowing fluently preempts that risk is managed by incentivizing business lines and consequently, it cannot be ensured that internal pricing reflects the current bear risk.

Disorders ... In Capital Levels = Inadequate Capital Levels

" ... if the capital level gets too low we'll see later on how to inject more from another source ... "

Within an increasingly regulated market, Banks and financial institutions could be forced to build-up capital and liquidity buffers in the good times to secure their survival in a Financial Crisis. Many companies which have gone bankrupt in the last years, incurred this mistake and failed to have such buffers filled at the required levels. Therefore this is a clear area where former industry players should have learned the lesson.

Uncovered Counterpart = Uncovered Counterpart Risk

" ... have you considered your counterpart risk? ... - Do I really need it? "

Regardless the risk management function should be independent of day-to-day operations, risk components are not something that can be left out of the daily operations – risk limits, stop-loss limits, exposure limits and counterparty limits should be key elements covered by any business line and considered when defining targets and objectives.

Too Complex ... = Complex Valuation of Structured Products

$$\text{" ...}\textit{Valuation Prod. A} = \left(\left[\sqrt[18]{x} \cdot \oiint y \right] \oplus \sum_{-\infty}^{\infty} \nabla \lambda z_i \right) \text{..."}$$

The role of structured products is mainly aimed at the design of investment products and customers' risk coverage. These products are highly subtle to market variations and therefore, too complex and time consuming methods for valuating these products allow more room for mistakes and less time to react to the volatility of the markets.

Extreme Scenarios = Lack of Extreme Scenarios

" ... - what if ...? - forget it; it will never happen.. "

In a high competitive and changing environment, such as the financial sector, it's an imperative for Banks and financial institutions to predict and prevent all potential challenges and threatening situations they may face at some point in time. Companies that have not defined severe, plausible and extreme scenarios in their management models have been more vulnerable and negatively affected by the crisis. Those organizations that have been better off, was because in the past the spectrum and range of possible risk scenarios they considered was more complete and consequently in difficult times they have had more margin to react and launch mitigation actions.

Having said this, the key to overcome such mistakes is based upon prudent management of risk, which entitles:

An organizational culture funded on prudent risk management

- Prudent and anti-cyclic policies as concerns to provisions
- Proactive risk management initiatives covering the whole credit life cycle; putting special emphasis on risk admission and monitoring processes

SIX QUICK WINS IN RISK MANAGEMENT

After analyzing the root causes of the economic downturn and the main mistakes, it is time to provide some tips that have proven to be successful for a leading European Bank that, despite the challenging environment, has managed to excel in performance and obtain the 2011 Best Bank Award.

For this player, the quality in risk management is one if its core identity signs and thus, a top 1 line of action. For over 150 years, The Bank has combined prudency in risk management and advanced risk management techniques which have fostered recurrent and healthy turnover and value creation for its stakeholders.

The balance between The Bank's appetite for risk vs. risk control is driven by its business model and core principles:

- The Retail Business is the bulk of The Bank's activity. The Bank is present worldwide and has significant market share (>10%) in all the main markets in which it operates. The Global Business practice is mainly developed in The Bank's core markets.
- Based upon strong capital and liquidity, The Bank's business model enables recurrent profits and financial results.
- The Bank formalizes its presence through autonomous subsidiaries, both in terms of capital and liquidity, compatible with a common corporate control model. The shareholders' structure looks to be simple, minimizing the number of non-operative or instrumental subsidiaries.
- The Bank relies on a powerful and advanced technology infrastructure and corporate tools – which enable an agile compilation and processing of the information – timely and in a standard format
- The Bank's activity is framed within its social and reputational commitment, fully aligned with its strategic objectives.

All these principles are the main levers of The Bank's risk management guidelines. These can be summarized in six quick wins that for other industry players have turned into best practices (Figure 5):

- Independent Risk Management Function
- Heavily involved Executive Board
- Vanguard tools and systems

- Integrated risk control and management
- Sustainable risk quality
- Objective decisions

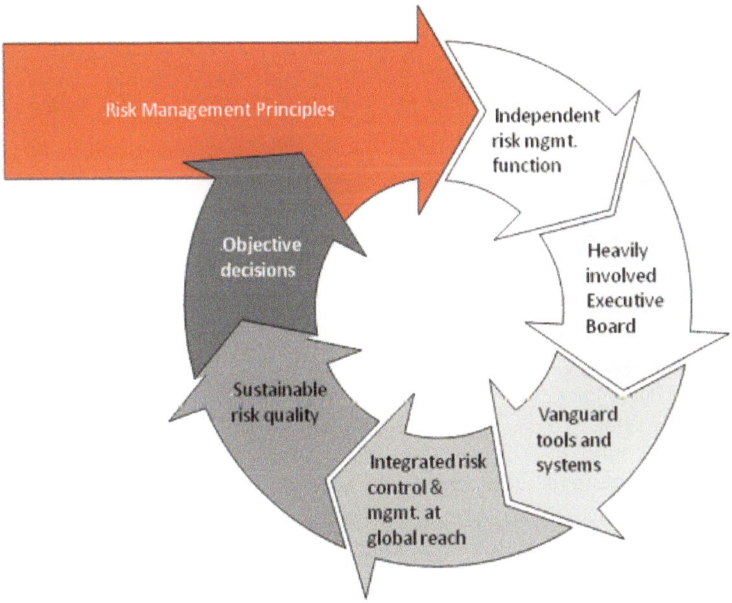

Figure 5: Quickwins in Risk Management.

Independent Risk Management Function

The Risk Management function has to be separated from daily operations. In this sense, The Bank counts on a Risks Management Unit, with its own Head of Department reporting directly to the Executive Board. Such Unit is responsible for risk admission and monitoring processes and acts on an autonomous way and thinking Global.

Heavily Involved Executive Board

The Senior Management of The Bank is aware of the importance of Risk Management and thus, inspires such culture and principles to the rest of the organization.

Vanguard Tools and Systems

One of The Bank's core principles is:

"Technology drives Operations"

Within the Risk Management arena, this translates into The Bank's keenness on the use of vanguard tools and systems. Having the right technology allows The Bank to analyze and measure risks at an acceptable confidence level.

Integrated Risk Control and Management

Risk must be identified, quantified and homogeneously managed according to a common magnitude (economic capital). The Bank tackles such risk control and management activities in an integrated way across the whole corporate structure:

- every risk
- in each Business line
- at all geographic markets

Sustainable Risk Quality

In the last 20 years, The Bank has applied proprietary risk scoring methods to evaluate the risk of its customers and operations. Ensuring that The Bank does not incur risk over a pre-defined threshold, guarantees the sustainable development of its business.

Objective Decisions

Decisions taken must be objective, taking into account contrast of opinions and avoiding decision making being exclusively restricted to an individual. The Bank pursues man-community decisions over credit operations both in the sales and risk areas.

As the objective of this chapter is not to describe in detail each of the aforementioned risk management guidelines, the main takeaway is that it is indeed critical for a firm to have in place some sort of core principles aligning its strategic objectives with its risk management model. Which specific principles are best suited at each particular organization is an open item that requires the organization an internal analysis.

For instance, although a risk management model could prove to be extremely successful for a leading player, it does not imply that the implementation of such guidelines by another competitor would prove the same degree of effectiveness.

In general, following industry best practices, lead to superior results than other techniques; nevertheless, the achievement of enhanced performance will only come by hand of ad-hoc and particularized risk management strategy.

CONCLUSIONS

This case study has outlined some reasons why Risk Management is important. Though the concept arised over a decade ago, the emergence of the economic crisis in 2008 has given thrust to organizations' adoption of risk management policies, specifically in the financial sector.

To date and during the downturn years we have evidenced common mistakes (the *"seven dreadful mistakes"*), that with the right risk management policies in place could have been avoided or at least ameliorated.

Nevertheless, in the midst of pessimism and underlying financial turmoil there is still room for hype and there are not only lessons to learn, but also quick wins that firms can put into practice to ease their recovery from the current situation.

ACKNOWLEDGEMENT

To my family and peer leaders - for their support and advice at all times.

REFERENCES

1. Grupo Santander2010Gestión del riesgo. 121157
2. El blog del riesgo y la estrategia empresarial2011Qué es la Gestión Integral de Riesgo Empresarial?. Available:http://riesgoyestrategia.wordpress.com.Accessed 2011 Dec 11.
3. LIMRA2009The Role of Advisors in Retirement Income Planning. 16 p.
4. Morgan Stanley2010Annuity Survey: Brighter Days Ahead … for Some. 5 p.
5. Financial Advisor Magazine2009Clients Demanding Insured Investments (referred to survey by Financial Research Corp.)
6. Prudential Financial2009Impact of the Market Crisis on Retirement preparedness. 4 p.
7. Moody MJ2010Enterprise Risk Management. The value proposition. The RoughNotes Company Inc. j. 4. Available:http://www.roughnotes.com/rnmagazine/2010/may2010/2010_05052 htm.Accessed 2012 Apr 15.
8. KPMG2011Placing a value on Enterprise Risk Management. Available:http://www.kpmg.com/CN/en/IssuesAndInsights/ArticlesPublications/documents/Placing-Value-ERM-201003.pdf.Accessed: 2012 Apr 15
9. JPMorgan Investment Analytics and Consulting2011Setting Up A Sound Risk Management Framework
10. J. M. Montero, Segundo. R. San, R. De Cordoba, Barcena. A. Marin la, Zlotnik, A(2009Strengthening Web Based Learning through Software Quality Analysis. 8th International Conference on Web-Based Learning. Aachen
11. K. Mathi, 2004Key Success Factors for Knowledge Management. Internationales Hochschulinstitut Lindau. Germany.
12. D. Marchand, 2004Information Strategy as a Key Success Factor for Enterprises and Universities. 7th International Bielefeld Conference. Germany
13. J. Philippe, at. Value, The. Risk, Benchmark. New, Managing. for, Risk. Financial, rd ed. McGraw-Hill. 978-0-07146-495-69780071464956
14. J. Marcareñas, 2008Introducción al VaR. Complutense University. Madrid
15. AIRMIC2002IRM. A Risk Management Standard
16. J. Sun, H. Li, 2008Data mining method for listed companies' financial distress prediction, Knowledge-Based Systems, 21 EOF5 EOF
17. J. Sun, H. Li, 2009Majority voting combination of multiple case-based reasoning for financial distress prediction. Expert Systems with Applications. j. 36343634373
18. J. Sun, H. Li, 2009Financial distress early warning based on group decision making. Computers & Operations Research. j. 363885906

19. J. Sun, H. Li, 2009Predicting business failure using multiple case-based reasoning combined with support vector machine. Expert Systems with Applications. j. 3661008510096

20. J. Sun, H. Li, 2009Gaussian case-based reasoning for business failure prediction with empirical data in China. Information Sciences. j. 179(1-2): 89 EOF108 EOF

21. J. Sun, H. Li, 2010Business failure prediction using hybrid2 case-based reasoning. Computers & Operations Research. j. 371137151

22. M. Aiken, 2001Competitive Intelligence through Neural Networks. Wiley Interscience. j. 1014953

23. J. C. Estepa, P. Lamothe, 2011La gestión del riesgo financieroy Basilea III. Universidad Autónoma de Madrid. Madrid

24. Las prácticas que nos hundieron en la crisis.Available: http://www.quequieres.es.Accessed 2011December 11.

25. Survey to Jesús Huerta de Soto2010Professor of Economy at Rey Juan Carlos University

26. BBC news2008Recession in the US has arrived

27. PriceWaterhhouse Coopers2011th Annual Global CEO Survey

8
CHAPTER

QUANTUM KEY DISTRIBUTION

Philip Chan Itzel Lucio-Martínez, Xiaofan Mo and Wolfgang Tittel

INTRODUCTION

This chapter describes the application of lasers, specifically diode lasers, in the area of quantum key distribution (QKD). First, we motivate the distribution of cryptographic keys based on quantum physical properties of light, give a brief introduction to QKD assuming the reader has no or very little knowledge about cryptography, and briefly present the state-of-the-art of QKD. In the second half of the chapter we describe, as an example of a real-world QKD system, the system deployed between the University of Calgary and SAIT Polytechnic. We conclude the chapter with a brief discussion of quantum networks and future steps.

MOTIVATION

The importance of communication networks has increased significantly in the last three decades. As an ever-growing fraction of our daily activities (including e-mail and e-banking) now depends on communication over public channels such as optical fibers, the security of the exchange of sensitive information also became an issue of high importance. Of special concern are credit card numbers, personal health records and business-related information, just to give some examples.

The problem of guaranteeing security is solved by encrypting the sensitive information (referred to as the plaintext and assumed to be in its binary form) before transmission. During encryption, the plaintext is processed using a key and a certain algorithm (the cipher or cryptosystem). The encrypted message is referred to as the cryptogram (or ciphertext), and the sender is typically denoted Alice. The cryptogram is sent through the communication channel to the receiver, Bob. If intercepted during transmission, it should be incomprehensible to an eavesdropper, typically called Eve. The encrypted message becomes meaningful only once it is decrypted. This requires a

Citation: Philip Chan, Itzel Lucio-Martínez, Xiaofan Mo and Wolfgang Tittel, Quantum Key Distribution, DOI: 10.5772/24468.

secret key, which must be known only to the legitimate receiver and, depending on the cryptosystem, the sender of the message. Different types of ciphers exist; they can be divided into two groups: symmetric and asymmetric ciphers.

- Asymmetric ciphers use two different keys: a public key with which anyone can encrypt a message and a private key that belongs to the receiver of the message. Only the private key allows decrypting the message.
- Symmetric ciphers use the same secret key for encryption and decryption.

Obviously, the encrypted message must not reveal any information about the plaintext. Hence, the secrecy of the encrypted message transmitted over a public channel relies on the secrecy of the key used for decryption. The security of a cryptosystem is generally assessed in terms of the time required to break it; two general categories exist:

- Computational security assumes the eavesdropper has limited computational power, and relies on assumptions about the difficulty to solve a certain mathematical problem. An example of a cryptosystem that provides computational security is RSA (named after the inventors Ronald Rivest, Adi Shamir and Leonard Adleman); its security relies on the difficulty to factorize a large number into its primes. In the factoring problem, the number of computational steps required increases exponentially with the number of bits used to represent the number to be factorized (Nielsen & Chuang (2004)). This is generally believed not to be computable for sufficiently large numbers. For instance, to factorize a 768-bit number, the best known classical algorithm has been estimated in 2010 to require on the order of 1500 years if a single-core, high-end processor is used (Kleinjung et al. (2010)). Furthermore, the factorization of a 1024-bit number, the current standard for RSA, is believed by the same authors to be 1000 times harder. This should suffice to safeguard any information one may want to encrypt.

However, the difficulty to factorize large numbers on a classical computer (a computer whose operation can be described using classical physics) is not proven, and less time-consuming algorithms may exist, or a large computer cluster may be used. Referring again to the example of a 768-bit number given above, this number has actually been factorized in 2010 using many hundreds of computers over a period of only two years (Kleinjung et al. (2010)). Furthermore, the researchers estimated that it is not unreasonable to expect that a 1024-bit RSA key can be factored within the next decade. Probably even more threatening, it is known that a quantum computer can factorize large numbers efficiently (i.e. in polynomial time – exponentially faster than the best known classical algorithm) by means of Shor's algorithm (Nielsen & Chuang (2004)). While these threats to RSA encryption do not yet exist (or rather, are currently not known to exist), today's eavesdropper could simply copy the encrypted information, wait for algorithmic or technological advances, and then decrypt the message efficiently.

We thus have to ask: when is it necessary to research alternative methods to safeguard information in transit? To answer this question, let us assume that the information has to remain encrypted for x years. Furthermore, let y be the time needed to retool the current secure-communication infrastructure. Hence, if disruptive technology appears in z years, where $z < x + y$, then a secret that has been encoded before the encryption infrastructure was improved becomes unprotected before the end of its lifetime. There is thus clear need to investigate and implement new encryption systems long before the old ones are broken (Stebila et al. (2010)).

- Information-theoretic security relies only on information-theoretic arguments. In particular, the security of the encrypted message does not depend on any assumptions about the computational power of an eavesdropper. The one-time pad satisfies this stringent condition. In the one-time pad the message is encrypted by combining it bit by bit with a random binary key, see figure 1. The key must be used only once, must be as long as the message that is to be encrypted, and, obviously, must only be known to the sender and the receiver. Then, regardless of the available time, an eavesdropper will never obtain the message from the ciphertext.

An important problem when using the one-time pad is thus the distribution of the secret key. This is generally accomplished using trusted couriers, a cumbersome solution that restricts its wide implementation and leaves a security loophole in the overall encryption procedure. Indeed, the key itself does not reveal if a non-trustworthy courier has duplicated it. This raises the question of whether alternative key distribution mechanisms exist that operate over standard communication channels and allow the detection of eavesdropping.

Table 1. Examples for two different cryptosystems

Cryptosystems		
Type	*Example*	*Security*
Asymmetric	RSA	Computational security
Symmetric	One-time pad	Information theoretic security

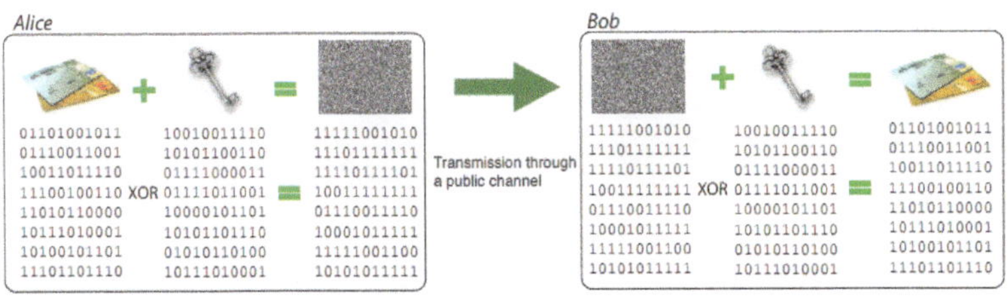

Figure 1: The one-time pad. Alice encodes her message with a random binary key using the XOR operation (i.e. 0+0=0, 0+1=1, 1+0=1, and 1+1=0). The encrypted message is then sent over a public channel to Bob. He decodes it with the same key, again using the XOR operation, and thereby obtains Alice's original message.

QUANTUM KEY DISTRIBUTION

Quantum key distribution (QKD) (Gisin et al. (2002); Scarani et al. (2009)) takes advantage of the peculiar properties of individual photons to provide two parties with arbitrarily long secret keys, provided a short key for authentication purposes is initially available. Hence, a more appropriate name for QKD would be quantum key growing.

Yet, as is common use, we will refer to this procedure as QKD. For QKD, information is encoded into one degree of freedom of photons (e.g. their polarization state), while all other degrees of freedom (phase, wavelength, etc.) must not contain any information. Each information-carrying photon then becomes a quantum bit (qubit) 2 . Due to their quantum nature, it is impossible for an eavesdropper to extract information about the encoded quantum states during transmission without altering them, which can be detected by Alice and Bob. Ignoring for the moment loopholes arising from imperfect implementations (we will discuss this problem later), the combination of QKD with one-time pad encoding provides information-theoretic secure communication3 that withstands any technological and algorithmic advances – even the development of the quantum computer.

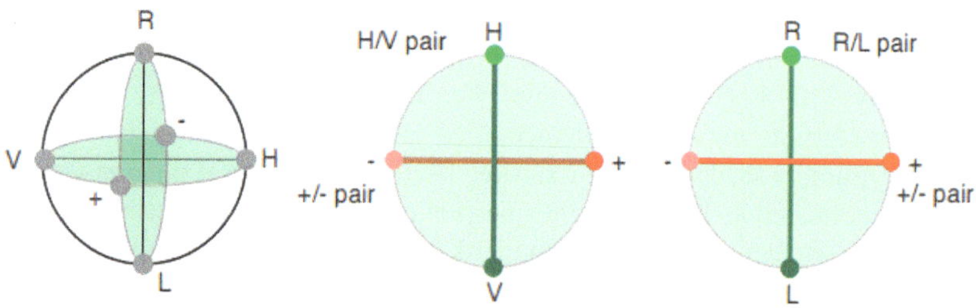

Figure 2: The Poincaré sphere (left-hand picture), and two examples of polarization states that are suitable for the BB84 protocol (center and right-hand picture). The first example comprises the |H, |V, |+ and |− linear polarization states, the second one comprises the |R, |L circular polarization states and the |+ and |− linear polarization states. Note that the states belonging to each example are arranged equally on two great circles around the Poincaré sphere.

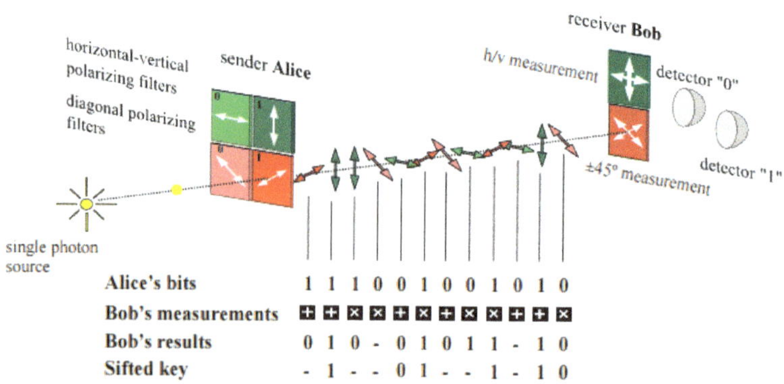

Figure 3: Illustration of the BB84 protocol.

For QKD, Alice and Bob share two communication channels: a quantum channel that is used to transmit qubits, and a classical (standard) channel to send classical messages. The quantum channel is generally an optical fiber or a free-space link connecting Alice and Bob, while the classical channel may be the Internet.

The BB84 protocol

Quantum key distribution was proposed in 1984 by Charles Bennett and Gilles Brassard (Bennett & Brassard (1984)). The first QKD protocol, generally referred to as the BB84 or four-state protocol, uses four different quantum states that form two pairs, chosen such that the difference (overlap) between any two states, one from each pair, is the same. A specific bit value is assigned to each state. For example, if the linear polarization states horizontal (|H), vertical (|V), +45° (|+) and -45° (|−) are used, |H and |V form one pair, |+ and |− form the other pair, then |H and |− correspond to bit 0, while |V and |+ correspond to bit 1, see figure 2[4] . For each photon Alice sends to Bob, she randomly selects one out of these four states. Bob, before receiving it, randomly decides whether to make a measurement that allows discriminating horizontally from vertically polarized photons, or +45° from -45° polarized photons. It is important to note that it is impossible to make a measurement that allows distinguishing between all four possible states (Nielsen & Chuang (2004)). Hence, whenever Bob picks the measurement that allows him to distinguish between the state that Alice sent and the orthogonal state, his measurement result indicates with certainty which state was originally prepared by Alice. Identifying states with bits, as described above, then obviously results in equal bits at Alice's and Bob's. Conversely, in the case where Bob choses to do the 'wrong' measurement, the measurement result as well as the associated bit value will be uncorrelated with the state sent by Alice.

Let us use the example of Alice sending state |H to make this concept more concrete: If Bob makes the 'correct' measurement (i.e. the measurement that distinguishes between |H and |V), he will find the result |H. Hence, Alice and Bob have sent and received the same bit value: 0. However, if Bob choses the measurement that distinguishes between |+ and |−, he will randomly obtain one of these two possible outcomes, and hence randomly obtain the bit value 0 or 1. From this point on all information exchange between Alice and Bob is performed over the classical channel, and the remaining steps in the protocol are known under the name of classical post-processing. These procedures are explained below.

Assume now that an eavesdropper intercepts photons during transmission from Alice to Bob. She (the eavesdropper) may duplicate each photon, keep one copy to measure it and obtain a bit value, and send the other copy to Bob. Fortunately, one of these steps is not allowed by quantum theory: the no-cloning theorem states that it is impossible to make a perfect copy of a photon in an unknown quantum state (Nielsen & Chuang (2004)). In fact, both 'duplicates' will only approximately resemble the original. Hence, the eavesdropper's attempt to eavesdrop inevitably leads to a modification of the state of the photon sent on to Bob, which results in errors in the bits that should be perfectly correlated and thereby reveals eavesdropping.

CLASSICAL POST-PROCESSING

Classical post-processing in QKD consists of four operations, as shown in Figure 4.

Sifting

Alice and Bob start by performing key sifting: Bob communicates which photons he detected, and which measurements he performed in these cases. However, he does not specify the results he obtained. Alice and Bob only keep those bits from their raw keys (i.e. the list of bits specifying the quantum states Alice sent and Bob detected, see figure 3) where Bob detected a photon, and that resulted from correct measurements (as defined above). All other bits are discarded. The result of this step is called the sifted key. Ideally, the sifted key would be error free, but in practice, no communication system is perfect and thus a small error rate, generally referred to as the quantum bit error rate (QBER), always remains. In addition, errors introduced by eavesdropping may also be present in the sifted key.

Error-correction

The next step is to perform error correction: Alice sends Bob additional information that allows him to generate an error-corrected key that is identical to Alice's. Furthermore, this procedure yields the QBER. Error correction in QKD is similar to error correction in classical communications, with the sifted key in QKD being analogous to the transmitted message. However, there is one important difference: rather than combining information that allows correcting errors directly into the message to be transmitted, this information is sent after key sifting is complete as it is only at this point that the message to be corrected is known. Furthermore, we need not worry about protecting the information for error correction against transmission errors as we can use existing protocols that provide error-free communication. With this in mind, the Cascade error correction protocol was originally designed for QKD (Bennett et al. (1992)). It requires many rounds of back-and-forth communication between Alice and Bob, which limits the maximum key rates that can be handled, due to communications delays. More recently, Low-Density Parity-Check codes (Gallager (1962); MacKay & Neal (1997)) have been adapted from classical communication protocols – they are capable of handling larger key rates (Pearson (2004)).

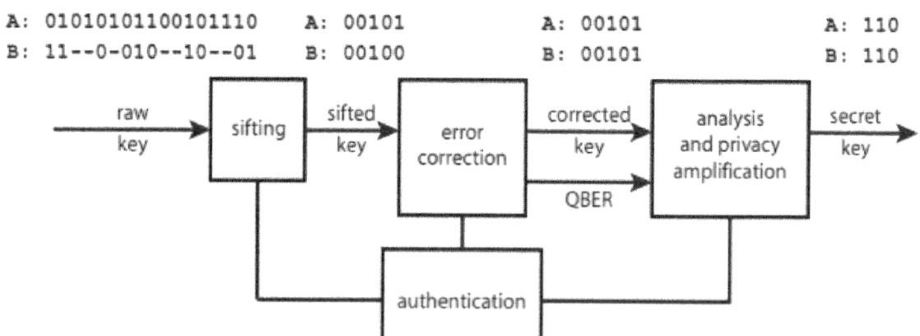

Figure 4: Post-processing in QKD. Example keys for Alice (A) and Bob (B) are shown. Only key bits resulting from correct measurements and photon detections are kept during sifting, yielding the sifted key. Remaining errors are corrected to form the error-corrected key. The eavesdropper's information about the error-corrected key is removed, yielding the secret key. Authentication is required for all steps.

Privacy amplification

Next, the amount of information that an eavesdropper may have obtained is estimated. The analysis considers several factors:

- First, the maximum amount of information Eve may have gained from measuring photons in transit, I_t, is evaluated from the error rate introduced into the sifted key (Gottesman et al. (2004)). Generally, all errors are attributed to eavesdropping as this is the worst-case scenario. If QKD is implemented using extremely faint laser pulses (containing on average less than one photon) instead of single photons, this procedure has to take into account the possibility of a so-called photon number splitting (PNS) attack (Brassard et al. (2000)). This attack exploits the fact that faint laser pulses sometimes contain more than one photon. It is generally thwarted by adding decoy states – qubits encoded into faint pulses with different mean photon number – to the signals used to establish the sifted key (Scarani et al. (2009)). This allows determining the information gained by the eavesdropper from PNS attacks, and makes implementations using faint laser pulses comparable to those using (much more difficult to generate) single photons.
- Second, the eavesdropper gains additional information by monitoring the error-correction procedure. The amount, I_{ec}, is directly given by the number of bits exchanged.
- Third, as we will discuss in more detail later, an implementation of QKD using imperfect devices can impact the security of the protocol. Sometimes, it is possible to quantify the information leakage Ileak (Lamas-Linares & Kurtsiefer (2007)).

Using these three contributions, the length of the secret key to be distilled from the corrected key is computed. Assuming for simplicity that Alice has used true single photons , the secret key per error-corrected bit amounts to

$$I_{secret} = 1 - I_t - I_{ec} - I_{leak}. \tag{1}$$

Privacy amplification, implemented by both Alice and Bob, then maps the error-corrected keys onto shorter secret keys in a way that knowledge of many bits in the corrected key is required to calculate any bit of the secret key. This step is typically performed by multiplication of the corrected key (expressed as a bit vector) with a suitably chosen binary Toeplitz matrix. This removes the eavesdropper's information about the key.

Authentication

An important consideration in all post-processing steps is to ensure that Alice and Bob are in fact going through this process with each other. Otherwise, an eavesdropper could simply block all quantum and classical communication between Alice and Bob and perform QKD with Alice while taking on Bob's role and vice versa. This is known as a man-in-the-middle attack, and would allow Eve to establish different secret keys with both Alice and Bob. She could then intercept a secret message, for example, being sent from Alice to Bob, decrypt it using the key she shares with Alice, read it, and then encrypt it again using the key she shares with Bob before forwarding it to him. She could thus read the entire message. To avoid man-in-the middle attacks, the classical channel has to be authenticated. In other words, Alice and Bob have to identify each message they send as originating from themselves. This can be achieved using a protocol known as Wegman-Carter authentication (Wegman & Carter (1981)). Hence, while the eavesdropper can listen to the conversation during post-processing (i.e. the classical channel is not required to be secure), she cannot modify or replace it. Authentication requires a short initial key, which is consumed during the first round of QKD. For subsequent rounds, it is replaced by some of the key generated during the key expansion.

SECURITY LOOPHOLES IN QKD

As introduced above, eavesdropping qubits encoded into individual photons during transmission is revealed through the observed error rate, regardless of the strategy. However, loopholes in the actual implementation of QKD may exist and can be exploited for attacks that are not reflected in the QBER. This was already noted in the very first implementation of QKD, where Charles Bennett realized that the noise emitted by the QKD system rendered the key only secure against an eavesdropper who happened to be deaf. Quantum hacking has become an important research field during the past five years, and various attacks have been proposed and experimentally studied. The most important ones are briefly introduced below.

- The already mentioned photon number splitting attack takes advantage of the fact that faint laser pulses sometimes contain more than one photon (Brassard et al. (2000)). This opens a security loophole when using the original BB84 protocol. Interestingly, this loophole can be closed by a small modification of the protocol, i.e. the addition of decoy states (Scarani et al. (2009)).
- In the Trojan-horse attack (Vakhitov et al. (2001)), Eve exploits the fact that every optical element reflects some of the incident light. It is then possible to analyze the status of optical components such as phase (polarization) modulators by reflecting short pulses of light from them, yielding for instance information about the qubit state that is being generated. This technique is called reflectometry and is well known to optical engineers. Counter measures include active monitoring of light at the input of Alice and Bob, and, for Alice, an optical isolator.
- QKD systems rely on single photon detectors. In the detector blinding attack, an eavesdropper exploits that these detectors can be prevented from detecting photons, and then forced to announce detections at will using various mechanisms (Makarov (2011)). In the time-shift attack (Lamas-Linares & Kurtsiefer (2007); Qi et al. (2007)) the eavesdropper exploits a possible detection efficiency mismatch between two detectors in the time domain. In this case, controlling the arrival time of each photon at Bob's device allows the eavesdropper to modify the probabilities for certain detectors to detect a given photon, and thereby

yields information about the key. Counter measures against attacks exploiting vulnerabilities of single photon detectors, often combining hardware and protocol modifications, have already been proposed and investigated (Makarov (2011); Yuan et al. (2010)).

It is of utmost importance to critically assess vulnerabilities of QKD systems and devise counter measures, either of theoretical nature or on the technological level, to remove the threat to security. Yet, even in the case of remaining potential loopholes, one should not underestimate that the security of QKD depends on the technological capabilities of the adversary at the time of the key exchange, in contrast to complexity-based cryptosystems that generate ciphertexts that can be recorded and decoded later. This point is important for secrets that should remain secure over many years.

STATE-OF-THE-ART

Quantum key distribution is the most mature application in the field of quantum information processing. For a few years, QKD systems have been commercially available (idQuantique (2011); MagiQ (2011); Quintessence (2011)) but research still continues to progress both theoretically and experimentally. Comparing different QKD systems is not a simple task, and trying to identify the 'best' system in a field that still evolves quickly is quite a pointless effort. Furthermore, it is unclear what figure of merit one should use. However, to give some idea about what is currently achievable, let us briefly summarize recent results that have advanced practical QKD in terms of maximum distance and key rate. Please note that, while these systems deliver secret keys if eavesdropping is restricted to measuring qubits in transit , we make no claim concerning their robustness against security loopholes such as those discussed above. QKD systems differ in terms of the type of quantum channel used (fiber or free space), the degree of freedom utilized to encode qubits (e.g. polarization or phase), and the nature of the quantum effect exploited (qubit states encoded into faint laser pulses, or so-called entangled qubits (Tittel & Weihs (2001))). Furthermore, they may employ single photon detectors based on avalanche photo diodes or on superconductors. As the state-of-the-art (in terms of distance and key rate) is only weakly system-dependent, we will not distinguish between different implementations.

Distances over which QKD systems operate can, in the best case, exceed ~200 km (Liu (2010); Schmitt-Manderbach et al. (2007); Stucki et al. (2009)). Due to the high channel loss experienced, the secret key rates are typically limited to ~10 bps. On the other hand, QKD systems have been demonstrated to deliver secret key rates up to ~1 Mpbs (Dixon et al. (2010); Restelli et al. (2009)). Obviously, the distances are reduced compared to those mentioned previously; the current maximum is 50 km. It is likely that these two benchmarks will not be improved significantly over the next few years, the only exception possibly being QKD over a free-space link between a ground station and a (very distant) satellite (Ursin et al. (2009)). An important concern in QKD systems, in particular in those clocked at high rates, is the generation of random numbers. For instance, in faint pulse based QKD, the security relies on Alice generating randomly selected qubit states encoded into laser pulses with average photon number chosen randomly from a small set. Furthermore, Bob has to randomly select which measurement to perform[9] and some randomness is required for privacy amplification. Hence, true random number generators, possibly exploiting randomness of certain quantum effects, are needed. A lot of progress has been made over the past years; quantum random number generators delivering random numbers at 16 Mbps are commercially available (idQuantique (2011)), and 50 Mbps rates have meanwhile been achieved in an academic effort (Fürst et al. (2010)). Yet, further improvement is required for QKD systems clocked at Gbps rates. Another possibility is the use of physical (non-quantum) RNGs for which Gbps rates have been reported (Honjo et al. (2009)).

OUR QKD SYSTEM - A CASE STUDY

The optical part of a QKD system consists of subsystems for signal generation, modulation, transmission, demodulation and detection, see figure 5. Figure 6 shows pictures of the sender and receiver of the QKD system that is currently being developed in our group (Lucio-Martinez et al. (2009)). Laser pulses generated by a standard telecommunication laser diode are attenuated to faint pulses and are used as carriers for qubits. Each of these laser pulses are modulated to a random polarization state (i.e. a qubit) and a random intensity level to implement the BB84 protocol supplemented with decoy states[10]. The pulses then pass through a standard, 12 km long telecommunication fiber and arrive at the receiver of the QKD system. On Bob's side, each qubit is measured using one out of two, randomly selected devices (see figure 3). The measurement results are post-processed, as described above, resulting in a shared secret key. The details of each subsystem are given below.

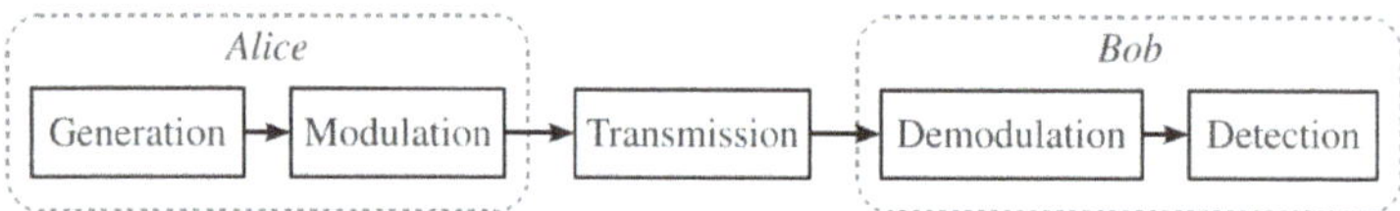

Figure 5: Diagram of the optical part of a QKD system, where Alice and Bob denote the sender and the receiver, respectively.

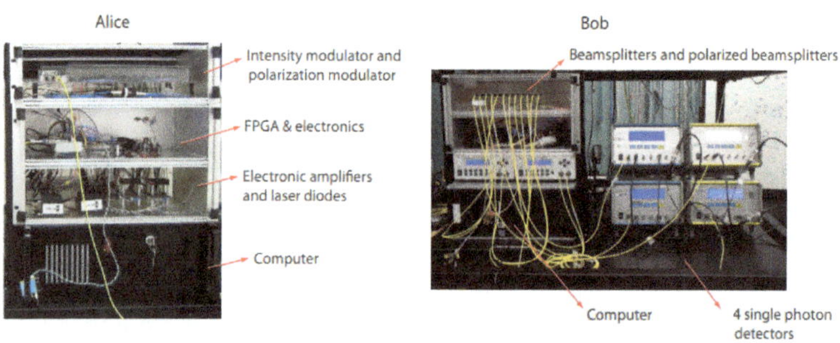

Figure 6: The QKD system currently being developed at the Quantum Communication and Cryptography (QC2) Lab at the University of Calgary. The left-hand picture shows Alice (located at SAIT Polytechnic), the right-hand one depicts Bob (located at the University of Calgary).

Generation

Figure 7 depicts the schematics of Alice's part of the QKD system. All fiber-optical components are polarization maintaining unless stated otherwise. We assume that the polarization beam splitter (PBS) transmits horizontal, and reflects vertical polarization. The laser diode LD_Q is driven by a homemade laser diode driver that is under the control of a field-programmable gate-array (FPGA)-based circuit. When the circuit sends a short digital signal to the driver, a 500 ps long, horizontally polarized laser pulse is generated. It features a central wavelength of 1548.07 nm, and a spectral width of 0.214 nm (full-width at half-maximum). The ratio between the power levels of a laser pulse and the background is around 100 to 1. An optical attenuator (ATT) reduces the energy of the laser pulse down to single-photon level; the background is reduced accordingly.

Modulation

The horizontally polarized laser pulse passes through the PBS, enters the subsequent polarization-maintaining fiber with its polarization aligned along one of the fiber's principal axes (slow, let's say), and arrives at an element denoted R_{45}. The axes of the polarization maintaining fibers on both sides of R_{45} are rotated by 45° with respect to each other. This rotation leads to a decomposition of the incoming laser pulse into two orthogonally polarized components with equal intensity, but randomly varying phase difference. The two components are polarized along the two polarization-maintaining axes of the second fiber, and arrive parallel to the slow (S) and the fast (F) axes of the subsequent $LiNbO_3$ phase modulator (PM). This modulator introduces a random and a controllable phase shift (φ_{in}) to one of the two components (slow, let's say), and another random phase shift to the component parallel to the other axis. Next, the Faraday mirror reflects the input light. Due to the Faraday effect, the polarization of the input light and that of the reflected light are orthogonal to each other, i.e. the component previously traveling along the slow axis of the modulator now travels along the fast one and vice versa. Hence, provided the random phase shifts introduced by the PM during the first passage of light have not changed before the second passage (a correct assumption given the small time difference of a few nanoseconds), the random phase shifts are equally present in both polarization components, and the phase difference is entirely due to the controllable phases (φ_{in} and φ_{out}) that are applied during the two passages. When arriving again at the PBS, the polarization of the reflected laser pulse can thus be expressed by the Jones vector

$$J_{out} = \begin{bmatrix} -i\sin\Delta\phi \\ \cos\Delta\phi \end{bmatrix}, \tag{2}$$

where $\Delta\phi = \frac{1}{2}(\phi_{out} - \phi_{in})$. The details of the calculation can be found in (Lucio-Martinez et al. (2009)). Equation 2 shows that the polarization of the reflected laser pulse varies as a function of $\Delta\varphi$, which is determined by the modulation voltages applied to the phase modulator. The horizontally polarized component of the laser pulse passes again through the PBS and is absorbed by the attenuator. The vertical polarization component is reflected by the PBS and is subsequently used to encode a qubit. By changing the polarization of the laser pulse, its intensity (or rather the average number of photons in the laser pulse) is modulated to a high or low value, as required by the decoy-state protocol. Furthermore, so-called vacuum states (pulses without photons) are generated by not triggering the laser diode.

Due to the use of a Faraday mirror, this intensity modulator has the following advantages compared to a standard modulator based on a Mach-Zehnder interferometer:

- The modulator is insensitive to changes in the environment, such as temperature and mechanical stress in the fiber. As an example, we have observed a variation of the output intensity of less than ±1.5% over 12 hours.
- The modulator is insensitive to polarization mode dispersion, which makes it suitable for use with a light source with large spectral width. As a second example, we routinely observe 20 dB power extinction ratio.

The faint laser pulses are then transmitted to the second, equally built polarization modulator. Depending on the value of the phase difference $\Delta\varphi$, we generate +45° ($\Delta\varphi = 0$), −45° ($\Delta\phi = \frac{\pi}{2}$), left-hand circular ($\Delta\phi = -\frac{\pi}{4}$) or right-hand circular ($\Delta\phi = \frac{\pi}{4}$) polarization. This is equivalent to the example given in the text above, as can be seen by comparing the center and right-hand parts of figure 7. We note that the second modulator comprises an optical circulator (CIR) instead of a PBS. Hence, both polarization components will exit the modulator, which then acts as a polarization modulator instead of an intensity modulator.

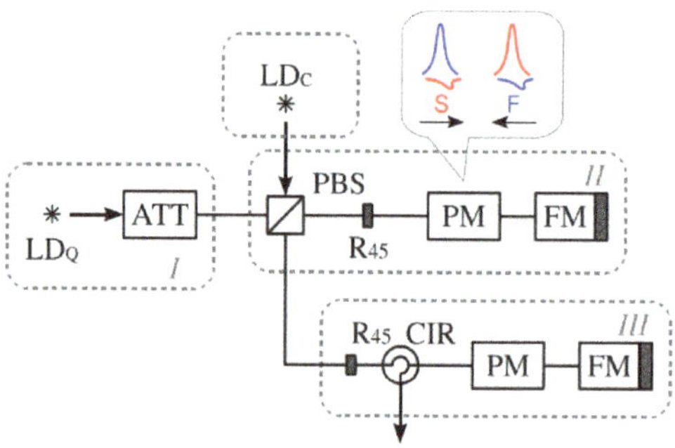

Figure 7: Schematics of Alice's system, which consists of sub-systems for signal generation (I), intensity modulation (II) and polarization modulation (III).

Transmission, demodulation and detection

The generated qubits are transmitted from Alice to Bob using a dedicated (dark) fiber, and then demodulated and detected using appropriate measurement devices. Before going into detail, we will briefly introduce the concept of quantum frames, which play an important role for selecting and maintaining quantum channels suitable for QKD.

The idea of quantum frames is inspired by the Ethernet protocol. A quantum frame consists of alternating sequences of high-intensity pulses (the classical control frame, providing a platform to include classical control information into quantum communication) and qubits encoded into faint laser pulses (the quantum data), see figure 8. Adding classical control frames (also referred to as data headers) allows for a variety of tasks related to establishing a link for QKD (e.g. in a network environment, which will be discussed below), and maintaining its properties:

- Routing: To allow all-optical routing of quantum data in a network, the classical control frames include information about the sender and the receiver. This information can be read using standard detectors, which, in turn, can activate optical switches to route entire quantum frames along specific optical paths. Work on quantum networks will be discussed briefly in section 8.
- Compatibility: In a future quantum network, it is likely that different types of QKD systems co-exist. They may vary in the degree of freedom chosen to encode quantum information into photons, or the protocol employed, which impacts on the way post-processing (in particular privacy amplification) is done. This information can be included into the classical control frames, and allows Bob to take appropriate action.
- Polarization compensation: Unfortunately, a fiber that maintains all polarization states required for the implementation of the BB84 protocol does not exist[11]. Hence, Bob will receive photons in states that differ from those sent by Alice. Moreover, the polarization change during transmission through the link varies with time (e.g. due to temperature fluctuations) rather than being constant. A feedback mechanism that tracks and compensates the change introduced by the link is thus required. We exploit strong pulses of light in specific polarization states to solve this problem. More precisely, the classical control frames contain information for Bob, which allows him to actively compensate for these polarization changes.
- Clock Synchronization: One of the challenges in QKD, especially in high-rate QKD, is clock synchronization between the two parties. This is needed to associate the generation with the corresponding detection of qubits. Information for clock synchronization is included into the classical control frames, allowing for periodic synchronization of Alice's and Bob's clocks.

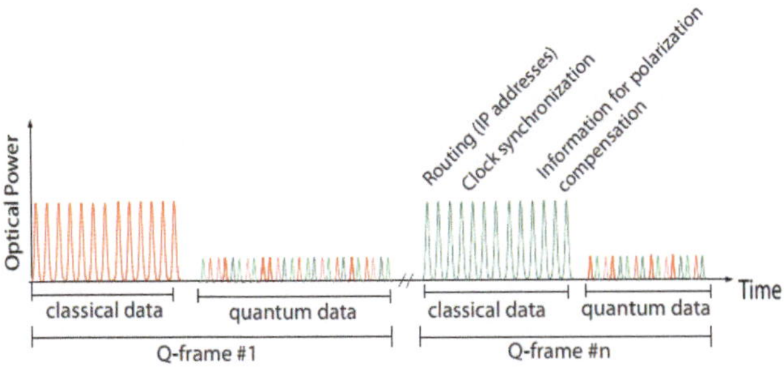

Figure 8: Structure of a quantum frame (not to scale). Classical information (high intensity pulses) are time-multiplexed with quantum bits (faint laser pulses). Each color in the quantum data indicates one of the four different polarization states required in the BB84 protocol.

The laser pulses constituting the classical control frames are generated by the laser diode LDC in figure 7: Horizontally polarized laser pulses pass through the PBS and are modulated to a specific polarization by the polarization modulator. On Bob's side, as shown in figure 9, 10% of the optical power is reflected towards a standard photodiode (PD), which detects the data header of the quantum frame to provide timing information for Bob's control circuit and thereby allow for clock synchronization. Ninety percent of the optical power is transmitted through a 10/90 beam splitter (BS_1) and is then equally divided by a 50/50 beam splitter (BS_2). The outputs of BS_2 are connected to two polarization measurement devices. Each device consists of a polarization controller (PC_1 , PC_2), a polarization beam splitter (PBS_1 , PBS_2) and two single photon detectors (SPD_{1a} , SPD2a and SPD_{1b} , SPD_{2b}).

PC_1 ensures that −45◦ polarized classical data, and hence qubits, emitted at Alice's arrive horizontally polarized at PBS1 and will be detected by SPD_{1a} . Similarly, PC_2 is set up such that right circular polarized classical data and qubits emitted at Alice's always impinge horizontally polarized on PBS2, and will thus be detected by SPD_{2a} . This directly implies that qubits prepared with +45◦ or left circular polarization arrive vertically polarized on PBS1 or PBS_2, respectively, and will thus be detected by SPD_{1b} and SPD2b . Hence, the two sets of PC, PBS and two SPDs allow compensation of unwanted polarization transformations in the quantum channel, and appropriate measurements of qubit states. At the end of each classical data header, the control circuit disables the polarization controller as well as the clock synchronization and starts gating single photon detectors based on InGaAs/InP avalanche photo-diodes operated in Geiger mode. The outputs of these detectors produce the raw key at Bob's, which is transmitted to a personal computer for classical post-processing.

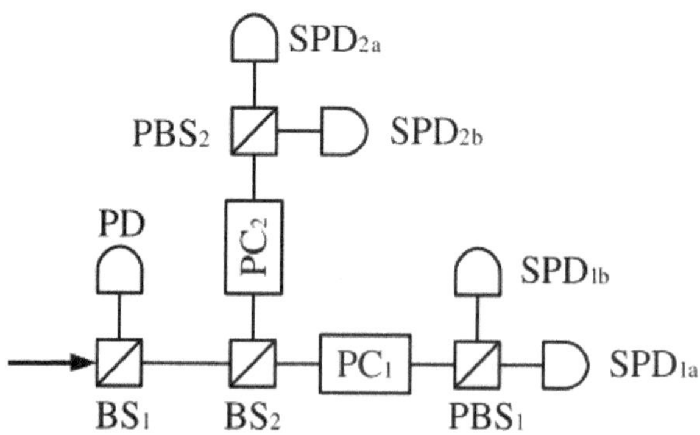

Figure 9: Schematics of Bob's system, which consists of demodulation and detection subsystems.

QKD performance

As described above, each deployed optical fiber introduces polarization changes to transmitted states of light (both quantum and classical) that vary over time. As shown in figure 10a, these variations are rapid during day-time (when the sun is out and the fiber heats up despite running through underground conduits) and are less pronounced during the night. However, even in the worst case, the polarization transformation is stable on a timescale of seconds. Due to the feedback system described above, our QKD system is able to perform continuously during ~30 hours: as depicted in figure 10b, the QBER remains at ~3% (a typical value for a QKD setup operating over ~10 km optical fiber), independent on the time of the day

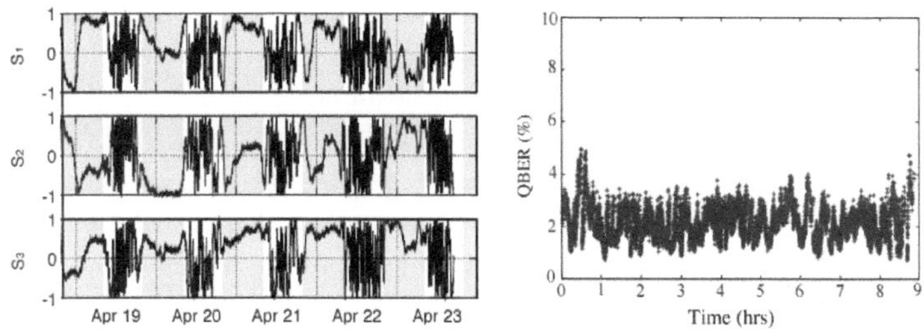

(a) Polarization variation

(b) QBER as a function of time

Figure 10: a) Plot of the polarization state of originally +45° polarized classical control frames arriving at Bob's as a function of time. The states are parametrized in terms of their Stokes vectors S_1 -S_3. A correlation between the time of the day and the polarization variation can be seen. b) QBER as a function of time, measured over a period of 9 hours.

Our QKD system currently features a raw key rate12 of ~0.5 KHz, which is sufficient to provide cryptographic keys for encoding using the Advanced Encryption Standard (AES)13 , but too small to provide keys for one-time pad encoding in real-time. The raw key rate is determined by the repetition rate at which qubits are produced or the single-photon detectors can be gated (whatever is smaller), the loss in the channel between Alice to Bob (~6.5dB), the fraction of time that is used for qubit generation and transmission (~10%; the remaining time is used for classical post-processing, which is currently done sequentially, and polarization compensation), loss in the optical components at Bob's (~3dB), and the quantum efficiency (i.e. the probability to detect a photon) of the single-photon detectors (~10%). The sifted key rate is ~0.25 KHz leading to a secret key rate of ~50 bps for an average of 0.5 photons per faint laser pulse. The performance can be improved by several orders of magnitude by employing high-rate single photon detectors14, and parallel implementation of classical post-processing using dedicated hardware.

QUANTUM NETWORKS

As described above, the no-cloning theorem prevents an eavesdropper from copying quantum data, but excludes at the same time broadcasting of identical quantum keys to several legitimate users. While QKD systems can thus operate only in point-to-point (P2P) fashion, it still benefits from being implemented in networks. This is due to the possibility to connect different users in a flexible and efficient way. Various types of quantum networks have been considered; the differences are determined by the available (or assumed) technology.

Trusted-node quantum networks

A trusted-node QKD network is composed of dedicated QKD links, each one connecting two neighboring locations or nodes. Secret keys for encoding messages (henceforth referred to as the message-encryption-key, MEK) are distributed between arbitrary (non-neighboring) nodes using a chain of QKD links. More precisely, the MEK is encrypted using the one-time pad and a key-encryption-key established with the neighboring node by means of QKD. The MEK is sent to the next node, attached with an authentication tag. Upon reception, the authentication tag is verified, and the MEK is decrypted. The process repeats until the MEK reaches its final destination. A potential drawback is that the security of the distribution of the MEK is only ensured if all intermediate nodes between the sender and receiver can be trusted as they posses full information about the MEK. However, on the other hand, the distribution of the MEK is not limited in distance as any distance can always be covered using many short-distance QKD links.

An example of a trusted-node quantum network is the SECOQC Network, implemented in October 2008 in Vienna, Austria (Peev et al. (2009)). This network comprised six nodes, connected by different QKD systems (or platforms). One of the main results of the deployment of this network was the development of an interface between a QKD system and existing (non-quantum) information and communication technology (ICT) systems. Also as a result of this project, an Industry Specification Group (ISG) of the European Telecommunications Standards Institute (ETSI) for QKD was put in operation to create universally accepted QKD standards (Langer & Lenhart (2009)). Another example is the Tokyo QKD Network, inaugurated in October 2010, also comprising six trusted-nodes connected by P2P QKD links forming the quantum backbone. The Tokyo Network includes a key management server for centralized management of the key life cycle and to determine the secure paths between two distant nodes (Sasaki et al. (2011)).

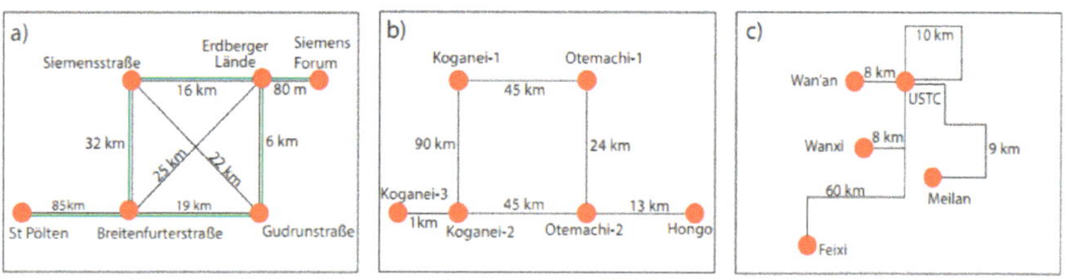

Figure 11: Examples for different quantum network topologies (all based on trusted nodes). a) SECOQC Network showing quantum channels (black) and classical channels (green) between the nodes. b) Tokyo Network. c) Hefei Network showing a star-type network.

Optically configurable quantum networks

An optically configurable quantum network utilizes passive or active optical devices (e.g. beam splitters, optical switches, wavelength multiplexers, etc.) in the quantum channel to allow QKD between multiple pairs of users. The benefit of this kind of network, in contrast to the previous kind, is that the nodes between the two parties that establish a secret key do not have to be trusted. Configurable quantum networks can be implemented with current technology. However, the distance over which a secret key can be established is limited to ~100 km, restricting its use to local or metropolitan areas. The first investigations towards optically configurable quantum networks were pursued within the framework of the DARPA Quantum Network (Elliot et al. (2005)) which was operational from 2004 to approximately 2008 in Massachusetts, USA. This network consisted of 8 nodes and employed various QKD platforms; 4 of these nodes were connected via active optical switches. A second example is the quantum network located in Hefei (Anhui), China. This hybrid network combines trusted relays and all-pass optical switches, allowing interconnection among all 5 nodes (Chen et al. (2010)).

Fully quantum-enabled networks

Fully quantum-enabled networks require technologies such as entanglement swapping, entanglement purification, quantum error correction and quantum memories (Kimble (2008)). These networks are not limited by the distance barrier imposed to optically configurable networks, and do not require trust in nodes, as opposed to trusted node networks. However, the technology required for fully quantum-enabled networks is not yet mature, even though all basic building blocks have meanwhile been demonstrated in proof-of-concept experiments (Lvovsky et al. (2009); Sangouard et al. (2011)).

THE FUTURE

To conclude this chapter, let us briefly address a few directions in which QKD is likely to evolve in the near future. First, QKD systems will be improved to deliver secret keys at Mbps rates, as has already been demonstrated in the QKD system developed by Toshiba. Progress beyond this rate can be expected to be slow, as many constituents, such as single photon detectors, face technical limitations that would require expensive and time-consuming engineering at the component level.

Next, the critical assessment of QKD implementations with respect to security loopholes will continue, and a lot of work will be devoted to the elimination of attacks through the development of better technology and the improvement of security proofs and protocols in the sense of making them more applicable to real-world devices. Key words here are squashing models (Lütkenhaus (2000)) and device-independent protocols (Masanes et al. (2011)). Squashing models allow the use of qubit-based security proofs for non-qubit-based implementations. Device-independent protocols go beyond squashing and attempt to remove not only all assumptions about the nature of the quantum systems used to transmit quantum information, but also those about the classical devices used by Alice and Bob. Furthermore, going beyond QKD, other quantum cryptography protocols that provide benefits compared to their classical analogs will receive more attention. Examples include quantum coin flipping (Berlin et al. (2009)) or quantum private database queries (Jakobi et al. (2011)). An interesting problem here is to devise protocols that can tolerate loss and errors, which are both present in real-world implementations. Finally, the integration of QKD into networks will be improved, and technologies required for breaking the distance barrier by means of quantum repeaters and for fully quantum-enabled networks will be further advanced.

This challenge is huge and immensely interesting, but progress over the past 5 years has been surprisingly rapid, and we believe that a fully quantum-enabled network will eventually be built.

ACKNOWLEDGEMENTS

The authors thank V. Kiselyov for technical support and S. Hosier for all the help with setting up the QKD system. This work is supported by General Dynamics Canada, Alberta's Informatics Circle of Research Excellence (iCORE, now part of Alberta Innovates Technology Futures), the National Science and Engineering Research Council of Canada (NSERC), QuantumWorks, Canada Foundation for Innovation (CFI), Alberta Advanced Education and Technology (AET), and the Mexican Consejo Nacional de Ciencia y Tecnología (CONACYT).

REFERENCES

1. Bennett, C. & Brassard, G. (1984). Quantum cryptography: Public key distribution and coin tossing, Proceedings of IEEE International Conference on Computers Systems and Signal Processing pp. 175–179.
2. Bennett, C. H., Bessette, F., Brassard, G., Salvail, L. & Smolin, J. (1992). Experimental quantum cryptography, Journal of Cryptology 5(3): 253–265.
3. Berlin, G., Brassard, G., Bussières, F. & Godbout, N. (2009). Fair loss-tolerant quantum coin flipping, Physical Review A 80(6):062321.
4. Brassard, G., Lütkenhaus, N., Mor, T. & Sanders, B. (2000). Limitation on practical quantum cryptography, Physical Review Letters 85: 1330–1333.
5. Chen, T., Wang, J., Liang, H., Liu, W.-Y., Liu, Y., Jiang, X., Wang, Y., Wan, X., Cai, W.-Q., Ju, L., Chen, L.-K., Wang, L.-J., Gao, Y., Chen, K., Peng, C.-Z., Chen, Z.-B. & Pan, J.-W. (2010). Metropolitan all-pass and inter-city quantum communication network, Optics Express 18(26): 27217–27225.
6. Dixon, A., Yuan, Z. L., Dynes, J., Sharpe, A. W. & Shields, A. (2010). Continuous operation of high bit rate quantum key distribution, Applied Physics Letters 96: 161102–161105.
7. Elliot, C., Colvin, A., Pearson, D., Pikalo, O., Schlafer, J. & Yeh, H. (2005). Current status of the DARPA quantum network, Proceedings of SPIE 5815: 138–149.
8. Fürst, M., Weier, H., Nauerth, S., Marangon, D. G., Kurtsiefer, C. & Weinfurter, H. (2010). High speed optical quantum random number generation, Optics Express 18(12): 13029–13037.
9. Gallager, R. (1962). Low-density parity-check codes, IRE Transactions on Information Theory 8(1): 21–28.
10. Gisin, N., Ribordy, G., Tittel, W. & Zbinden, H. (2002). Quantum cryptography, Review Modern Physics 74: 145–195.

11. Gottesman, D., Lo, H., Lütkenhaus, N. & Preskill, J. (2004). Security of quantum key distribution with imperfect devices, Quantum Information and Computation 4: 325.

12. Honjo, T., Uchida, A., Amano, K., Hirano, K., Someya, H., Okumura, H., Yoshimura, K., Davis, P. & Tokura, Y. (2009). Differential-phase-shift quantum key disitrbution experiment using fast physical random bit generator with chaotic semiconductor lasers, Optics Express 17(11): 9053–9061.

13. idQuantique (2011). www.idQuantique.com.

14. Jakobi, M., Simon, C., Gisin, N., Bancal, J.-D., Branciard, C., Walenta, N. & Zbinden, H. (2011). Practical private database queries based on a quantum-key-distribution protocol, Physical Review A 83(2): 022301.

15. Kimble, H. J. (2008). The quantum internet, Nature 453: 1023–1030.

16. Kleinjung, T., Aoki, K., Franke, J., Lenstra, A., Thomé, E., Bos, J., Gaudry, P., Kruppa, A., Montgomery, P., Osvik, D., te Riele, H., Timofeev, A. & Zimmermann, P. (2010). Factorization of a 768-bit RSA modulus, in T. Rabin (ed.), Advances in Cryptology – CRYPTO 2010, Vol. 6223 of Lecture Notes in Computer Science, Springer Berlin / Heidelberg, pp. 333–350.

17. Lamas-Linares, A. & Kurtsiefer, C. (2007). Breaking a quantum key distribution system through a timing side channel, Optics Express 15(15): 9388–9393.

18. Langer, T. & Lenhart, G. (2009). Standarization of quantum key distribution and the ETSI standarization initiative ISG-QKD, New Journal of Physics 11(5): 055051.

19. Liu, Y. (2010). Decoy-state quantum key distribution with polarized photons over 200 km, Optics Express 18(8): 8587.

20. Lucio-Martinez, I., Chan, P., Mo, X.-F., Hosier, S. & Tittel, W. (2009). Proof-of-concept of real world quantum key distribution with quantum frames, New Journal of Physics 11(9): 095001.

21. Lütkenhaus, N. (2000). Security against individual attacks for realistic quantum key distribution, Physical Review A 61: 052304.

22. Lvovsky, A. I., Sanders, B. C. & Tittel, W. (2009). Optical quantum memory, Nature Photonics 3: 706–714.

23. MacKay, D. & Neal, R. (1997). Near Shannon limit performance of low density parity check codes, Electronics Letters 33(6): 457–458.

24. MagiQ (2011). http://www.magiqtech.com/MagiQ/Home.html.

25. Makarov (2011). Secure gated detection scheme for quantum cryptography, Physical Review A 83(3): 032306.

26. Masanes, L., Pironio, S. & Acín, A. (2011). Secure device-independent quantum key distribution with causally independent measurement devices, Nat. Commun. 2(238).

27. Nielsen, M. A. & Chuang, I. L. (2004). Quantum Computation and Quantum Information (Cambridge Series on Information and the Natural Sciences), 1 edn, Cambridge University Press.

28. Pearson, D. (2004). High-speed QKD reconciliation using forward error correction, Proc. 7th International Conference on Quantum Communication, Measurement and Computing (QCMC), Vol. 734, pp. 299–302.

29. Peev, M., Pacher, C., Alléaume, R., Barreiro, C., Bouda, J., Boxleitner, W., Debuisschert, T., Diamanti, E., Dianati, M., Dynes, J. F., Fasel, S., Fossier, S., Fürst, M., Gautier, J.-D., Gay, O., Gisin, N., Grangier, P., Happe, A., Hasani, Y., Hentschel, M., Hübel, H., Länger, G. H. T., Legré, M., Lieger, R., Lodewyck, J., Lorünser, T., Lütkenhaus, N., Marhold, A., Matyus, T., Maurhart, O., Monat, L., Nauerth, S., Page, J.-B., Poppe, A., Querasser, E., Ribordy, G., Robyr, S., Salvail, L., Sharpe, A. W., Shields, A. J., Stucki, D., Suda, M., Tamas, C., Themel, T., Thew, R. T., Thoma, Y., Treiber, A., Trinkler, P., Tualle-Brouri, R., Vannel, F., Walenta, N., Weier, H., Weinfurter, H., Wimberger, I., Yuan, Z. L., Zbinden, H. & Zeilinger, A. (2009). The SECOQC quantum key distribution network in Vienna, New Journal of Physics 11: 075001.

30. Qi, B., Zhao, Y., Ma, X., Lo, H.-K. & Qian, L. (2007). QKD Quantum key distribution with dual detectors, Physical Review A 75(5): 052304–052314.

31. Quintessence (2011). http://www.quintessencelabs.com/.

32. Restelli, A., Bienfang, J. C., Mink, A. & Clark, C. W. (2009). Quanutm key distribution at GHz transmission rates, Proceedings of SPIE 7236(72360L): 1–7.

33. Sangouard, N., Simon, C., de Riedmatten, H. & Gisin, N. (2011). Quantum repeaters based on atomic ensembles and linear optics, Review Modern Physics 83(1): 33–80.

34. Sasaki, M., Fujiwara, M., Ishizuka, H., Klaus, W., Wakui, K., Takeoka, M., Tanaka, A., Yoshino, K., Nambu, Y., Takahashi, S., Tajima, A., Tomita, A., Domeki, T., Hasegawa, T., Sakai, Y., Kobayashi, H., Asai, T., Shimizu, K., Tokura, T., Tsurumaru, T., Matsui, M., Honjo, T., Tamaki, K., Takesue, H., Tokura, Y., Dynes, J. F., Dixon, A. R., Sharpe, A. W., Yuan, Z. L., Shields, A. J., Uchikoga, S., Legré, M., Robyr, S., Trinkler, P., Monat, L., J.-B., Ribordy, G., Poppe, A., Allacher, A., Maurhart, O., Länger, T., Peev, M. & Zeilinger, A. (2011). Field test of quantum key distribution in the Tokyo QKD network, Optics Express 19(11): 10387–10409.

35. Scarani, V., Bechmann-Pasquinucci, H., Cerf, N. J., Dušek, M., Lütkenhaus, N. & Peev, M. (2009). The security of practical quantum key distribution, Review Modern Physics 81: 1301.

36. Schmitt-Manderbach, T., Weier, H., Furst, M., Ursin, R., Tiefenbacher, F., Sheidl, T., Perdigues, J., Sodnik, Z., Kurtsiefer, C., Rarity, J. G., Zeilinger, A. & Weinfurter, H. (2007). Experimental demonstration of free-space decoy-state quantum key distribution over 144 km, Physical Review Letters 98(1): 010504.

37. Stebila, D., Mosca, M. & Lütkenhaus, N. (2010). The case for quantum key distribution, Lecture Notes of the Institute for Computer Sciences, Social Informatics and Telecommunications Engineering 36: 283–296.

38. Stucki, D., Walenta, N., Vannel, F., Thew, R. T., Gisin, N., Zbinden, H., Gray, S., Towery, C. R. & Ten, S. (2009). High rate, long-distance quantum key distribution over 250 km of ultra low loss fibers, New Journal of Physics 11: 075003.

39. Tittel, W. & Weihs, G. (2001). Photonic entanglement for fundamental tests and quantum communication, Quantum Information and Computation 1(2): 3–56.

40. Ursin, R., Jennewein, T., Kofler, J., Perdigues, J., Cacciapuoti, L., de Matos, C., Aspelmeyer, M., Valencia, A., Scheidl, T., Acin, A., Barbieri, C., Bianco, G., Brukner, C., Capmany, J., Cova, S., Giggenbach, D., Leeb, W., Hadfield, R., Laflamme, R., Lütkenhaus, N., Milburn, G., Peev, M., Ralph, T., Rarity, J., Renner, R., Samain, E., Solomos, N., Tittel, W., Torres, J., Toyoshima, M., Ortigosa-Blanch, A., Pruneri, V., Villoresi, P., Walmsley, I., Weihs, G., Weinfurter, H., Zukowski, M. & Zeilinger, A. (2009). Space-quest, experiments with quantum entanglement in space, Europhysics News 40(3): 26–29.

41. Vakhitov, A., Makarov, V. & Hjelme, D. (2001). Large pulse attack as a method of conventional optical eavesdropping in quantum cryptography, Journal of Modern Optics 48: 2023–2038.

42. Wegman, M. & Carter, J. L. (1981). New hash function and their use in authentication and set equality, Journal of Computer and System Sciences 22(3): 265–279.

43. Yuan, Z. L., Dynes, J. & Shields, A. J. (2010). Avoiding the blinding attack in qkd, Nature Photonics 4: 800–801.

9
CHAPTER

CHINESE CUSTOMERS' BANKING HABITS AND E-BANKING BARRIERS

Xiao Ling Qiu

Keywords: Chinese customer, Banking, Habit, Barrier

INTRODUCTION

With the development of the Internet, more knowledge is accessible to people anywhere at anytime. Facilitating communication, data transmission, and global interaction, the Internet is a playing field unlike any other. Transcending the traditional barriers of time and space, the Internet is redefining the world of banking. The Internet has created new methods for carrying out a variety of financial transactions. With these developments, a new era of banking has emerged which has come to be known as "E-banking". E-banking encompasses an array of financial transactions, once done through the tangible exchange of information, now are done electronically. While the benefits of such advancements have been welcomed by most of the American customers, many Chinese customers are still uncomfortable with E-banking. The reason is that there are some drawbacks such as computer illiteracy, security, fraud, and theft have deterred Chinese customers from participating in E-banking. Many Chinese customers are still accustomed to tangible banking transactions. Some of the E-banking activities include the transactions of buying and selling goods, paying bills, transferring funds, and managing investments.

The psychological barriers involved with computer literacy, age, financial status, education, and the level of uncertainty avoidance are in relation to an individual's comfort level towards E-banking. The study was conducted in New York City Chinatown area to investigate the Chinese customers' banking habits and the major barriers which prevent them from participating in E-banking. It is important for the American financial institutions to understand the E-banking behaviors of the Chinese

Citation: Xiao Ling Qiu, Chinese Customers' Banking Habits and E-banking Barriers, ISSN 1833-3850.

customers, because the Chinese population growing up fast in the United States. It is also important for the financial institutions in China to understand the local Chinese customers' E-banking behaviors, because the huge population with Internet access in China provides an attractive market for E-banking business. The findings in the study can help marketers understand more about Chinese customers' E-banking behaviors. It is obvious that the development of a successful E-banking system is based on the understanding of the banking customers' behaviors.

LITERATURE REVIEW

Today, the Internet is providing unlimited access to resources with real-time quality. More and more people are using the Internet to carry out actions that would have otherwise been done in person. "The online procurement industry is reportedly at least doubling in size every year" (World Almanac & Book of Facts, 2001). In efforts to keep up with technological advancements, banks all over the world are offering E-banking as an appealing alternative to the traditional styles of banking with the intentions of luring potential customers. "Internet banking appears as a response both to the technical drawbacks of previous Home banking systems and to the growing demands of consumers" (Giannakoudi, 1999, p. 205). Despite the barriers associated with E-banking and the Internet, the advancements and benefits of E-banking to consumers as well as banking institutions is irreplaceable. From the consumer's perspective, E-banking has provided them with the ability to pay bills, manage accounts, and shop all from the convenience of their homes. This alternative has also reduced cost for the banking institutions that offer the service, "an online transaction costs the bank much less than a face-to-face interaction with a bank's teller" (World Almanac & Book of Facts, 2001). With less paperwork to process every month and the money that is being saved, banks have been able to concentrate their efforts on improving other aspects of their organization.

As technology infiltrates the financial market, banks are anxious to capitalize on the spoils of technological advancements. Initially, banks implemented new systems internally improving communication and fostering standardization between branch offices. Later, banks began to use technology externally to promote interaction and increase transactions with customers. The developments of automated systems allow banks to more efficiently and effectively conduct common banking practices. With the introduction of Automated Teller Machines (ATM), the time-honored tradition of going into the bank to withdraw money or transfer funds, for example, becomes a method of the past. Through the use of ATMs, customers carry out activities such as withdrawing, transferring, or even depositing funds without having to speak to a teller. This self-service machine was a first step in the development of electronic banking.

As customers become more accustomed to ATMs and the variety of functions they can conduct on their own, the appeal for self-service automation grows. The Internet brings the bank to the customer replacing the old ideals of the customer needing to go to the bank. Customers are not the only beneficiaries from the transition to point and click banks. With the Internet in full swing, the banking sector is taking advantage of the new possibilities introduced to them. Norway is the first country in the world to offer Internet banking services (Ebersohn & Henning, 2001). After this, the rest of the world follows, making Internet banking a worldwide phenomenon. A recent study by the American Bankers Association (ABA) and Grant Thornton found that nearly 20% of bankers believe the Internet will the dominant banking channel by the year 2005 (Poquette, 2002). With increased appeal to offer services on the Internet, banks are seeking out and finding clients in many areas of the world. The Internet has provided banks with limitless freedom in offering services and establishing partnerships. While opening a branch in a foreign market can be a surefire way to make its presence known, a bank could loose a considerable amount of its investment if the branch is not successful in generating business. The freedom banks are experiencing in their attempts at cross-border banking is what Goutzinis (2001) calls a freedom of establishment and the freedom to provide services through the Internet.

This freedom, however attractive and beneficial, may present some challenge. Although the Internet has opened new possibilities for private and commercial banks, it also has opened the door to some challenges. Banks are becoming increasingly advanced and interconnected offering a variety of self-service banking options online and subscribing to a global payment systems and global structures. In an attempt to remain on the cutting edge in the evolutionary world, banks and bank managers are challenged by the new technology and software systems used to make the finance world run smoothly (Stewart, 2000). With constant upgrades and improvements, banks are having difficulty keeping up with the latest trends and technologies, while remaining competitive in the global marketplace. The second challenge Stewart points out is deciding what services to provide. In an effort to remain competitive in the global payment system the banking world now operates in, banks are challenged in deciding if they want to offer simple, traditional services or something completely new and radical to gain and retain customers. Often driven by corporate visions and organizational structures, banks are finding that they need to revise these strategies and cooperate with one another, working towards common interests in a cross-border situation to deter nontraditional competitors from penetrating the market. The third challenge Stewart cites is the bank's ability to manage a complex new variety of business relationships coupled with the organizational and cultural differences that will make these relationships more difficult. Stewart questions how a bank will deal with newly formed nonbank competitors, new technology partners, and an array of service providers. He advises banks to seek partnerships and alliances in the emerging cross-border banking systems.

While banks are responding to one of Stewart's challenges by deciding what services to offer, customers are familiarizing themselves with these very same services. Whether it is the traditional options such as account management or balance inquiry, or the more elaborate options such as loan applications or automated clearinghouse transactions, customers have a responsibility to know what options are available to them. Balance inquiry and account management are two of the more basic options available to an online customer. Balance inquiry refers mainly to watching the overall balance of an account and checking the daily balance. Account management implies the handling of assets such as transferring funds between accounts and general account maintenance such as balancing checkbooks and maintaining savings accounts. According to Poquette

(2002), check balances (90.6%), cash management (81.1%) and wire transfers (73%) are the most popular of the 19 reviewed services offered to small-business customers. In addition to these common and traditional services, bill presentment and payment are two other common elements found in the online banking package (Spiotto, 2001).

Not only are customers finding new ways to pay their bills, they are able to pay them from different places. Wireless or mobile banking has put banking transactions on the move. People are checking e-mail, receiving real-time stock quotes, and conducting conversations all with one little handheld device. With its convenience and utility, cellular phones have optimized the flow of banking information for wireless users (West, 2002). The impact that wireless phones with Internet access have on remote banking channels can be seen through the increasing improvements and new features being offered to cellular customers, while also targeting those customers who would conduct their finances from a wireless or Internet-based medium.

The benefits that Internet banking have brought to the modernized world does not come without a price. In the increasingly interconnected marketplace, anyone can have access to nearly anything from anywhere. People who engage in these online practices are vulnerable to a myriad of risks. The emergence of a whole new category of crimes has given both, the banking industry and customers something, to think about. Many problems affect one side of the partnership more than the other. Some of the more common problems include, but are not limited to, unauthorized access and the redirection of websites or e-mail, identity theft, credit card fraud, and phony organizations. These technology risks, as well as several others, have prompted the development of a category of safety measures for Internet transactions. Both banks and customers are expected to maintain certain levels of safety in addition to following and implementing procedures that help keep them safe. With customers accessing their money and making transactions from new places and spending in new ways, e-banking has taken them to new levels in their financial pursuits and abilities. Resulting from these new transactional capabilities is great responsibility (Jain, Hong, & Pankanti, 2000). Other problems facing e-banking customers are vulnerability to hackers and viruses and knowing with whom they are communication when they logon to a website. Many personal computer users are familiar with and have experienced viruses. These pathogens come from a multitude of sources, through e-mail, file downloads, and illegitimate software programs. They can cause damage in a variety of ways, weakening a computer and allowing a hacker access to personal information stored on the hard drive (Katyal, 2001).

In everyday life, credit cards fraud is an issue of concern. Verifying signatures and identification is a relatively common practice for in-store purchases, but what about online? While this is a somewhat effective technique for in-store purchases, credit card fraud still continues despite all efforts to the contrary. Credit cards fraud becomes increasing more possible and extremely easier to carry out (Bruno, 2001). With online shopping, the most common way to "check out" of a website is by using a credit card to purchase the selected items and complete the transaction. Mills (2002) reported that "One recent report says credit card fraud is now 12 times higher online than in-store, while another report pegs online fraud at four times as frequent as the oldfashioned kind" (p.7). Another result of credit card fraud online is identity theft. Using a stolen credit card number, the defrauder pretending to be the cardholder steals and assumes the victim's identity, passing off his or her actions as those of the cardholder.

Though there are several security concerns that the consumer must take into consideration to ensure their safety on the Internet, the burden to provide a safer online environment lies more so in the banking industry's hands. Banks are faced with the responsibility of making e-banking a safe venture, not only for themselves, but for their consumers as well. Key elements for establishing a security plan include reviewing intrusion detection systems, maintaining well-trained staff to handle any computer issues and protect the integrity of the data, and employee verification, including background checks if necessary. Since a customer can manage nearly all of their finances online, banks are faced with the obligations, as service providers, to guarantee their clients' security. Banks must assess the risk involved to the consumer and the companies, establish a plan for security, and analyze possible solutions and monitor their implementation to alleviate security concerns about e-banking. Banks, however are not perfect entities, and like their customers, they may make mistakes. There are generally seven management and security shortcomings that are attributed to a bank's security problems (Levitt, 2001). Carlson, Furst, Lang, and Nolle (2001) explain that this lack of consumer confidence can not only lead to large financial losses, but the lack of confidence in the security measures can lead to the slowing of company development.

Successful E-banking Strategies

The Internal Banking Strategies

The responsibility for safety lies heavier in the hands of banking institutions. Since they are the service providers in most cases, they have equal if not more responsibility in making their websites, databases, and networks safe for the Internet and handing e-commerce transactions. Banks should subscribe to certain requirements and prevent themselves from falling into the most common pitfalls. Some of these problem areas include the potential of internal threat and minimizing the importance of small network problems that if ignored may become larger and more damaging (McCarthy & Campbell 2001). Some suggestions made by Pray and McCoppin (2001) for regulating internal security include staying away from passwords that are linked to an employee's name, address, or social security number, and programs that offer to store a password for easy, repeat access.

The External Liability

Another area for concern is the use of third party providers. Increasingly, most large banking institutions contract with third party service providers to handle issues outside their realm of knowledge. Banks should verify the integrity and identity of the companies they are dealing with, and address any and all concerns when dealing with these agencies.

Technological Developments for Safety

Authentication, identification, and authorization are three big areas that information technology developments have profoundly affected. Other security concerns that compose banks' strategies for a safer banking environment are encryption and the use of tangible identification methods. Messages that travel over the Internet are susceptible to interception by someone other than the individual at the intended destination. For this reason, sending sensitive information such as bank account numbers and credit card numbers over the Internet is troubling for some consumers. Encryption techniques exist to counter these security weaknesses. In another effort at customer security, some banks are using techniques such as tangible devices, or something a customer possess to ensure their safety (Middlemiss, 2002).

Legislation

The absence of territorial boundaries in cyberspace is causing challenges for legislation that depends on the well-defined perimeter of time and space and separation of agencies and people (Shanmugam, Suganthi, & Balachander, 2002). Banks have the responsibility to maintain a set of goals attained through well designed security measures or a "security architecture" which provides the roadmap to an organization's strategic safety vision (Patilla, 2001). This roadmap should lead to compliance with government regulations, their best interests, and the needs of their customers to provide and promote a safe E-banking atmosphere. To that end, protecting the consumer is of vital importance for services such as e-banking and e-commerce which are dependent on continuous customer interest and usage. While it is important that a customer take responsibility for their own safety, consumers must be made aware and educated, if necessary, about the levels of security protection available to them. Customers should understand their rights and obligations as Internet users, costs they may incur and risks they may be vulnerable to by participating in actions such e-banking (Giannakoudi, 1999).

E-banking is popular in the United State today. Both the banks and the customers take the advantages of E-banking. The United State is a country with diverse cultures. People with different cultural backgrounds might have different behaviors. According to the encyclopedia Wikipedia (2006), the Chinese population in the United States is more than 3.5 millions, some of them are American-born-Chinese, and some of them are first generation of immigrants. Most of them are located in some big cities such as New York, Los Angeles, San Francisco, Boston, Washington DC, and Philadelphia. The study was conducted in New York City to investigate the Chinese customers' banking habits and the major barriers which prevent them from participating in E-banking.

METHODOLOGY

The overall purpose of this study was to investigate the Chinese customers' banking habits and the major barriers which prevent them from participating in E-banking. The findings of the study can help marketers understand more about the Chinese customers' banking behaviors, and can help financial institutions implement effective strategies to attract and serve the customers. The respondents in the study were contacted at bank branches in Chinatown area in New York City. The data collection activities were permitted by the bank branch managers. Convenient sampling technique was applied in the study. The instrument used in this study was questionnaire. The survey was comprised of two questions and the respondent's demographic information. These data were used to determine the respondents' banking habits and the major barriers which prevent them from participating in E-banking.

FINDINGS

The survey was conducted at six bank branches in Chinatown area in New York City during fall 2007. Two branches were Citibank branches, two branches were Chase bank branches, and two branches were HSBC branches. Totally, there were 110 questionnaires had been completed and submitted. Table 1 shows the respondents' demographic information. Regarding the question "With what medium do you do most of your banking transactions?" There were 62 (56%) respondents reported they did most transactions with teller station, there were 32 (29%) respondents reported they did most transactions with ATM, and there were only 16 (15%) respondents reported they did most transactions with Internet (shown in table 2, table 3, and table 3).

Table 1: Respondents' demographic information

Gender	Age	Education	Annual Income	Total respondents
Male 62 Female 48	< 30 years : 41 30-50 years: 38 > 50 years: 31	High school level: 34 College level: 62 Professional school level: 14	< $25,000: 25 $25,000 to $50,000: 65 > $50,000: 20	110

Table 2: I do most teller station transaction: respondents' demographic information

Gender	Age	Education	Annual Income	Total numbers of respondents and percentage
Male: 35 Female: 27	<30 years: 15 30-50 years: 22 > 50 years: 25	High school level: 20 College level: 35 Professional school level: 7	< $25,000: 15 $25,000 to $50,000: 37 > $50,000: 10	62 (56%)

Table 3: I do most ATM transaction: respondents' demographic information

Gender	Age	Education	Annual Income	Total numbers of respondents and percentage
Male: 17 Female: 15	<30 years: 16 30-50 years: 12 > 50 years: 4	High school level: 10 College level: 18 Professional school level: 4	< $25,000: 8 $25,000 to $50,000: 19 > $50,000: 5	32 (29%)

Regarding the question "What are the major barriers prevent you from participating in E-banking?" There were 99 (90%) respondents reported "security concern", there were 64 (58%) respondents reported "without technical assistance from bank staffs", there were 21 (19%) respondents reported "computer illiteracy", and there were 8 (7%) respondents reported "without computer or Internet access" (shown in table 5). The 99 "security concern" respondents and 64 "without technical assistance from bank staffs" respondents were from any gender group, any age group, and education level group, and any income level group. The 21 "computer illiteracy" respondents were from at least one of the following two groups: "over 50 years old" group and "high school dropout and high school diploma" group. All the 8 "without computer or Internet access" respondents were from "annual income under $25,000" group.

Table 4: I do most Internet transaction: respondents' demographic information

Gender	Age	Education	Annual Income	Total numbers of respondents and percentage
Male: 10 Female: 6	<30 years: 10 30-50 years: 4 > 50 years: 2	High school level: 4 College level: 9 Professional school level: 3	< $25,000: 2 $25,000 to $50,000: 9 > $50,000: 5	16 (15%)

Table 5: barriers of using online transaction

Security concern	Without technical assistance	Computer illiteracy	Without computer or Internet access	
99	64	21	8	Number of respondents
90%	58%	19%	7%	Percentage of respondents

SUMMARY AND CONCLUSIONS

The study shows most of the Chinese customers in New York City still prefer to do banking transactions with teller station, irrespective of their gender, age, education level, and income level. A couple reasons account for this phenomenon. First, many banks set branches in Chinatown area in New York City. It is very convenient for customers to do banking because of the location. Second, customers prefer the high-touch service channel, because they can request services or ask questions when they need. Third, customers consider on-site banking is more secure. Hofstede (1980) identified four cultural dimensions that could differentiate countries; one of the dimensions was weak versus strong uncertainty avoidance. Many Chinese customers are strong uncertainty avoidance oriented. Compared to the on-site banking (56%) and the ATM banking (29%), there are only 15% of the Chinese customers prefer the online banking. Most of these 15% customers are featured with relative young age (under 30 years old), relative high education (college level education), and relative high income (annual income ranges from $25,000 to $50,000). Those customers, featured with relative old age (over 50 years old), relative low education (high school dropout and high school diploma), and relative low income (annual income under $25,000), account for only a small portion of the group prefer online banking. The findings indicate that aging people with low education and low income are less likely to participate in online banking.

Fall in the middle between on-site banking and online banking, there are 29% of the Chinese customers prefer ATM banking. The reason accounts of this phenomenon could be: ATM banking combines the features of relative convenience (the location), relative high tough service channel (customers can ask bank staffs for assistance if they need during the business hours), and relative safety (security). Regarding the major barriers which prevent Chinese customers from participating in E-banking, the "security concern" is the single most important barrier. There are 99 (90%) respondents report that they consider the safety of the online banking. The second most important barrier is "without technical assistance from bank staffs". The findings indicate that when the Chinese customers participate in online banking, they consider the security issue and technical issue. They are afraid that their information is obtained by third party or misused by the financial institutions; and they are afraid that they can not get assistances from bank staffs when they suffer from computer technical problems at home. The "computer illiteracy" is an online banking barrier for those aging and low-educated Chinese customers, especially those aging customers. The "without computer and Internet access" is an online banking barrier for those low income Chinese customers. It is surprised that only 8% respondents report "without computer and Internet access", while 25% respondents report "computer illiteracy". That means there are 17% of the respondents who own computers but they are computer illiteracy. The reason is that other family member(s) rather than the respondent uses the computer at home. For example, it is the respondents' spouses, the children, or the grandchildren who use the computers.

It doesn't make sense for financial institutions to promote the E-banking to those customers without computer or computer illiteracy. On the contrary, the computer-skilled customers with Internet access are the financial institutions' target market of E-banking. The major task for the financial institutions is to remove the online banking barriers and convince customers to participate in E-banking. How to protect customers' information and how to set up call center to support customers are the two major concerns for many financial institutions. Although the study was conducted in New York City, however, all the respondents were Chinese. The findings are useful for financial institutions which try to promote E-banking to Chinese customers in China. It is estimated that, by 2007, there are 162 millions Chinese people with Internet access in China, it accounts for more than 12% of its population (Miniwatts Marketing Group, 2007).

The major limitation of the study is the sampling. The nonprobability sampling technique and the relative small amount of samples prevent the findings from being generalized. Although all the respondents in the study are China, however, the first generation of Chinese immigrants might have different characteristics as the American-born-Chinese generation does. It is believed that the first generation of Chinese immigrants is more Chinese culture oriented, while the American-born-Chinese generation is more American culture oriented. The researcher didn't identify the generation difference of those respondents created another limitation of the study.

REFERENCES

1. Bruno, M. (2001). Microsoft gives boost to surrogate card numbers. Bank Technology News, 14(10), 31, 34.
2. Carlson, J., Furst, K., Lang, W., & Nolle, D. (2001, revised). Internet banking: Market Development and Regulatory issues. In Society of Government Economists Conference 2000. The new economy: What has Changed, and the challenges for Economic policy. Washington, DC: Office of the Comptroller of the Currency.
3. Giannakoudi, S. (1999). Internet banking: The digital voyage of banking and money in Cyberspace. Information & communications Technology Law, 8(3), 205-244.
4. Goutzinis, A. (2001). European banks and the cross-border provision of services vie the Internet: Commercial practices and regulatory concerns. Journal of International Banking Regulation, 3(3), 208-229.
5. Hofstede, G. (1980). Culture's Consequences. Beverley Hills, CA: Sage.
6. Henning, J. J. & Ebersohn, G. J. (2001) Risk to the South African financial markets. Journal of International Banking Regulation, 3(3), 269- 290.
7. Jain, A., Hong, L. & Pankanti, S. (2000). Biometric identification. Association for Computing Machinery, Communications of the ACM, 43(2), 90-98.
8. Katyak, N.K., (2001). Criminal law in cyberspace. University of Pennsylvania Law Review, 149(4).
9. Levitt, J. (2001). Security—the enemy within. Information Week, (834), 67-70.
10. McCarthy, P., & Campbell, S. (2001).Taking e-security to a higher level. Financial Executive, 17(9), 50-51.
11. Middlemiss, J. Banks get smart about computer chip cards. (2002, April 8). Retrieved September 19, 2007, from http://www.banktech.com/story/techfoucus/bnk20020408s0027
12. Mills, S. (2002). Web security must not stop a firm from doing business. American Banker, 167(137), 7.

13. Miniwatts Marketing Group (2007). China Internet usage Stats and Telecommunications Market Report.

14. Retrieved November 24, 2007, from http://www.internetworldstats.com/asia/cn.htm

15. Patilla, J. (2001). Designing an e-commerce security architecture. Software Magazine, 21(2).

16. Poquette, B. (2002). Consumers flip to the Internet channel for financial services Bank News, 102(4), 18-22.

17. Pray, A., & McCoppin, P. (2001). More convenience – more risk: Internet security Challenges to successful Treasury management. AFP Exchange, 21(2), 50-54.

18. Shanmugam, B., Suganthi, R., & Balachandher, K. (2002). Malaysian regulation versus E-banking. Journal of International Banking Regulation, 4(1), 84-95.

19. Spiotto, A. (2001). Electronic bill payment and resentment: A primer. The Business Lawyer, 57(1), 447-473.

20. Stewart, J. Jr. (2000). Changing technology and the payment system. Current Issues in Economics and Finance, 6(11), 1-5.

21. West, L. (2002). Dial M for money: Western European banks are buying into wireless Technology. Bank Technology News. Retrieved August 26, 2007, from http://www.futurebanker.com/btn/articles/btnjan01-3.shtml

22. World Almanac Education Group Inc. (2001). Internet Basics. World Almanac & Book of Facts, 566-569.

23. Wikipedia. (2006). Chinese American. Retrieved November 20, 2007, from http://en.wikipedia.org/wiki/Chinese_American

10
CHAPTER

MAPPING E-BANKING MODELS TO NEW TECHNOLOGIES

Ismail M. Romi

INTRODUCTION

Financial institutions are facing significant pressure to make their operations and processes more efficient and effective. Meanwhile, banks play a crucial role among these institutions, therefore; banks are required to provide solutions, and to cope with the variable changes in the economy, technology, and business and financial laws. Traditional banking models are no longer sustainable, and unable to meet the changing needs of customers [1]. Where, the shift towards e-banking produces many challenges. KPMG [2] report those challenges in four main areas, mainly, regulations and regulators, economic environment, changing customers, and the march of technology. Where, those challenges implies that banking sector have to operate in a dynamic environment in which information systems plays a vital role. Therefore, modern banking has tendency of dynamic evolution, adapting its business to valuable changes occurring in the global marketplace. Milan et al. [3] suggests that banks require new philosophy, new strategies, new structures, and new banking models based on new technologies can provide sustainability to banking system. To achieve that; banks are required to map its business models and strategies with the latest technologies, in order to compete well in the marketplace, and satisfy its customers. Meanwhile, empirical results about this type of mapping are inconsistent; because prior researches didn't take all aspects of e-banking as a whole, but focuses on some aspects of e-banking such as models, or technology, or management, and so forth. Therefore, the main objective of this study is to provide further insight into e-banking, the latest technologies, and then find out e-banking requirements that enable banks to cope the dynamic evolutions in its environments.

Citation: Ismail M Romi (2015) Mapping E-banking Models to New Technologies. ISSN: 1204-5357.

BACKGROUND AND LITERATURE REVIEW

E-banking

The review by Oyewole et al. [4] to the study of Egland et al. [5] suggested that; e-banking or internet banking is the employment of a remote delivery channel in performing banking services. Angelakopoulos and Mihiotis [6] indicate that; e banking covers a wide spectrum of banking transactions, which the customer can perform electronically without the need to visit a brick-and-mortar branch. According to this broad definition a lot of services and technologies constitute what is known as e-banking. Rusu and Shen [7] added that; the Internet has been used to support many traditional banking services, such as managing an account and transferring funds among different accounts. It also enables some new services, such as electronic bill payments and online investment. Where; Devi [8] suggested that the ranges of services provided by the e-banking are: internet banking, electronic transfer fund (ETF), electronic clearing services (ECS), telebanking, mobile banking, electronic data interchange (EDI), automated teller machine (ATM) and so on. Milan et al. [3] added that a new banks model were emerged, this type of banks is called virtual banks; which have a business model that provides online services with a lower operating costs.

The reported statistics in the past few years show that the online banking grows up rapidly. Statista [9] shows that 423.5 million people accessed online banking sites in 2012 from internet audience, i.e. 28.7% of the internet audience worldwide accessed online banking. Where, 45% in internet audience accessed online banking in North America, 37.8% from Europe, 25.1% from Latin America, 22% from Asia, and 8.8% from the Middle Ease and Africa. In 2013, Pew Research Center reported that 51% of U.S. adults, or 61% of internet users accessed online banking, meanwhile, in Europe the percentage reaches 43%. Eurostate [10] statistics show that 45% of the European internet users accessed the online banking. Factbrowser [11] shows that online users willing to conduct online banking are 46% from Asia Pacific, 45% from Africa and the Middle East, and 36% from Latin America.

The interest with e-banking came from the tremendous amount of benefits from the services covered when using such systems. Salehi and Alipour [12] classified those benefits from several viewpoints, bank's point of view, customers' point of view, economical benefits, and society perspective. From the banks' view point; the benefits are: better branding and better responsiveness to the market, enjoying a better brand image, and offering a perfect opportunity for maximizing profits. From the customers' point of view, the benefits are: increased comfort and timesaving, quick and continuous access to information, better cash management, and providing faster, easier and more reliable services. Meanwhile, the economic benefits are lower operational costs of banks, potentially lower margins, and expand reach through selfservice. From society perspective e-banking business makes access to finance from banks attractive. E-Finance offers the following attractive benefits for society: ease of use, lower costs of financing, convenience, timesaving's, and operational efficiency.

E-banking business models

Romi [13] reviewed the definition of business model in the literature, and find out that a business model is architecture of a business for creating value that incorporates the business strategy and its alignment with information technology that produces value to stakeholders. Table 1 shows the definitions provided by Laudon and Traver [14] to the components of a business model. Milan et al. [3], determined a set of factors that affect the development of e-banking; which are developing information systems using Internet and Web technologies that is suitable for financial transactions, conducting financial transactions digitally, developing business models depending on knowledge and new technologies, enabling financial business systems to operate globally, implementing ISO standards which concerned with safety and information protection.

Table 1: Business Model Components [14]

Business Model Components	Question to ask
Value proposition	Why should the customer buy from the firm?
Revenue model	How will the firm earn money?
Market Opportunity	What marketspace does the firm intend to serve and what is its size?
Competitive Environment	Who else occupies the firm's intended marketspace?
Competitive Advantage	What special advantages does the firm bring to the marketspace?
Market Strategy	How does the firm plan to promote its products or services to attract its target audience?
Organizational Development	What types of organizational structures within the firm are necessary to carry out the business plan?
Management Team	What kind of backgrounds should the firm's leaders have?

KPMG [2] argues that banks needs new business models that enables banks to reduce costs, cope with complex value chain, standardized data requirements, and delivers distinctive customer service. KPGM [2] shows that some banks start to implement the horizontally-integrated model; which uses business process that cross functional areas in the bank to provide common services, rather than products, thus the model operates by dividing the value chain into a particular parts across the whole product.

Table 2: Key Components of Accenture Models [1]

Model	Definition	Key Components
1. Intelligent Multichannel Bank	Engaging with customers on their financial needs effectively. • Integrated multichannel architecture, powered by analytics. • Advanced digital advisory. • Need-based offerings optimized by channels.	• Advanced multichannel integration focusing on digital channels and an integrated architecture. • Pervasive analytics based on effective customer data collection, micro-segmentation and predictive modeling to determine the most effective basket of products. • Real-time interactions management that can increase conversion rates from inbound and outbound contacts. • Advanced advisory services leveraging digital channels and personal analytics. • Product offerings and related pricing schemes based on micro-segments and optimized by channel.
2. Socially Engaging Bank	Interacting with customer to increase customer intimacy. • Customer engagement.	• Social media monitoring to identify opportunities to engage customers, mitigate risks and promptly react to issues • Social digital marketing building on clustering to enable the bank to

	• Leverage influencers. • Co-creation based on increased customer intimacy.	better defines the best content for individual customer profiles and attracts them. • Social CRM enriching customer data with social media data, thus facilitating more effective propositions.
3. Financial/Non-Financial Digital Ecosystem Bank	An ecosystem selling financial and non-financial services, leveraging in particular the power of mobile technology. • Bank with an extended proposition (financial and non-financial). • M-payment services	• Mobile payments based on Near Field Communication (NFC) or mobile wallet, that enhances bank competitiveness in the payment arena and helps retain existing customers • Enriched propositions through mobile commerce focused on financial and non-financial offerings, mobile marketing, m-loyalty and m-analytics • Alliances and partnerships with non-banking operators and creation of related content.
4. The "do the basics right" Bank	• Optimized branch network and contact center. • Enhanced digital channels. • Need-based offerings and consistent sales behaviors.	• Branch network optimization (number and size of branches), reviewing network architecture (i.e. hub and spoke model) • Basic multichannel integration, alignment of channels and integrated governance processes for real-time banking • Proactive and reactive

	• Basic multichannel integration.	management interaction based on customer needs • Operational customer segmentation driven by a needs-based offering structure • Sales force effectiveness powered by consistent sales behaviors and tools • Simple and clear communication with customers • Performance management (new customer-oriented metrics) and tailored compensation schemes.

Accenture [1] suggest three business models for banking and called them the next generation banking models. Those models are intelligent multichannel model, socially engaging model, and financial/ non-financial digital ecosystem model. Where banks have to consider these models when defining their own models. Accenture provides the definitions and key components Table 2 to each of the suggested models, besides the definition and components of the traditional banking which they called it the "do the basics right" bank model-model 4 in Table 2. Accenture [1] adds that; the selection from the specified models depends on bank potential capabilities, and suggests the capabilities matrix to measure bank capabilities.

E-banking technological features

E-banking and e-commerce formulated as the use of Internet, the Web, and other features to conduct transactions electronically. Therefore, the required features for e-commerce can be settled to e-banking. Researchers [14,15] found out the features of e-commerce technology. Those features include ubiquity; which refers to the availability everywhere, and at any time, global reach; which refers to the ability of e-banking technology to permit transactions to cross cultural and national boundaries, universal standards; which refers to the technical standards of the Internet, richness is the complexity and content of a message, interactivity; which refers to conducting online dialogues with the consumer, information Density; which refers to the total amount and quality of information available to all consumers, and stakeholders, personalization/and Customization; this component refers to allowing personalized messages to be delivered to consumers., and social technology; which refers to using content generation, distribution, and supporting social networks [14,15].

To achieve those requirements, Laudon and Traver [14] suggests that implementing e-banking requires the banking transactions to be conducted everywhere, at all times, and cross cultural national boundaries taking into consideration global banking and internet standards. In addition to the ability of technology to handle with customer dialogues and messages; which may include all types of presentations, video, audio, and so forth. Laudon and Traver [14] adds that; the used technology must have the ability to handle with huge amount of data in all time including peak time using scalability, and handle with the changes of the delivered message based on a user's preferences.

KPMG [2] provides a clear image of the cross-cultural banking. Where, any proposed model must take into consideration the decentralized and fragmented structure, cutting cost, and using complex IT architecture. Therefore, IT architecture must be capable to operate in a dynamic environment, taking into consideration to operate using service oriented architecture (SOA) principles, standardization and subdivide value chain activities, reporting requirements [2].

E-banking success factors

E-banking can be classified as an information system; which consists of computer hardware, software, databases, procedures, and users. Researchers classified information systems success factors, and hence, e-banking success factors as a set of dimensions and aspects that produce the net benefits of information system. Those dimensions include the e-banking system quality, the quality of the produced information, and the quality of the services provided by e-banking, e-banking use, user satisfaction, and net benefits produced from using e-banking [16-20]. Romi [21], tests (Figure 1) the impact of information systems quality, the quality of the produced information, the quality of the services provided by the information systems on the stakeholders requirements, mainly; information system use, information systems user satisfaction and net benefits in the financial institutions, and find out that system quality, and service quality explains 78.2% of the variance in system use, the service quality, and information quality explains 77.2% of the variance in user satisfaction, and the system use, and user satisfaction explains 54.9% of the variance in the net benefits. Therefore, the model (Figure 1) provides a good explanation of information systems success,and thus e-banking success. These results implies that e-banking success depends on many factors, mainly, systems quality, service quality, and information quality. Table 3 provides the definition of Delone and Mclean [17] to these factors, and the constructs of each factor, which are tested by Romi [13].

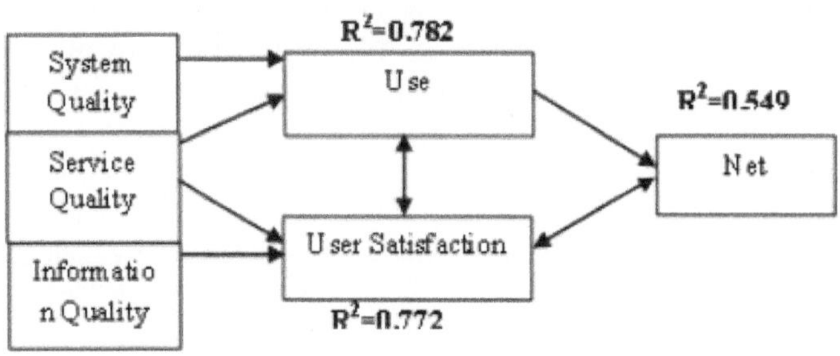

Figure 1: Information Systems Success Model [13].

Table 3: E-Banking Success Factors [13,17]

Success Factor	Definition	Factors Constructs
System Quality	Defined as a set of constructs related to information system that determines the quality of the systems.	System reliability, easy to learn, ease of use, user preemptive, flexibility, and integration with another systems,
Information Quality	The degree to which information presents the required benefits.	Availability, timeliness, relevancy, accuracy, appropriateness, completeness, concise representation, interpretability.
Service Quality	A set of characteristics related to services submitted by information systems to customers.	Services reliability, assurance, empathy, and security.

E-banking requirements and features

The literature provides answers to some questions that are essential to use the best technology in banking operation "e-banking". Meanwhile there are many challenges that have to be considered while implementing this type of banking. Those challenges are reported by KPMG [2], which includes the efforts by regulators to produce a new regulations to avoid new banking crises (regulations and regulators), economic environment; where banks are required to operate in the reduced economy growth and any other expected economic situation, changing customers behavior towards banks; where they are more warily and less trust to banks, and the changing technology; where banks are required to upgrade their information systems to cope with the complicated and rapid changes in technology. Addressing those challenges requires an insight analysis to all aspects of banking processes and operations, as well as the banking environment. Where, the literature provides an analysis to some aspects to e-banking requirements. Accenture [1] suggested three models (Table 2) that can be implemented in banking operations depending on bank capabilities. Where, the key components of the predefined models provide the functionalities of banks. Meanwhile, the study of Rusu and Shen [7], and Devi [8] provides banking functions that are required by customers, such as managing accounts, electronic bill payments, online investment, internet banking, electronic transfer fund (ETF), electronic clearing services (ECS), telebanking, mobile banking, electronic data interchange (EDI), automated teller machine (ATM) and so on. Meanwhile, e-commerce technological features; are determined by Laudon and Traver [14] and Shafiyah et al. [15]; which include global reach, ubiquity, richness, interactivity, personalization/ and customization, information density, universal standards, and social technology. Depending on the success factors provided by Delone and Mclean [17], and tested by Romi [13] in the financial institutions, E-banking success factors include three main constructs (Table 3), mainly; e-banking system quality, the quality of the produced information, the quality of the services provided by e-banking. The provided analysis shows that; even if banks achieve all given requirements, the challenges still need more investigation and analysis. This is consistent with the results of Milan et al [3], which argues that; banks require new philosophy, new strategies, new structures, and new banking models based on new technologies can provide sustainability to banking system.

MAPPING E-BANKING TO NEW TECHNOLOGIES

Figure 2 presents a proposed model for e-banking. Where the model is composed of five main domains, mainly; bank functional and non-functional requirements, customer functional and non-functional requirements, bank technological capabilities, customers technological capabilities, and suppliers technological capabilities.

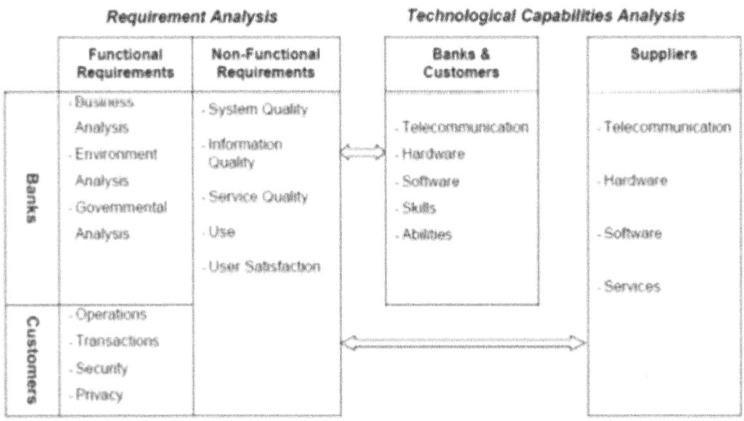

Figure 2: E-Banking Model.

The e-banking model based on five key domains

Banks requirements: Determining banks requirements requires an insight analysis to business, environment, and regulations.

a. Business analysis

This phase includes analyzing banks scope, vision, mission, strategy, policies, procedures, programs, daily operations, synergies, core competences, and all aspects of banks daily work. To achieve the best in this step, analysts have to take into consideration the suggested banking models in the literature [1,2].

b. Environmental analysis

Analyzing the stakeholders, who have direct or indirect impact on banking, in order to determine alliances, economical situations, and so forth.

c. Governmental analysis

This phase includes analyzing governmental and international laws and standards related to financial operations.

Customer requirements:

Identifying the target customers (individual, business corporations, and governmental) who will use e-banking, and their characteristics. Then determining customer's goals in the form of functional and non-functional requirements.

a. Functional requirements

This type of requirements, incorporate all required operations and transactions that the customer needs from banks.

b. Non-functional requirements

Non-functional requirements, affect customer satisfaction. Therefore, an analysis to these requirements must be conducted. In general, common non-functional requirements can be considered that have a direct or indirect impact on customers acceptance to e-banking. The information systems success model (Figure 1) presents the main dimension of the user acceptance to an information system, and hence, to e-banking, which includes; system quality, information quality, service quality, use, and user satisfaction.

Banks technological resources and capabilities: Information technology (IT) can be defined as all sources of technology, which is used to create, store, disseminate, exchange, and use information, which includes hardware, software, and telecommunications. Meanwhile, IT capabilities include the skills and abilities of IT-workforce, which includes technical skills, management skills, and relationship skills [22]. In this phase, an analysis must be conducted to all technological resource available at banks, and then analyzing the available capabilities.

Customers technological resource and capabilities: The information technology resources available to customers; which includes hardware, software, and telecommunications. The customer capabilities include the skills and abilities of customer to use e banking. In this phase, a survey, and analysis must be performed to intended customers, and then analyzing the available capabilities of customers.

Information technology supplies: An Information technology supply is the market, where, banks can collect IT requirements and services. This phase includes analyzing the available hardware, software, and telecommunications in the market.

Requirements Bidirectional Fit to Technological Capabilities

To develop an e-banking system that matches between banks and customer's capabilities that matches the latest technologies, two type of bidirectional fit take place. First, the requirements bidirectional fit to supplier's technological capabilities. Second; the requirements bidirectional fit to banks and customers Capabilities.

Requirements bidirectional fit to suppliers technological capabilities

Achieving this type of bidirectional fit requires developers to analyze the latest technologies in the market, and then analyze banks and customers requirements as if they use this latest technology. This is an essential step that enables banks to keep up to date with technology. In case the current requirements are less than latest technology capabilities, developers can take into consideration the current requirements, and leave the remaining requirements for future work as a plan.

Requirements bidirectional fit to banks and customers capabilities

Prior researches find out that the successful system is the one that accepted by customers. Therefore, developers have to match between bank and customers functional and non-functional requirements from one side, and match between banks and customers capabilities from the other side. After that, a match must be conducted between the requirements and actual capabilities.

Conclusion and Recommendations

This study reviews the literature that is concerned with e-banking requirements, and then conducted an analysis to the available requirements. This can be summarized in:

- E-banking requirements, which can be determined from the banking models, mainly; intelligent multichannel bank, socially engaging bank, financial/non-financial digital ecosystem bank, and the do the basics right" bank.
- Customer requirements, which includes managing accounts, electronic bill payments, online investment, internet banking, electronic transfer fund (ETF), electronic clearing services (ECS), telebanking, mobile banking, electronic data interchange (EDI), automated teller machine (ATM) and so on.
- E-banking features to be considered during the implementation of e-banking, which include global reach, ubiquity, richness, interactivity, personalization/and customization, information density, universal standards, and social technology.
- E-banking success factors, which includes e-banking system quality, the quality of the produced information, the quality of the services provided by e-banking.
- The results show that prior researches focused on some aspects of e-banking; some of these researches works on banking requirements, others' works on technology, meanwhile; the rest works on customer requirements.
- The current study, proposed a model for e-banking, which is composed of five main domains, mainly; bank functional and non-functional requirements, customer functional and non-functional requirements, bank technological capabilities, customers technological capabilities, and suppliers technological capabilities. And then, matches e-banking systems to latest technologies. Where, two types of bidirectional fit take place; first, the requirements bidirectional fit to

supplier's technological capabilities, and second, the requirements bidirectional fit to banks and customers Capabilities.

REFERENCES

1. Accenture (2012) Banking 2016: Accelerating growth and optimizing costs in distribution and marketing.
2. KPMG (2012) Optimizing banking operating models- from strategy to implementation.
3. Milan DN, Jelena V, Sava S (2011) Electronic banking models.International journal of economics and law 1: 24-37.
4. Oyewole O, Abbe M, El-muade, Gambo J, Arikpo, Abam I (2013) E-banking and Bank Performance: Evidence from Nigeria.International Journal of Scientific Engineering and Technology 2: 766-771.
5. Egland KL, Furst K, Nolle DE, Robertson DD (1998) Banking over the Internet. Quarterly Journal 17.
6. Angelakopoulos G, Mihiotis A (2011) E-banking: challenges and opportunities in the Greek banking sector. Electronic Commerce Research 11: 297-319.
7. Rusu RF, Shen K (2012)An empirical study on E-Banking acceptance in the United Arab Emirates (UAE).Journal of Electronic Banking Systems2012: 1-9.
8. Devi PA (2010) Customers' Perception of E-Banking: Factor Analysis. The IUP Journal of Management Research 6: 1-14.
9. Statista (2015) Global online banking penetration in April 2012, by region.
10. Eurostat (2015) Individuals using the internet for internet banking.
11. Factbrowser (2015) Online Banking Facts and Statistics.
12. Salehi M, Alipour M (2010) E-Banking in Emerging Economy: Empirical Evidence of Iran. International Journal of Economics & Finance 2: 201-209.
13. Romi IM (2013) Testing Delone and Mclean's Model in Financial. American Academic & Scholarly Research Journal 5: 121-129.
14. Laudon KC, Traver CG (2014) E-commerce 2014: business, technology, society (10thedn.).
15. Shafiyah N, Alsaqour R., Shaker H, AlsaqourUddin O (2013) Review on Electronic Commerce. Middle-East Journal of Scientific Research 18: 1357-1365.
16. Delone WH, Mclean ER (2003) The Delone and Mclean Model of Information Systems Success: a Ten- Year Update. Journal of Information Systems 19: 9-30.
17. Delone WH, McLean ER (1992) Information systems success: The quest for the dependent variable. Information Systems Research 3: 60-95.
18. DeLone WH, McLean ER, Petter S (2008) Measuring information systems success: models, dimensions, measures, and interrelationships. European Journal of Information Systems 17: 236-263.

19. Seddon PB (1994) A partial Test Development of Delone and Mclean's Model of IS Success. ICIS 1994 Proceedings. Paper 2.The international Conference of Information Systems, Vanconver.

20. Seddon PB (1997)A Re-specification and Extension of the Delone and Mclean's Model of IS Success. Information Systems Research 18: 240-253.

21. Romi IM (2012) Mobile Commerce Success Factors for the Various Business Models. Proceedings of 2ndComputer Science On-line Conference in 2012, Open Publish Proceedings series, Czech Republic.

22. Ravarini, Aurelio (2010) Information technology capability within small-medium enterprises PhD thesis,School of Computer and Security Science, Edith Cowan University,Australia .

11
CHAPTER

STRATEGIC CONTEXT FOR INTERNET BANKING

Stephen Kent Callaway and Sandeep Bhailalbhai Jagani

Keywords: Strategic context; strategic control systems; e-commerce

INTRODUCTION

The resource-based view of the firm (RBV) argues that resources are the source of firm competitive advantage (Barney, 1991; Wernerfelt, 1984). Therefore, firm performance depends upon how the firm manages and directs its resources. The issue of managing resource flows of new ventures is particularly important in the case of traditional banks pursuing e-commerce. The strategic role of the e-commerce venture is termed its strategic context. The strategic context of the e-commerce unit indicates the extent of resource flows to and from the banking unit (Callaway, 2006). The concept of strategic context may be used to identify and assess critical information about the strategic management of the unit, and directly relates to the control of resource flows. Therefore, organizational control systems are critical for how firms manage resources such as IT. Specific archetypes of strategic control systems include input-based (focused on recruiting and training), clan control (informal norms and values), output-based (focused on incentives for achieving certain outcomes), or behavior-based (focused on following particular policies and procedures) (Kirsch, 1996; Ouchi, 1979, 1980; Snell, 1992).

The case of high internal and external resource flows, indicating the venture demonstrates greater strategic importance, means the unit is important and influential to the bank, yet also connected to and influenced by external constituents (Pfeffer & Salancik, 1978). Therefore the greater strategic context is associated with a greater use

Citation: Stephen Kent Callaway and Sandeep Bhailalbhai Jagani, Strategic Context for Internet Banking, ISSN: 1204-5357.

of all the aforementioned strategic control systems. Furthermore, the e-commerce unit may use existing corporate IT resources to help launch the e-commerce unit, and the ecommerce unit can then be used to help develop further IT resources that can be used throughout the corporation, leading to the development of IT capabilities. IT capabilities are an outcome of how a firm leverages its website and e-commerce operations. In short, a well-developed and successful website constitutes an IT capability. Organizations must excel at two extremes simultaneously; they must generate both structure and improvisation, exploit the current source of competitive advantage while continually adapting and creating new ones, and generate both scale and flexibility (Beinhocker, 1997; Brown & Eisenhardt, 1998). Some IT resources and control systems may be extremely codified and explicit, establishing formal rules and targets, where explicit tasks are prescribed, emphasizing efficiency. Other systems may be rather more flexible, allowing substantial authority and empowerment at the local level (Hedlund, 1994). In short, these strategic controls are essential for banks to balance these competing demands, and therefore lead to the development of IT capabilities.

Moreover, the strategic context also relates to how the bank balances efficiency and innovation. That is, the context may relate to key goals like efficiency or innovation. A more aggressive strategic context clearly demonstrates a higher strategic priority, reflecting maximum flow of internal and external resources. This approach maximizes the balance between efficiency and innovation. Because the e-commerce creates substantial opportunities both for cost reduction and presenting new sources of revenue, banks with a well-developed e-commerce unit will likely demonstrate superior performance; measured by revenue enhancement and cost efficiency (intermediate performance metrics). As a result, banks that develop a strong website, meaning they have developed IT capabilities, may expand their business and generate new sources of income, while utilizing a lower cost delivery medium (Callaway, 2011). Of course, these intermediate performance dimensions, revenue enhancement and cost reduction, are associated with final performance, measured by profitability and returns. Finally, ecommerce offers a low cost way for banks to expand market reach and product breadth (Pyun et al., 2002), meaning IT capabilities (i.e., a successful website) leads to improved final performance. Therefore, the central research questions for this paper are: How does the strategic context of a bank's e-commerce unit influence the strategic control systems utilized, and therefore the development of IT capabilities associated with that website? How do those IT capabilities influence firm performance? First, current research on strategic context, strategic controls, and IT capabilities is described, and hypotheses are created. The methodology and results sections are described next. Finally, a discussion concludes the paper, including research and managerial implications.

THEORY AND HYPOTHESES

Strategic Context and Control System

The resource-based view of the firm (RBV) argues that resources are the source of firm competitive advantage (Barney, 1991; Wernerfelt, 1984). Therefore, firm performance depends upon the firm managing its resources effectively. In particular, firms must be able to manage its resource flows between subsidiaries or units, which have ramifications for the strategic importance of those subsidiaries. As such, Gupta & Govindarajan (1991) posed a typology of subsidiary context by focusing on knowledge flows between units within a corporation. Following, Callaway (2006) presented a matrix depicting a unit's strategic context in relation to how a traditional firm may develop a new technology or business, such as in the case of internal corporate ventures (Burgelman, 1983; Burgelman & Sayles, 1986).

The matrix posed the two dimensions of resource flows as the inflow of resources from corporate to the new unit, and the outflow of resources from the unit to corporate (Callaway, 2006). Brown & Eisenhardt (1998) argued that organizations need to blend the past and the present, that is, to utilize the old (an established, legitimated architecture) and the new (a novel contribution). Even firms developing innovative new technologies may get into trouble by ignoring the past, such as an accepted standard, thereby demonstrating too much disconnect. Furthermore, firms must strike an ideal balance of internal collaboration within the organization, using a standard technology, sharing a distribution channel, sharing knowledge, etc.; along with seeking out external resources. Overall, strategic context relates to the dependence of the venture on the corporation as well as the contribution of the venture to the corporation, and gets to the heart of strategically balancing "the old and the new" (Brown & Eisenhardt, 1998). The greater the flow of resources both to and from the new venture, the greater its strategic context.

These issues of balancing the old and the new are particularly important in the case of established banks that pursue Internet Banking along with their traditional branch business. Indeed all bank units must continue to develop innovative products in order to keep up with changing technologies and customer demands, as traditional banks have pioneered the development of many innovative delivery channels including telephone banking, drive-through banking, and ATMs (Booz, Allen & Hamilton, 1999; Gopalakrishnan, Wischnevsky & Damanpour, 2003). Moreover, the relationship of Internet Banking units to headquarters has shifted to a more integrated role over the last few years, as many banks view Internet Banking simply as a remote delivery channel (Gopalakrishnan, Wischnevsky & Damanpour, 2003). According to Callaway (2006), strategic context of the e-commerce unit indicates the extent of resource flows to and from the banking unit. A more independent unit, indicating minimal resource flows, serves to accumulate just enough external resources to survive, but does not disseminate these resources throughout the rest of the organization. The external resources are only those that the unit requires in order to survive and carry out its mission, so the unit relies little on traditional resources from the organization to complement these new resources. A more integrated unit, indicating maximum resource flows, serves to acquire external resources for the purpose of disseminating them across the corporation; however the unit is not self-sufficient in those resources needed to carry out this mission. In this sense, the overall goal of the corporation, through this integrated unit, is to combine the best of the old with the best of the new. The unit acts to combine the traditional knowledge and resources with new knowledge and resources associated with the e-commerce venture (Callaway, 2006).

The concept of strategic context may be used to identify and assess critical information about the strategic management of ventures vs. traditional units. Therefore, organizational control systems are critical for how firms manage resources such as IT. Specific archetypes of strategic control systems are typically utilized for achieving management of resource flows. For example, Kirsch (1996), Ouchi (1979, 1980) and Snell (1992) argued that a firm's strategic controls may be input-based (focused on recruiting and training), clan control (informal ritual and norms), output-based (focused on incentives for achieving certain outcomes), or behavior-based (focused on following particular policies and procedures). Various external factors affect which controls are most appropriate (Kirsch, 1996; Ouchi, 1979, 1980; Snell, 1992). A venture with a greater strategic importance demonstrates greater IT resource flows, and so these flows must be effectively managed. This situation of high internal and external resource flows means the unit is important and influential to the bank, yet connected to and influenced by external constituents (Pfeffer & Salancik, 1978) as well.

As such, Internet Banking plays a critical role in combining traditional bank IT with creating new technologies from e-commerce. According to Callaway & Jagani (2015), Internet Banking allows for the creation of new technology-driven products and services, and increases a bank's demographic reach to new and unfamiliar markets, requiring new and different banking practices (Furst, Lang, & Nolle, 2000; Gopalakrishnan et al., 2003). Internet banking is changing the global banking industry, blurring the traditional lines between product, market, and customer base (Pyun, Scruggs, & Nam, 2002) (Sullivan, 2000). Indeed Gopalakrishnan et al. (2003) identified the key benefits of internet banking as the reduction of transaction costs, the expansion of market reach, the extension of product tailoring, and enhancing customer convenience. The relative importance of these benefits depends upon the unit's strategic context. First, one key success factor for banking, including internet banking, is efficiency and cost reduction. Using innovative technologies to reach out to customers reduces cost and improves overall efficiency. Efficiency is critical for bank performance, including making more productive loans (Fries & Taci, 2005). Advanced technologies enable communication with customers faster and at lower cost, and provide them the information and services they seek more efficiently (Booz, Allen & Hamilton, 1999; Gopalakrishnan, Wischnevsky & Damanpour, 2003). Banks may use e-commerce for cost reduction purposes, and so focus on efficient implementation of objectives, emphasizing goal specificity and formalization of rules (Scott, 1992). In this context, formal rules are particularly effective. That is, behavioral controls (formal rules, policies, procedures) are useful for standardizing efficiency and establishing consistency (Kirsch, 1996; Ouchi, 1979).

Second, banks face pressures for achieving growth objectives. Major US banks face a critical challenge: given reduced opportunities for growth through acquisitions, it is essential to find ways to grow organically, that is, to expand its existing business by attracting more customers, and fulfilling a greater share of their banking needs (offering more products and services to them) (Thomke, 2003). This necessary aggressive growth strategy likely will likely require a substantial increase in sales requirements for unit managers, with the corresponding needed rewards and incentive programs. That is, individual units may face competition to achieve sales goals, requiring incentives for meeting formal targets. However, this emphasis on sales quotas does not replace the traditional emphasis on efficiency and rules, rather it complements it (Callaway & Jagani, 2015; Thomke, 2003.) Third, a greater strategic importance is associated with greater utilization of both input strategic controls (recruiting and training) and informal rules. This argument is premised upon the importance of the management of the lateral interdependence of the banking units. Greater resource flows, both internal and external, lead to more give and take, and mutual reliance, leading to more emphasis on recruiting and training programs (Callaway, 2006). The more extensive resource flows also create greater uncertainty. The emphasis on recruiting and training managers reflects a greater emphasis on the empowerment of local managers, important for encouraging innovation and entrepreneurship. Informal rules are also important for strategic context. The adoption of informal rules, norms and values, and the dissemination of external institutionalized norms, may be particularly important for banking ventures facing this substantial uncertainty (DiMaggio & Powell, 1983; Meyer & Rowan, 1977). The informal rules and norms provide an effective way to encourage teamwork, coordination and sharing.

According to Thomke (2003), a major global bank illustrates each of these approaches to strategic control. The bank created an innovation market within the bank's existing network of branches. These units provided "a test bed for creative ideas" designed to increase customer satisfaction and increase revenue. In this sense, unit managers became individual entrepreneurs, while the key to success for the bank relied upon substantial knowledge sharing among all the bank managers and the corporate level. A key point, though, is that the bank's innovation and experimentation had to be conducted efficiently, at a reasonable cost, and its results had to be accurately measured. Even with the local innovation, managers at the branches still earned a substantial portion of their total pay from performance bonuses related to metrics such as meeting various targets: sales quotas, the number of different products sold, the branch's customer satisfaction levels, market demographics, and incentives based upon team performance (Callaway & Jagani, 2015; Thomke, 2003). Standardizing processes for cost efficiency, offering rewards for meeting targets, investing in managers and associates with recruiting and training, and creating a culture of teamwork and sharing through informal rules, all were critical for this bank. So, a more important strategic context, demonstrating greater flows of internal and external resources, is associated with a greater use of all the aforementioned strategic control systems. Thus,

H1: A greater strategic context is positively associated with greater utilization of strategic control systems.

IT Capabilities

IT resource flows are critical for a firm to develop IT capabilities. It is important to note the difference between IT resources and IT capabilities. IT resources itself will not necessarily lead to sustained competitive advantage (Bharadwaj, 2000; Santhnam & Hartono, 2003). According to Mata et al. (1995), value resides more in the firm's ability to utilize IT than in the technology resource itself. Rather firms innovatively and creatively integrate the resources and accordingly develop unique capabilities from these core IT resources. Therefore, IT resources are the input, which eventually leads to the development of IT capabilities (the output), which is the source of superior firm performance (Muhanna et al., 2010). However, how the firm manages the flow of IT resources to and from the e-commerce venture is the first step toward developing IT capabilities. As such, the e-commerce unit may use existing critical corporate IT resources to help launch the e-commerce unit, while the e-commerce unit can then be used to help develop further IT resources that can be used throughout the corporation. If these resource flows are managed correctly, the firm should be able to develop IT capabilities associated with the e-commerce unit. A firm's IT capability, the outcome of IT resources, specifically refers to "the firm's capacity to leverage the potential of information technology by effectively deploying IT resources in combination or co-present with other resources in the organization" (Bharadwaj, 2000; Santhnam & Hartono, 2003). As firms innovatively and creatively integrate various resources, they are more likely to develop unique capabilities from these core IT resources (Zhang, et al., 2005).

Indeed, the website of a company engaged in e-commerce is critical, since it comprises the critical interface between buyer and seller (Bitner, Stephen and Meuter, 2000). That is, a well-developed website is a key part of delivering customer value (Bitner, Stephen and Meuter 2000; Saeed, Grover and Yujong 2005). A company with a good ecommerce strategy can leverage website technologies in order to enhance customer value as it is then able to provide superior customer service (Saeed, Grover and Yujong 2005), by innovatively integrating its various firm resources. That is, IT capabilities are an outcome of how a firm leverages its website and e-commerce operations. In short, a well-developed and successful website constitutes a capability. Because the strategic context is critical to this process, a greater strategic context is associated with the development of greater IT capabilities. Thus,

H2: A greater strategic context is positively associated with IT capabilities

According to Callaway, et al. (2009), a major investment in information technology may be associated with a lock-in to a particular technology (Reddy 2006; Shapiro and Varian 1999). These past information technology systems, or legacy systems, while very efficient, potentially may reduce a firm's strategic flexibility if not controlled properly (Reddy 2006). Strategic control systems are essential for balancing this efficiency and flexibility. The information technology lock-in has special implications for intra-firm and inter-firm relationships, particularly in an increasingly dynamic external environment where creativity and innovation is so essential, as well as cost efficiency (Hitt et al.1998). Therefore, the strategic control systems, critical for driving efficiency, growth, and / or innovation, are essential for these relationships to develop into actual IT capabilities. That is, strategic control systems are essential for firms to innovatively and creatively integrate various resources, which in turn is what leads to the development of IT capabilities.

IT resources are associated with streamlined procedures and improving communication. At the same time, however, according to Batra (2006), IT systems offer organizations the opportunity for functional integration, multi-skilled staff, rapid and flexible decision making structures, greater autonomy of operating units, and a more flexible and organic approach. That is, while IT processes and resources are associated with monitoring and governance systems, they can also be a part of participative management, rationalize personnel strength, and reduce the number of hierarchical levels. This approach emphasizes the importance of employees, whereby managers delegate tasks and push decision making to lower levels (Batra, 2006). Recruiting and training (critical for individual empowerment), as well as informal norms and rules (critical for teamwork and cooperation), are an essential part of the potential for IT to achieve these benefits. Overall, some IT resources and control systems may be extremely codified and explicit, establishing formal rules and targets, where explicit tasks are prescribed, emphasizing efficiency. Other control systems may be rather more flexible, allowing substantial authority and empowerment at the local level (Hedlund, 1994). The interaction between organization training and the use of technology is considered an integral part of the structuring and control of organizations (Child, 1972; Foo, 1995). Formal processes along with investments in people to promote employee empowerment work together. Firms establish both formal structure and flexibility in incorporating technologies, while instituting training, standardized processes, electronic communication, and leadership (Curlee, 2008). That is, organizations must excel at two extremes simultaneously; they must pursue focused and robust strategies, generate both structure and improvisation, exploit the current source of competitive advantage while continually adapting and creating new ones, and generate both scale and flexibility (Beinhocker, 1997; Brown & Eisenhardt, 1998). In short, all of these strategic control systems are essential for organizations to balance these competing demands, thereby leading to the development of IT capabilities (demonstrated in a successful website). In sum,

H3: Greater utilization of strategic control systems is positively associated with IT capabilities

Performance implications

Greater utilization of control systems reflects a greater strategic context. A greater utilization of control systems is also necessary for firm performance. That is, the strategic context requires control systems to make sure that goals and objectives are met. Greater control systems means greater standardizing processes for cost efficiency, offering more rewards for meeting targets, investing more in managers and associates with recruiting and training, and creating a culture of teamwork and sharing through informal rules, all are a critical part of ensuring the successful execution of strategy. Strategic control systems are what enable the aforementioned functional integration, rapid and flexible decision making structures, and a more flexible and organic approach, along with efficiency and standardization. Strategic controls emphasize the importance of employees, whereby managers delegate tasks and push decision making to lower levels, all the while establishing rigid governance systems (Batra, 2006). The success of both standardization and creativity are necessary for firm performance. That is, an aggressive utilization of strategic control systems, including both standardizing processes for efficiency, and encouraging innovation and teamwork, clearly demonstrates the greatest commitment to immediate cost control and future growth. This approach maximizes balancing and maximizing both efficiency and innovation, that is, balancing the old and the new. This approach reflects maximum coordination between the unit and the traditional bank to drive efficiency, as well as maximum flexibility and innovation. In this sense, the strategic control systems are essential for the e-commerce unit to create new technology-driven products and services, and increase the bank's demographic reach to new and unfamiliar markets, requiring different banking practices, but still in a cost efficient manner (Furst, Lang, & Nolle, 2000; Gopalakrishnan et al., 2003).

Because the e-commerce unit creates substantial opportunities both for cost reduction and presenting new sources of revenue, banks with strong strategic control systems have the potential to demonstrate superior performance. To understand why, it is important to examine performance outcomes comprehensively, addressing not only typical measures of performance for banking – net income and return on assets (e.g., Hernando and Nieto 2007; Reynolds, Ratanakomut and Gander 2000), but also noninterest income (revenue enhancement) and noninterest expenses (cost reduction) (Callaway, 2011). As such, intermediate performance metrics constitute the two critical dimensions of revenue enhancement and cost efficiency. In short, final performance as measured by profitability or returns, indicates what the bank is achieving on the bottom line. Key intermediate performance metrics indicate at a deeper level of understanding why the bank is achieving those numbers. In sum,

H4: Greater utilization of strategic control systems is positively associated with intermediate performance (revenue enhancement and cost efficiency).

Tallon and Kraemer (2003) argued that many firms make considerable investments in IT resources in order to build static capabilities, such as reducing operating costs, perhaps related to a particular product or supplier (Prahalad and Krishnan 2002). IT capabilities should also lower external coordination and internal organization costs by reducing search costs and enabling firms along the value chain to collaborate more closely, helping to make the firm more flexible (Gurbaxani and Whang 1991). That is, according to Reddy (2006), the impact of IT on performance relates to two perspectives: Coordination theory, which focuses on reducing transaction costs for current relationships; and resource-based theory, which focuses on how IT is a dynamic capability (see also Malone and Smith 1988;Malone et al. 1987; as well as Bharadwaj 2000; Byrd 2001; Hitt et al. 1998). As such, IT capabilities achieve two benefits: Superior coordination of current transactions; and building dynamic capabilities to better manage complex and changing business relationships for future innovation and growth (see, also Callaway, Celuch & Murphy, 2009). Indeed, Xue et al. (2012) addressed the impact of IT on the two critical dimensions of organizational performance; innovation (new products and exploring revenue growth opportunities) and efficiency (cost reduction).

A successful website indeed can be a critical part of a firm's efficiency and flexibility, leading to both revenue enhancement and cost reduction. E-commerce has the potential to improve both noninterest income (revenue enhancement) and noninterest expenses (cost reduction). According to the FDIC, noninterest income indicates the ability of the bank to generate additional sources of income beyond traditional interest-bearing assets (such as loans), and includes items such as brokerage and underwriting fees, securitization income, service fees, insurance commissions, fees, and income. Noninterest expenses may include items such as salaries, benefits, premises and equipment expenses (http://www2.fdic.gov). That is, a bank which has successfully integrated its website operations into other business processes may be able to reduce costs by using staff and physical branches more efficiently, and reduce costs for postage, printing, or paper supplies. As a result, banks that develop a popular website with a strong reputation have the potential to expand their business and generate new sources of income, while utilizing a lower cost delivery medium (Callaway, 2011). Thus,

H5: IT capabilities are positively associated with intermediate performance (revenue enhancement and cost reduction).

For a firm to achieve long term competitive advantage, it is essential to demonstrate superior profits and returns. There are fundamentally two critical ways a firm may achieve greater profitability. One is to find new ways to better meet customer needs (create customer value now and in the future), the other is to do so efficiently. This necessity relates to effectiveness (doing the right things for customers) vs. efficiency (driving down costs) (Xue et al., 2012). One dimension constitutes growth objectives (revenue enhancement); the other dimension constitutes cost objectives (cost reduction). Similarly, a comprehensive way to measure organizational performance, the balanced scorecard, addresses the customer and innovation perspectives (i.e., customer satisfaction and innovation), as well as the internal business processes perspective (i.e., efficiency in managing organizational assets), which then drive financial performance (i.e., profitability) (Kaplan & Norton 1992). Furthermore, a study by Batem & Begum (2014) addressed the impact of cost efficiency on final profit efficiency for banks. Indeed, key banking studies already view bank performance as the result of both revenue enhancement and cost reduction (see, for example, Cornett, et al., 2006). Thus,

H6: Intermediate performance (revenue enhancement and cost reduction) is positively associated with final performance.

Information technology (IT) has long been recognized for its potential role in contributing to sustained competitive advantage for firms (Barney, 1991; Feeny & Ives, 1990; Swierczek & Shrestha, 2003; Vargas, Hernandez, & Bruque, 2003). According to Batra (2006), IT has created an information society where a substantial amount of information is available, bringing increased power and greater choices. Research has shown that IT investments are related to the development of important capabilities that in turn have been shown to improve firm performance (Bharadwaj, 2000; Powell & Dent-Metcalf, 1997; Santhanam & Hartono, 2003). These skills involve management's ability to develop and leverage IT applications to support and contribute to other business functions. Integrating and coordinating the core IT resources (i.e., developing IT capabilities) serves as a source of sustainable competitive advantage owing to their nature and development (achieving more complex coordination across the IT function, other business functions, customers, etc., over time) (Mata et al., 1995). A well-developed and well-coordinated e-commerce unit, of course, reflects these capabilities. Internet business facilitates external knowledge acquisition and intra-firm knowledge dissemination needs, improving the firm's absorptive capacity (Liao et al., 2003). Specifically, a company's e-commerce website is also essential for delivering customer value (Bitner et al., 2000). Moreover, e-commerce offers a low cost way for banks to expand market reach and product breadth, and bank websites offer portals connecting customers to a host of financial products, increasing cross-selling opportunities (Pyun et al., 2002). For example, Kaur (2012) found that better utilization of IT improved branch productivity for banks. As such, IT capabilities, demonstrated in a successful website, should lead to improved bottom line performance (measured by profitability / returns).

H7: IT capabilities are positively associated with final performance.

METHODOLOGY

Sample

We used three different sources of data for this research: Primary data collected from a survey, secondary data as performance collected from the FDIC website, and secondary data from Alexa.com for IT capabilities. A database was first created by downloading data of 8304 FDIC-registered banks as of 2009. From this database, 731 banks were contacted by telephone, and information regarding their willingness to participate in the survey was obtained. Of these contacts, 375 banks showed their willingness to participate in the survey. Emails were sent to these participants that contained a link to the online survey and the explanation of the survey. We obtained 101 completed responses from these participants. This reflected a 27% response rate of those agreeing to participate in the survey, having actually completed it; which is 13.8% of the total banks contacted (McFadden, Henagan, & Gowen III, 2009). In the current era of survey-based research, this response rate we obtained is adequate. Revealing the identity of respondent was optional. Those who revealed it were kept in sample, so we could match to secondary data, leaving 71 responses. Using this methodological approach, the secondary data included in this study constituted objective measures of the corresponding important constructs like ITcapabilities, intermediate performance and final performance. As stated earlier, data were collected from three different sources; as the IT-capabilities (ITRank and ITReach) variables came from Alexa.com while the performance variables came from the FDIC. Utilization of multiple sources of data eliminates mono-method bias (Podsakoff, MacKenzie, Lee, & Podsakoff, 2003).

Measures

Callaway (2006) depicted strategic context of bank units to explain the management of internal corporate venture as compared to traditional units. Strategic Context in our study is measured with two items. First, SC1– the respondent banks were asked to rate the importance of their IT-resources for developing e-commerce site. The scale anchor of 1 indicated that their existing IT-resources were not very relevant for developing ecommerce site and scale anchor of 7 indicated that well established IT-resources of their financial firm were instrumental in developing their e-commerce site. Then, SC2 – the respondents were asked whether the development of their e-commerce site has created any IT-resources. Scale anchor of 1 indicated that the development of their e-commerce site has not created any IT-resources which are relevant to the rest of their financial business and scale anchor of 7 indicated that development of their e-commerce site has created a significant IT-resource important to the rest of their financial services business.

We use Formal Rules, Formal Targets, Informal rules and Input Control System as a measure of strategic control systems of a firm. Three items were used to measure Formal Rules (these items had been tested in Daft & Macintosh, 1981; Kirsch, 1996). The measurement items were: FR1 – there is an understandable, written sequence of steps to be followed, FR2 – established materials (manuals, standards, directives, technical and professional books, etc.) exist, and FR3 – we are required to know a lot of existing, written procedures and standard practices. The scale anchors of 1 indicated the statement is not true at all and 7 indicated that it is very strongly true. Three items were used to measure Formal Targets (Snell, 1992). The measurement items were: FT1 – performance evaluations place primary weight on results, FT2 – pay consists of performance based rewards, and FT3 – rewards are linked to concrete results. The scale anchors of 1 indicated the statement is not true at all and 7 indicated that it is very strongly true. Three items were used to measure Informal Rules (concepts and items tested in prior studies from Fleishman, 1953; Shakeela, 2004). The measurement items were: IR1 – we push the staff for greater effort, IR2 – we emphasize meeting deadlines, and IR3 – we ensure that the staff is working up to capacity. The scale anchors of 1 indicated the statement is not true at all and 7 indicated that it is very strongly true.

Four items from Snell (1992), which were tested in prior studies, were used to measure Input Control Systems which. The measurement items were: IC1 – we have gone to great lengths to establish the best staffing procedures possible, IC2 – we take pride in the fact that we hire the very best people for a job, IC3 – we have a strong commitment to training and developing skilled managers, and IC4 – managers receive substantial training before they assume responsibility. The scale anchors of 1 indicated the statement is not true at all and 7 indicated that it is very strongly true. IT-capabilities was measured in terms of the logarithm of IT Rank and the logarithm of IT Reach. Website rank and reach for each of these banks' websites were obtained from Alexa. com. The global traffic rank is a measure of the website's popularity. www.alexa.com calculates rank using data over the past 3 months of daily visitors to the site and page views on the site. We call this variable ITRank. Finally, the percent of global Internet users who visit the bank's website is termed website reach. We call this variable ITRank.

Finally, definitions of Return on assets (ROA), Return on Equity (ROE), Noninterest income to earning assets (NONIIY) and noninterest expense to earning assets (NONIXY) are adopted from FDIC website. ROA is defined as "Bank net income (including gains or losses on securities and extraordinary items) as a percentage of average total assets. The basic yardstick of bank profitability." ROE is defined as "Bank net income (including gains or losses on securities and extraordinary items) as a percentage of average total equity capital." (http://www2.fdic.gov/qbp/Glossary.asp). Section 5.1 of Risk Management Manual of Examination Policies (RMMEP) of FDIC defines Noninterest income to earning assets (NIIEA) as "annualized income from bank services and sources other than interest-bearing assets, divided by average assets". Noninterest income is largely of service charges on deposits, trust department income, mortgage servicing fees, and certain types of loan and commitment fees. Noninterest expense to earning assets (NIEEA) also termed as overhead ratio at FDIC website is defined as "annualizing expenses related to salaries and employees benefits, expenses of premises and fixed assets, and other noninterest expenses, divided by average assets". Some of the expenses that are included in NIEEA are excessive salaries and bonuses, sizable management fees paid to the bank holding company, and high net occupancy expenses caused by the purchase or construction of a new bank building. (FDIC, 2005)

RESULTS AND ANALYSIS

Using SPSS, factor analysis with varimax rotation was carried out producing five variables as shown in Table 1. As predicted, SC1 and SC2 produced Strategic Context. Formal Rules consisted of FR1, FR2 and FR3, Formal Targets consisted of FT1, FT2 and FT, Informal Rules consisted of IR1, IR2 and IR3 and, Input Control Systems consisted of IC1, IC2, IC3 and IC4. Each factor had an eigenvalue over 1.0. For Strategic Context, Input Control System, Informal Rules, Formal Rules and Formal Targets, Average Variance Extracted (AVE) was 0.800, 0.778, 0.761, 0.781 and 0.751 respectively. Cronbachs Alpha was 0.751, 0.906, 0.847, 0.861 and 0.834 respectively. Next, correlations were run on these variables plus ITRank, ITReach, NIIEA, NIEEA, ROA and ROE. Table 2 shows the correlation results.

Next, the hypotheses were tested using linear and multiple regression using SPSS. The results are shown in Tables 3-8. The first hypothesis indicated that Strategic Context is positively associated with Strategic Control Systems. Linear regression was carried out with the Strategic Control Systems variables Formal Rules (FR), Formal Targets (FT), Informal Rules (IR) and Input control system (IC) regressed one by one, with the independent variable Strategic Context. All the Strategic Controls variables generated strong regression coefficients with FR and IC significant at 0.01 level, and FT and IR significant at 0.05 level. F-values also showed significant results. The results strongly supported Hypothesis 1. ITRank and ITReach, measures of IT Capabilities, were similarly regressed with Strategic Context, one by one. However, non-significant regression coefficients and Fvalues were obtained. Hypothesis 2, which indicated that Strategic Context is associated with IT Capabilities, is not supported. Table 3 shows tests results for Hypotheses 1 and 2.

Hypothesis 3 indicated that Strategic Controls are associated with IT Capabilities. Two sets of multiple regression analyses were done to test this hypothesis. FR, FT, IR and IC were the independent variables and regressed with both ITRank and ITReach, one by one. A check for multicollinearily was done. Variance Inflation Factor (VIF) in all the cases tested is under 2. If VIF is above 10 then multicollinearily is an issue (Aiken & West, 1991). For ITRank, a strong regression coefficient was generated significant at .05 level. Similarly, all the variables of Strategic Controls were regressed with ITReach. Again, VIF was in an acceptable range to eliminate multicollinearily concerns. However the regression coefficient was not significant. Strategic Controls cannot predict ITReach. Thus, Hypothesis 3 was partially supported. Table 4a and 4b shows test results for Hypothesis 3. Intermediate Performance consisted of two observed variables, noninterest income to earning assets (NIIEA) and noninterest expense to earning assets (NIEEA). Multiple regression was carried out with Strategic Controls variables as the independent variables and NIIEA as first dependent variable and then NIEEA as the second dependent variable. Since VIF was around 2.0, multicollinearily was not an issue. However, the regression coefficients were not significant, so we cannot conclude that Strategic Controls predicts Intermediate Performance. Therefore, Hypothesis 4 is not supported. Table 5a and 5b shows test results for Hypothesis 4.

Hypothesis 5 argued that IT Capabilities is associated with Intermediate Performance (revenue enhancement and cost reduction). Linear regressions were individually carried out with ITRank and ITReach as independent variables turn by turn, and NIIEA and NIEEA as the dependent variables. The results indicated that ITRank significantly predicted NIIEA while failing to predict NIEEA. However, ITReach did not significantly predict NIIEA or NIEEA. Thus, Hypothesis 5 was partially supported. Table 6a and 6b shows test results for Hypothesis 5 Hypothesis 6 argued that Intermediate Performance predicts Final Performance. Multiple linear regression was performed with NIIEA and NIEEA as the independent variables and ROA and ROA as the dependent variables, one by one. Results generated high regression coefficients indicating Intermediate Performance is associated with Final Performance. Thus, we find strong support for Hypothesis 6. Table 7a and 7b shows test results for Hypothesis 6.

Finally, Hypothesis 7 argued that IT Capabilities is associated with Final Performance. Therefore, to test this, ITRank and ITReach were regressed turn by turn with ROE and ROA as dependent variables. However the regression coefficients were not strong enough to conclude that IT Capabilities significantly predicts Final Performance. Thus, Hypothesis 7 was not supported. Table 8a and 8b shows test results for Hypothesis 7.

DISCUSSION AND CONCLUSION

This study examines the relationship of strategic context and strategic controls on the development of IT capabilities in banking institutions, and the corresponding impact on performance. Many studies have undertaken to show the impact of e-commerce on firm performance, but with mixed results. Therefore this study has developed a comprehensive model showing the particular strategic role of the e-commerce unit, the strategic control systems employed, and the nature of IT capabilities developed, in order to explain firm performance. Given that firm performance depends upon both revenue growth and efficiency in operations, and that e-commerce is well-established to be able to achieve both, this study is important. Further, given that control systems have the important function of encouraging creativity and innovation (important for future growth) as well as controlling costs, and that IT systems have the function of improving efficiency and offering greater information to encourage local innovation (Batra & Reddy), this study is important. As such, this study has found that a more aggressive strategic context is associated with greater usage of strategic control systems, which comprise input controls, informal controls, formal targets and formal processes. Further strategic controls is partly associated with IT capabilities, IT capabilities is partly associated with intermediate performance metrics (revenue enhancement, but not cost reduction), and intermediate performance metrics are associated with final firm profitability. This study shows that effectively managing resource flows is critical for firms to achieve competitive advantage.

Scholarly implications

This paper makes both theoretical and empirical contributions. A key theoretical contribution is explaining firm performance for banks pursuing e-commerce. Many studies have undertaken to show the impact of internet banking on performance, but with mixed results. Simply assessing the extent of internet commerce and the impact on performance fails to explain firm performance adequately. Many other variables are essential for understanding e-commerce. Therefore this study developed a comprehensive model showing the particular strategic role (termed the strategic context) of the e-commerce unit, the relation of strategic context to strategic control systems utilized, and the nature of IT capabilities developed, in order to explain firm performance.

This paper also makes an important empirical contribution. Data were collected from three different sources, comprising both primary and secondary data. Regarding secondary data, the IT-capabilities variable came from Alexa.com and the performance variables came from the FDIC. The strategic controls and strategic context constructs came from questionnaire data, including new items as well as items that had been verified in prior research. It is particularly important that the outcome variables came from secondary sources and different sources than the antecedent variables. Overall, this utilization of multiple sources of data eliminates mono-method bias (Podsakoff, MacKenzie, Lee, & Podsakoff, 2003). For this reason, the performance implications are quite robust.

The results of this study shed light on how firms pursuing new ventures, particularly ecommerce ventures, can improve performance. First, the strategic context of the venture is critical. This strategic context (role) comprises two dimensions, inflow of external resources and outflow of internal resources. Interestingly, these two dimensions were highly correlated. That is, the strategic role seemed to indicate how independent or integrated the venture was, meaning both high inflow and outflow, or both low inflow and outflow. A unit pursuing pure cost reduction, such as utilizing internal resources as a platform just to implement the banking strategy via the internet; or a venture focusing purely on innovation, attempting to transform the bank by bringing in substantial external knowledge, but with few corporate ties initially; were rather atypical. It seemed that strategic context simply measured how aggressive the internet banking unit was. A second interesting insight gained from this study, was that all four strategic control archetypes, input controls, informal rules, formal targets, and formal rules, typically complement one another rather than some replacing others. This observation likely is related to the first. A more aggressive strategic context did not lead to more controls focusing on innovation (such as informal rules and input controls) and less on standardization and cost reduction controls (such as formal rules), but instead the more aggressive context was associated with a greater utilization of all the controls. Control simply became more important. A case illustration from Thomke (2003) indicated that a major bank's aggressive venturing had to be conducted efficiently and at a reasonable cost. That is, even while local managers were empowered to pursue innovation at their local branches, they still earned substantial pay from performance bonuses tied to sales quotas, the number of different products sold, as well as incentives based upon team performance (Thomke, 2003). That is, standardizing rules for cost reduction, offering incentives for meeting targets, investing in local managers through recruiting and training, and creating a culture of teamwork and sharing, all are important to improve banking performance.

Third, and related to performance implications, it is interesting that IT capabilities were associated with greater revenue, but was not associated with reduced cost. This finding may be a key problem facing traditional firms that are pursuing e-commerce. That is, according to Callaway (2011), positive findings regarding noninterest income suggests that greater e-commerce is associated with a greater ability to find new and different sources of revenue beyond traditional loans. That is, banks apparently have used ecommerce to cross-sell other products successfully, by bundling banking, investments, and insurance products at one convenient place. However, the fact that e-commerce was not associated with reduced noninterest expenses indicate that the promise of reduced costs and greater efficiency has yet to materialize. There are fixed costs associated with establishing online banking and technical support, before being able to reduce transaction costs. However, many banks utilize Internet banking to complement rather than reduce or replace traditional branch activities (Hernando and Nieto 2007; Holloway 2009). That is, if these institutions continue to build and staff branches, the cost-reduction potential of online banking may never show up in final performance (Holloway 2009). Spending more on e-commerce may not necessarily mean reduced overhead with traditional branches, so greater efficiencies and cost reduction has yet to materialize (Callaway, 2011).

Managerial implications

This study also provides important insights for managers. First, more banks are creating new products, designing new services, entering into new customer segments, and expanding globally (Gopalakrishnan, Wischnevsky & Damanpour, 2003). As such, top level managers and local branch managers must be able to manage the abundance of increasingly diverse information (Grandori, 2001). The more aggressive context creates substantial opportunities for creativity and innovation, as financial institutions have had to be very creative and innovative in developing IT capabilities (Gopalakrishnan, Wischnevsky & Damanpour, 2003). Therefore, it is essential for these institutions to standardize processes for designing financial products and interacting with customers, yet maintain the level of innovation necessary for improved firm performance (Reddy, 2006). For example, the current findings may emphasize the importance of investing in people who deal with important industry regulations, so that they are equipped to handle local accountability and decision making. Again, standardization and innovation go hand in hand.

The fact that the promise of reduced costs and greater efficiency has yet to occur also has important implications for banking managers. The fixed costs from establishing online banking and providing technical support must be recouped, by being able to reduce transaction costs in the longer term. Bank executives must reconsider whether they want to utilize Internet banking to complement rather than reduce traditional branch activities, as was detailed by Hernando and Nieto (2007) and Holloway (2009). That is, more banking institutions, in order to improve firm performance, may need to find a way to reduce traditional branch activities while developing their e-commerce sites, drawing a new focus on cost reduction. Managers have already found a way to enhance revenue, now they must focus on reducing costs.

LIMITATIONS AND FUTURE RESEARCH

There are some limitations to this study. First, there is a need to establish more complete measures of IT capabilities. This study only examined the reach and rank of the website. While that may be a good measure of the popularity of the website, IT capabilities are a much more comprehensive construct. Therefore multi-item measures spanning all facets of IT should be incorporated in future studies. For example, future research could follow the approach of Roche (2014) and Paschaloudis & Tsourela (2014) in examining Internet Service Quality as a particular form of IT capabilities for Internet Banking.

Second, future research could further develop the model and extend the methodology utilized in this study. There is a need to use simultaneous equations in assessing the model posed here. Structural equations modeling would enhance the model greatly, as a way to ascertain how these relationships are mediated. For this reason, a much larger sample size is required, perhaps 200-300 observations. Furthermore, this study used cross sectional data. Future research could test causality, perhaps utilizing time series data. Doing so would go beyond simply testing associations, and would actually shed some light on the direction of the relationships in the model.

Finally, this study intentionally looked only at banking institutions. As a result of this limited sample, however, interpretations regarding the generalizability of the study should be made cautiously. Future studies should examine other financial services industries beyond banking, and other industries beyond financial services. Hopefully this study will be the start of many addressing the strategic control of new ventures that help firms develop the capabilities necessary to improve performance. Much more research is still warranted to understand the role of strategic context, strategic controls systems, and the development of IT capabilities, in this process.

REFERENCES

1. Aiken, L. S., & West, S. G. (1991). Multiple regression: testing and interpretinginteractions. Newbury Park, CA: Sage Publications.
2. J. Barney. Firm resources and sustained competitive advantage. Journal ofManagement 1991; 17: 99-120.
3. Baten, A. (2014, April). Stochastic Fronteir Model for Cost and Profit Efficieny of IslamicOnline Banks.Journal of Internet Banking and Commerce, 19(1).
4. Batra, S. (2006), "Impact of information technology on organizational effectiveness: Aconceptual framework incorporating organizational flexibility", Global Journal ofFlexible Systems Management, Vol. 7 No. 1 / 2, 15-25.
5. Beinhocker, E. (1997). Strategy at the edge of chaos. The McKinsey Quarterly, 1: 25-39.
6. Bharadwaj. A resource-based perspective on information technology capability andfirm performance: An empirical investigation. MIS Quarterly 2000; 24: 169-196.
7. Bitner, M., Stephen, W., and Meuter, M. 2000. Technology infusion in serviceencounters. Journal of the Academy of Marketing Science 28 (1): 138-149.
8. Booz, Allen & Hamilton Rep., 1999.Going for broke: The battle for online events. Online(www.hp.com/Ebusiness/financial.html).
9. Brown, S. L. and Eisenhardt, K. M. (1998) Competing on the Edge: Strategy asStructured Chaos. Boston: Harvard Business School Press.
10. Burgelman, R. (1983) A process model of internal corporate venturing in a majordiversified firm. Administrative Science Quarterly, 28: 223-244.
11. Burgelman, R. and Sayles, L. (1986) Inside Corporate Innovation: Strategy, Structure,and Managerial Skills. New York: Free Press.
12. Byrd, T. 2001. Information technology: Core competencies, and sustained competitiveadvantage. Information Resources Management Journal 14: 27–36.
13. Callaway, S. K. (2006). Strategic context for bank units: Comparing resource flows forInternet ventures and traditional branches. The Journal of High TechnologyManagement Research, 17(1), 1–15. doi:10.1016/j.hitech.2006.05.001
14. Callaway, S. (2011). Internet banking and performance: the relationship of web sitetraffic rank and bank performance. American Journal of Business, 26: 12-25.
15. Callaway, S., Celuch, K., & Murphy, C. 2009. Strategic Flexibility and SMEs: The Roleof Information Technology for Managing Internal and External Relations.
16. Callaway S. and Jagani, S. 2015. The impact of banks' entrepreneurial orientation onstrategic control systems.American Journal of Business.forthcoming.
17. Child, J. (1972), "Organisational structure and strategies of control: A replication of theAston Study", Administrative Science Quarterly, Vol. 17, 163-167.
18. Cornett, M., McNutt, J., Tehranian, H. 2006. Performance Changes Around BankMergers: Revenue Enhancements versus Cost Reductions. Journal of Money,Credit & Banking. 38 (4): 1013-1050.

19. Curlee, W. (2008), "Modern Virtual Project Management: The Effects of a Centralizedand Decentralized Project Management Office", Project Management Journal,Vol. 39 (Supplement), 83–96.

20. Daft, R. L., & Macintosh, N. B. (1981).A tentative exploration into the amount andequivocality of information processing in organizational work units. AdministrativeScience Quarterly, 207–224. DiMaggio, P. J. and Powell, W. W. (1983) The iron cage revisited: Institutionalisomorphism and collective rationality in organizational fields. AmericanSociological Review, 48: 147-160.

21. FDIC.(2005). Risk Management Manual of Examination Policies. Retrieved fromhttp://www.fdic.gov/regulations/safety/manual/index_pdf.html

22. Feeny, D. F., & Ives, B. (1990). In search of sustainability: Reaping long-term advantagefrom investments in information technology. Journal of Management InformationSystems, 7(1), 27−46.

23. Fleishman, E. A. (1953). Leadership climate, human relations training, and supervisorybehavior. Personnel Psychology, 6(2), 205–222.

24. Foo, C. (1995), "Organization HRD and technology: towards a bureaucratic theory ofstrategic control", The International Journal of Human Resource Management,Vol. 6 No. 1, 127-141.

25. Fries, S., &Taci, A. (2005). Cost efficiency of banks in transition: Evidence from 289banks in 15 post-communist countries. Journal of Banking and Finance, 29, 55–81. doi:10.1016/j.jbankfin.2004.06.016

26. Furst, K., Lang, W., &Nolle, D. (2000). Internet banking: developments and prospects.Office of the Comptroller of the Currency Economic and Policy Analysis WorkingPaper, (2000-9).

27. Gopalakrishnan, S., Wischnevsky, J., Damanpour, F. 2003.A multilevel analysis offactors influencing the adoption of internet banking. IEEE Transactions onEngineering Management, 50, 413-425.

28. Grandori. Neither hierarchy nor identity: Knowledge-governance mechanisms and thetheory of the firm. Journal of Management and Governance 2001; 5: 381-399.

29. Gupta, A. K. and Govindarajan, V. (1991) Knowledge flows and the structure of controlwithin multinational corporations. Academy of Management Review, 16 (4): 768-792.

30. Gurbaxani, V., and S. Whang. 1991. The impact of information systems on organizationsand markets. Communications of the ACM 34: 59–73.

31. Hedlund, G. (1994), "A model of knowledge management and the n-form corporation",Strategic Management Journal, Vol. 15, 73-90.

32. Hernando, I. and Nieto, M. 2007. Is the Internet delivery channel changing banks'performance? The case of Spanish banks. Journal of Banking and Finance 31(4): 1083-1099.

33. Hitt, M., B.Keats, and S. DeMarie. 1998. Navigating in the new competitive landscape:Building strategic flexibility and competitive advantage in the 21st century.Academy of Management Executive 12: 22–42.

34. Holloway, J. 2009. Real test for online banking is how it hits the bottom line. Credit UnionTimes, August 12, 20 (32): 16.

35. Kaplan, R.S., Norton, P., 1992, Th e Balanced Scorecard – Measures The at DrivePerformance, Harvard Business Review, 70 (1), 71–79. http://ehis.ebscohost.com/eds/.

36. Kaur, R. (2012, December). An Impact of IT on Branch Productivity of Indian Banking inthe Era of Transformation.Journal of Internet Banking and Commerce, 17(3).

37. Kirsch, L. J. (1996). The management of complex tasks in organizations: Controlling thesystems development process. Organization Science, 7(1), 1–21.

38. Liao, J., Welsch, H., &Stocia, M. (2003). Organizational absorptive capacity andresponsiveness: An empirical investigation of growth-oriented SMEs. Entrepreneurship, Theory and Practice, 28(1): 63-85.

39. Malone, T., and S. Smith. 1988. Modeling the performance of organizational structures.Operations Research 36: 421–436.

40. Malone, T., J. Yates, and R. Benjamin. 1987. Electronic markets and electronichierarchies. Communications of the ACM 30: 484–497.

41. Mata, J. Francisco, Fuerst, L.William, Barney, B. Jay. Information Technology andSustained Competitive Advantage: A Resource-Based Analysis. MIS Quarterly1995; 19: 487-505.

42. McFadden, K. L., Henagan, S. C., &Gowen III, C. R. (2009). The patient safety chain:Transformational leadership's effect on patient safety culture, initiatives, andoutcomes. Journal of Operations Management, 27(5), 390–404.

43. Meyer, J. W. and Rowan, B. (1977) Institutionalized organizations: Formal structure asmyth and ceremony. American Journal of Sociology, 83: 340-363.

44. Muhanna, A. Waleed, M. Stoel, Dale. How Do Investors Value IT? An EmpiricalInvestigation of the Value Relevance of IT Capability and IT Spending AcrossIndustries. Journal of Information Systems 2010; 24: 43-66.

45. Paschaloudis, D. (2014, April). Using E-S-QUAL to Measure Internet Service Quality ofEBanking Web Sites in Greece.Journal of Internet Banking and Commerce,19(2).

46. Pfeffer, J., &Salancik. (1978) The external control of organizations: A resourcedependence perspective. Reading, MA: Addison Wesley Educational Publishers.

47. Podsakoff, P. M., MacKenzie, S. B., Lee, J.-Y., &Podsakoff, N. P. (2003). Commonmethod biases in behavioral research: A critical review of the literature andrecommended remedies. Journal of Applied Psychology, 88(5), 879–903.

48. Powell T.C., and A. Dent-Metcalf. 1997. Information technology as competitiveadvantage: The role of human, business, and technology resources. StrategicManagement Journal 18: 375–405.

49. Prahalad, C., and M. Krishnan. 2002. The dynamic synchronization of strategy andinformation technology. MIT Sloan Management Review 43: 24–33.

50. Pyun, C. S., Scruggs, L., & Nam, K. (2002).Internet banking in the US, Japan andEurope. Multinational Business Review, 10, 72–81.

51. Reddy, S. (2006), "Strategic flexibility and information technology properties:Competitive advantage and asset specificity", ACR, Vol. 14 No. 1, 16-43.

52. Reynolds, S., Ratanakomut, S., and Gander, J. 2000.Bank financial structure in precrisisEast and Southeast Asia. Journal of Asian Economics 11 (3): 319-332.

53. Roche, I. D. (2014, August). An Empirical Investigation of Internet Banking ServiceQuality, Corporate Image and the Impact on Customer Satisfaction. Journal ofInternet Banking and Commerce, 19(2).

54. Saeed, K., Grover, V., and Yujong, H. 2005. The relationship of e-commercecompetence to customer value and firm performance: An empirical investigation.Journal of Management Information Systems 22 (1): 223-256.

55. R. Santhanam, E. Hartono. Issues in linking information technology capability to firmperformance. Management Information Systems Quarterly 2003; 27: 125–153.

56. Shakeela, M. (2004). A Measure of Leadership Behaviour: Does the Age–Old MeasureRequire Redefining? Research and Practice in Human Resource Management,12(2), 140–151.

57. Scott, W. R. (1992). Organizations : rational, natural, and open systems (3rd ed., p. xii,414 p.). Englewood Cliffs, N.J.: Prentice Hall.

58. Shapiro, C., and H.Varian. 1999. Information rules: A strategic guide to the networkeconomy. Boston, MA: Harvard Business School Press.

59. Snell, S. A. (1992). Control theory in strategic human resource management: Themediating effect of administrative information. Academy of Management Journal,292–327.

60. Sullivan, R. J. (2000). How has the adoption of Internet banking affected performanceand risk in banks? Financial Industry Perspectives, (Dec), 1–16.

61. Swierczek, F. W., &Shrestha, P. K. (2003). Information technology and productivity: Acomparison of Japanese and Asia-Pacific banks. Journal of High TechnologyManagement Research, 14(2), 269–288.

62. Tallon P. P., and K. L. Kraemer. 2003. Investigating the relationship between strategicalignment and IT business value: The discovery of a paradox. In Shin Namchul,ed..Creating Business Value with Information Technology: Challenges andSolutions. Hershey, PA: Idea Group Publishing, 1–22.

63. Tallon and Kraemer, Thomke, S. H. (2003). Experimentation matters: unlocking the potential of newtechnologies for innovation. Boston: Harvard Business Press.

64. Vargas, A., Hernandez, M. J., &Bruque, S. (2003). Determinants of informationtechnology competitive value: Evidence from a western European industry.Journal of High Technology Management Research, 14(2), 245–268.

65. B. Wernerfelt. An Organizational Resource Based View of the Firm, StrategicManagement Journal 1984; 5: 171-180.

66. Xue, L., Ray, G., Sambamurthy, V. (2012). Efficiency or Innovation: How Do IndustryEnvironments Moderate the Effects of Firms' IT Asset Portfolios? MIS Quarterly.36 (2): 509-528.

67. Z. Zhang, M. K.O. Lee, P. Huang, L. Zhang, X. Huang. A framework of ERP systemsimplementation success in China: An empirical study. International Journal ofProduction Economics 2005; 98: 56-80.

12

CHAPTER

AN INTEGRATED DATA ENVELOPMENT ANALYSIS–ARTIFICIAL NEURAL NETWORK APPROACH FOR BENCHMARKING OF BANK BRANCHES

Elsa Shokrollahpour, Farhad Hosseinzadeh Lotfiand Mostafa Zandieh

Keywords: Data envelopment analysisArtificial neural networkBenchmarking

INTRODUCTION

Since banking industry is highly competitive, the performance assessment has been receiving more attention recently. The banking sector is in a race to see which banks offer the better or the best services. This results in an intensified competition in the market place. Therefore, bank management involves identifying and eliminating the underlying causes of inefficiencies to help firms improve their efficiency. In the literature, data envelopment analysis (DEA) is a leading approach in terms of performance analysis and discovering newer benchmarks. Various models of DEA are widely used for evaluating bank efficiency, such as Sherman and Gold (1985), Soteriou and Zenios (1999), Golany and Storbeck (1999), Athanassopoulos and Giokas (2000), thick frontier approach (TFA) as in Berger and Humphrey (1991), Clark (1996) and Deyoung (1998), free disposal hull (FDH) as in Tulkens (1993) and Chang (1999), stochastic frontier approach (SFA), also called econometric frontier approach (EFA) as in Kaparakis et al. (1994), Berger and Humphrey (1997) and Hao et al.(2001), and distribution free approach (DFA) as in Berger et al. (1993), and Deyoung (1997).

As DEA can hardly predict the performance of other decision-making units, Wang (2003) used artificial neural network (ANN) to assist in estimating efficiency. Athanassopoulos and Curram (1996) firstly introduced the combination of neural networks and DEA for classification and/or prediction. They used DEA in bank with multi-output: four inputs, three outputs to monitor training cases in a study. The

Citation: Elsa Shokrollahpour, Farhad Hosseinzadeh Lotfi and Mostafa Zandieh, An integrated data envelopment analysis–artificial neural network approach for benchmarking of bank branches, DOI 10.1007/s40092-015-0125-7.

comparison between DEA and ANN demonstrates that DEA is superior to ANN for measurement purposes. Azadeh et al. (2006), (2007a, b) utilized a highly flexible ANN algorithm to measure and rank the performance of decision-making units (DMUs). They defined an application of an algorithm in efficiency calculation of Iran steam power plants in 2004. Results demonstrate that the proposed algorithm estimates the values of efficiency closer to the ideal efficiency. Finally they displayed that the results of the proposed algorithm are more robust than the conventional approach as better performance patterns were explored. Furthermore, they proposed a method to integrate their pervious algorithm (Azadeh et al. 2007a, b). Azadeh et al. (2011), also used the combination of DEA, ANN and rough set theory (RST) for determining the impact of critical personnel attributes on efficiency. Wu et al. (2006) combined DEA and ANN for measuring the performance of a large Canadian bank. They came to the conclusion that the DEA–ANN method produces a more robust frontier and helps to identify more efficient units. Furthermore for inefficient units, it provides the guidance on how to improve their performance to different efficiency ratings. Finally, they concluded there was no need to make assumptions according to the production function in the ANN approach (the major drawback of the parametric approach) and that it is highly flexible, and that the weakness of the DEA in forecasting is the reason to use ANN (Wu et al. 2006).

On the other hand, Rahimi and Behmanesh (2012) employed the combined method to predict the DMU's evaluation performance. Recently, Gutierrez and Lozano (2010) mixed DEA and ANN to enhance the traditional Taguchi method for estimating quality loss measures for unobserved factor combinations and the non-parametric character of the performance evaluation of all the factor combinations. Consequently, Bashiri et al. (2013) combined DEA and ANN to optimize a Taguchi-based multi-response optimization problem for the processes where controllable factors are the smaller-the-better (STB)- type variables and the analyzer desires to find an optimal solution with smaller amount of controllable factors.

The classic DEA methods did not have the ability to demonstrate benchmarks for the future. ANN has been viewed as a useful tool for managers in predicting system behaviors. This paper integrates DEA and neural networks to cover for the shortcomings we were faced with while using DEA. Therefore, benchmarks are based on the future data and inefficient MDUs have better performance patterns to improve their efficiencies. The paper is organized as follows. "Problem definition" section briefly reviews neural networks and DEA. "ANN– DEA" section demonstrates the models and methodology utilized in this paper. The DEA results and further discussion is given in "Computational results" section. Finally, our conclusions and future work are offered in "Conclusions and future works" section.

PROBLEM DEFINITION

Data envelopment analysis

DEA is a non-parametric method, which uses linear programming to calculate the efficiency in a given set of decision-making units (DMUs).

The DMUs that make up a frontier envelope are scored as 1. The less efficient firms and the relative efficiency of the firms are calculated in terms of scores on a scale of 0–1. Envelopment surface that represents best practices can give an indication of how inefficient DMUs can improve to become efficient. DEA provides a comprehensive analysis of relative efficiencies for multiple input–multiple output situations by evaluating each DMU's performance relative to an envelopment surface composed of efficient DMUs. Units that lie on the surface are known as efficient according to DEA, while those units that do not are named inefficient. The efficient reference set includes DMUs, which are the peer group for the inefficient units.

The projection of inefficient units on an envelopment surface is called a benchmark. Benchmarks are the indication of how the inefficient DMU can improve to be efficient. Benchmarks prove that once the evaluated DMU includes these inputs and outputs, it could become efficient.

Assume input and outputs for j = 1,…,n DMUs (X_j,Y_j) where $X_j = (x_{1j},\dots,x_{ij},\dots,x_{mj})$ is a vector of observed inputs and $Y_j = (y_{1j},\dots,y_{rj},\dots,y_{sj})$ is a vector of observed outputs for DMUj.

The production possibility set is as below:

$$T = \{(X,Y)|Y \geq 0 \text{ can be produced from } X \geq 0\}$$

The input possibility L(Y), for each Y, and the output possibility P(X), for each X, are defined as below:

$$L(Y) = \{X|(X,Y) \in T\}$$

$$P(X) = \{X|(X,Y) \in T\}$$

For achieving production possibility set, T, the following proprieties were postulated:

1. Convexity:

If $(X_j, Y_j) \in T$, $j = 1,\dots,n$, and $\lambda_j \geq 0$

are nonnegative scalars such that $\sum_{j=1}^{n} \lambda_j = 1$, then

$$\left(\sum_{j=1}^{n} \lambda_j X_j, \sum_{j=1}^{n} \lambda_j Y_j\right) \in T$$

where λ is a vector of coefficients.

2. Inefficiency postulate:

(a) If $(X,Y) \in T$ and $\overline{X} \geq X$, then $(\overline{X},Y) \in T$
(b) If $(X,Y) \in T$ and $\overline{Y} \leq Y$, then $(X,\overline{Y}) \in T$

3. Ray unboundedness:

If $(X,Y) \in T$ then $(KX,KY) \in T$ for any $k > 0$

4. Minimum extrapolation: T is the intersection set of $\hat{T}$ satisfying postulates 1,2, and 3 and subject to condition that each of observed vectors $(X_j, Y_j) \in \hat{T},\ j = 1, \ldots, n.$. With mentioned assumptions Tv as below:

$$Tv = \left\{ \begin{pmatrix} X \\ Y \end{pmatrix} \middle| X \geq \sum_{j=1}^{n} X_{ij}\lambda_j \&\ Y \leq \sum_{j=1}^{n} Y_{ij}\lambda_j \&\ \sum_{j=1}^{n} \lambda_j \&\ \lambda \geq 0 \right\}$$

Different models for calculating efficiency were introduced, the oldest model is BCC (Banker et al. 1984) model: Input-oriented BCC Model

Minimize $\theta - \varepsilon(1s^{+} + 1s^{-})$

Subject to,

$$\sum_{j=1}^{n} x_{ij}\lambda_j + s_i^{-} = \theta x_{iq} \quad i = 1, 2, \ldots, m$$

$$\sum_{j=1}^{n} y_{ij}\lambda_j - s_r^{+} = y_{rq} \quad r = 1, 2, \ldots, s$$

$$\sum_{j=1}^{n} \lambda_j = 1 \quad j = 1, \ldots, n$$

$$\lambda_j, s_i^{-}, s_r^{+} \geq 0 \quad i = 1, 2, \ldots, m \quad r = 1, 2, \ldots s \quad j = 1, \ldots, n$$

A DMU is called efficient, if it has $\theta^{*} = 1,\ s_i^{-*} = 0,\ s_r^{+*} = 0.$. Otherwise, it is called inefficient.

For inefficient DMUs (ex. DMU_q), the DEA model calculates the benchmark. The benchmark is as follows:

$$\begin{pmatrix} X_q \cdot \theta^{*} - s^{-*} \\ Y_q + s^{+*} \end{pmatrix} = \begin{pmatrix} \sum_{j=1}^{n} \lambda_j^{*} X_j \\ \sum_{j=1}^{n} \lambda_j^{*} Y_j \end{pmatrix}$$

Benchmarks are like alerts when it comes to designing new strategies or changing old strategies. For each DMU, two parts should be taken into account:

1. Eliminate the distance between each DMU and its peer group
2. Display the frontier in a specific time horizon

As the benchmarks were based on the past data, they could not help in showing the frontier in specific time horizon and they may be still less efficient compared to the future benchmarks. Therefore, ANN is used to mitigate this issue and to indicate the envelope surface.

Artificial neural networks

The original inspiration for the structure of the neural networks comes from the human brain functions. The key factor of this paradigm is the novel structure of the information processing systems. A system consists of a large number of highly interconnected processing neurons working together to solve specific problems. Similar to people, ANNs learn by example. Neural network is trained by adjusting weights between neurons, so that an input leads to a target output.

The fast growth of ANN over the last decade has introduced a new dimension into the field of performance measurement especially in business application. One of the major application areas of ANNs is forecasting (Sharda 1994). Many different ANN models have been proposed since 1980s. Multilayer perceptron (MLP), Hopfield networks, and Kohonen's self-organizing networks are the most influential models.

The MLP networks are used in several problems especially in forecasting because of their inherent capability of arbitrary input–output mapping. Several layers of nodes are included in an MLP. The information receiver layer is an input layer, which is the lowest layer. The last or the highest layer is an output layer in which the problem solution is obtained. The hidden layers are the intermediate layers where the input and output layers are separated. Acyclic arcs from a lower layer to a higher layer connect the nodes in adjacent layers. Figure 1 shows an example of a fully connected MLP with one hidden layer.

Most multilayer networks are trained using the back propagation (BP) algorithm for forecasting. BP neural networks consist of a collection of inputs and processing units known as neurons.

BP networks are a class of feed-forward neural networks, which refers to the direction of information flow from the input to the output layer, with supervised learning rules. In such learning, each network's forecasts are compared with the known correct answer and the weights are adjusted based on the resulting forecast error to minimize the error function.

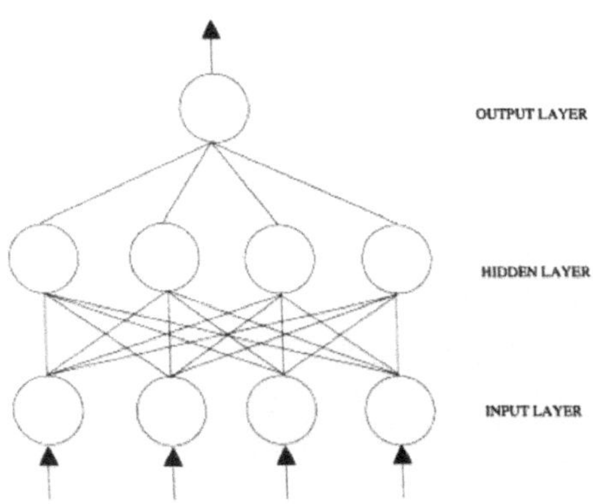

Figure 1: The structure of three-layer MLP network.

For example, for forecasting the value of x(t + 1) in x(1)...x(t) time series, x(t – k + 1)...x(t) is chosen as the inputs to multilayer network and the output will be the forecast. The network uses the data, which are extracted from the historical time series for the sake of training and testing on large training and testing sets.

Before an ANN can be used to perform any desired task, it must be trained to do so. Basically, training is the process of demonstrating the arc weights, which are the key factors of an ANN. Arcs and nodes are saving the learned knowledge in the form of arc weights and node biases. The MLP training is a method of training, in which the desired response of the network (target value) for each input pattern (example) is always available. The steps of the training process are usually as following. Firstly, examples of the training set are entered into the input nodes. Secondly, the activation values of the input nodes are weighted and accumulated at each node in the first hidden layer. Lastly, activation value is obtained by an activation function, which is transforming the total into an activation value. The value becomes an input into the nodes in the next layer. This process works until the output activation values are found. The training algorithm is tried to the weights that minimize the mean squared errors (MSE) or the sum of squared errors (SSE).

ANN–DEA

During this research, multilayer ANN has been applied to forecast the input and outputs of each DMU in 5 years. After the preliminary analyses and trial, the Levenberg–Marquardt algorithm (the fastest training algorithm) was chosen for the proposed MLP network. Levenberg–Marquardt algorithm can be considered as a trust-region modification of the Gauss–Newton algorithm. Two operations must be considered in MLP networks: training and prediction. MLP uses two data sets, the training set for the training of the MLP and the test set for the prediction.

Arbitrary values of the weights, which might be random numbers, are the beginning of the training mode. In each epoch, the iteration of the complete training set in the network adjusts the weights. Adjusting the weights results in reducing errors. The prediction mode begins with information flowing from the inputs to the outputs. The network produces an estimation of the output according to the input values. The resulting error demonstrates the quality of prediction of the trained network. The parameters of the estimated artificial neural network can be seen in Table 1.

Table 1: Estimated neural network parameters

Concept	Result
Data	Input 6000 past data/output predicted data
Network architecture	2–3–1
Algorithm	Levenberg–Marquardt
Epochs (max)	10,000
R^2	0.99
Learning rate	0.7
Mean square error	0.001

The estimated neural network includes a hidden layer and the Levenberg–Marquardt algorithm has been selected for the training. Figure 2 shows the two samples of the test and the train regression charts for the proposed ANN. Figure 2 displays the good quality of the trained network prediction. After forecasting the inputs and outputs by the ANN, the DEA model must be selected for calculating the efficiency and benchmarks.

Since some inputs and outputs in this study could be negative, the selected DEA model for efficiency measurement and benchmarking should not be sensitive to negative data. One of the best models, which could be used to deal with negative data, is the SBM model.

The SBM model is as follows:

$$\text{Minimize } \rho = \frac{1 - \frac{1}{m}\sum_{i=1}^{m}\left(s_i^- / R_i^-\right)}{1 + \frac{1}{s}\sum_{r=1}^{s}\left(s_r^+ / R_r^+\right)}$$

Subject to;

$$\sum_{j=1}^{n} x_{ij}\lambda_j + s_i^- = x_{iq} \quad i = 1, 2, \ldots, m$$

$$\sum_{j=1}^{n} y_{ij}\lambda_j - s_r^+ = y_{rq} \quad r = 1, 2, \ldots, s$$

$$\sum_{j=1}^{n} \lambda_j = 1 \quad j = 1, \ldots, n$$

$$\lambda_j, s_i^-, s_r^+ \geq 0 \quad i = 1, 2, \ldots, m \quad r = 1, 2, \ldots, s$$
$$j = 1, \ldots, n$$

where, $R_j^- = \max\{x_{ij} : j = 1, \ldots, n\} - \min\{x_{ij} : j = 1, \ldots, n\}$. The variables s^+ and s^- measure the distance of inputs $X\lambda$ and outputs $Y\lambda$ of a virtual unit from those of the unit evaluated (X_q). The numerator and the denominator of the objective function of model measure the average distance of inputs and outputs, respectively, from the efficiency threshold. For variable returns to scale, condition $\sum_{j=1}^{n} \lambda_j = 1$ is added. The stages involved in the proposed algorithm are illustrated in Fig. 3.

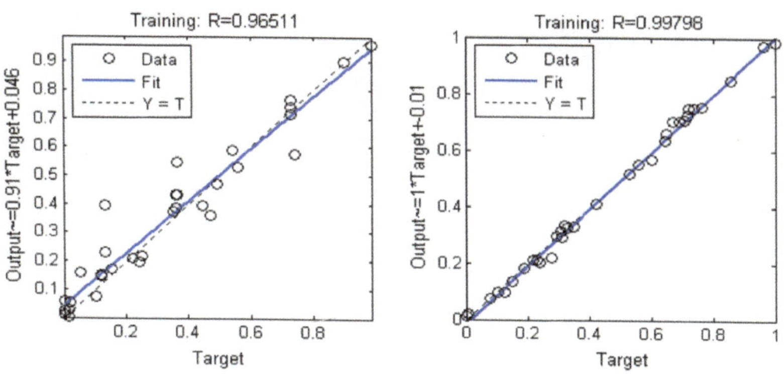

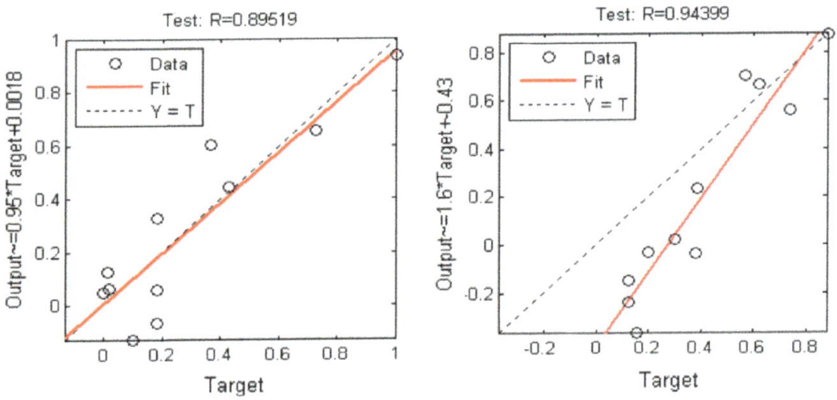

Figure 2: Training and testing charts.

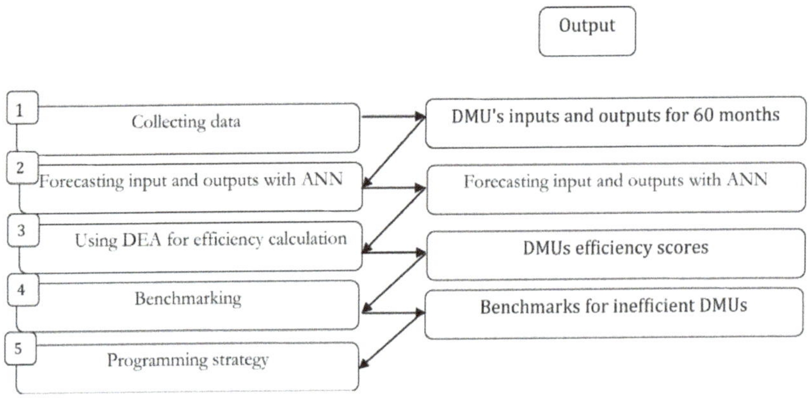

Figure 3: The steps of ANN–DEA.

COMPUTATIONAL RESULTS

100 branches of one of the Iranian commercial banks were selected and the related data were collected. The data cover the period of March to February during the years 2006–2011. Each branch demonstrates a decision-making unit (DMU) and uses two inputs to produce seven outputs as is shown in Table 2. After implementing the ANN and computing the efficiencies by the SBM model, the efficiency and the benchmark that are calculated for the 11th DMU are as follows:

$$\rho = 0.005$$

$$\text{Benchmark}: \begin{pmatrix} \sum_{j=1}^{100} \lambda_j X_j \\ \sum_{j=1}^{100} \lambda_j Y_j \end{pmatrix}$$

Table 2: Inputs and outputs of branches

Outputs	Inputs
	1. Income condominium (Y_1)
1. Deposit's paid profit (X_1)	2. Fee (commission) (Y_2)
2. Expenses (personnel and official) (X_2)	3. Other income (Y_3)
	4. Main deposits (Y_4)
	5. Other deposits (Y_5)
	6. Current deposit (Y_6)
	7. Loan granted account (Y_7)

Table 3: Distance between DMU11 and its benchmark

Inputs and outputs	Benchmark	DMU11	Difference
X_1	3.81E + 09	7.27E + 09	−3.47E + 09
X_2	7.21E + 08	7.21E + 08	0
Y_1	7.13E + 09	1.64E + 09	5.49E + 09
Y_2	3.31E + 09	6.4E + 07	3.25E + 09
Y_3	7.12E + 11	6.14E + 11	9.83E + 10
Y_4	1.35E + 12	1.09E + 12	2.64E + 11
Y_5	9.14E + 10	2.28E + 10	6.86E + 10
Y_6	8.32E + 09	0	8.32E + 09
Y_7	6.6E + 11	1.14E + 11	5.46E + 11

As is shown in Table 3, the 11th DMU should decrease its inputs and increase its outputs within a 5-year time horizon. Hence, the 11th DMU will be efficient in 5 years. For DMU 38, the benchmark is displayed in Table 4. For being efficient in 5 years, the 38th DMU should increase the inputs and outputs (q = 0.737).

The efficient DMUs included in the reference set are the peer group for the inefficient units. Therefore, the benchmark and DMU are the same. For superefficient DMUs, like DMU1, the benchmark is as Table 5 (q = 1). Annual prediction could help each bank branch to have a strategic improvement plan. Hence, the bank management can plan due to this guide, and reach the 5-year goal.

CONCLUSIONS AND FUTURE WORKS

This paper presents an ANN–DEA study to the branches in one of the Iranian commercial banks. The result helps DMUs to improve their efficiency and gives them a useful strategic plan for future developments. Unlike DEA, the ANN–DEA approach guides weaker performers on how to improve their performance to different efficiency ratings for the future. We can also list the following directions for future researches. First, ranking DMUs can be considered for future work. Second, Malmquist productivity index can be used for calculating the DMU's progress or regress. Third, other prediction methods can be utilized for estimating. Forth, combinatorial method can be used to find the most productive scale size.

Table 4: Distance between DMU38 and its benchmark

Inputs and outputs	Benchmark	DMU38	Difference
X_1	1.71E + 12	1.54E + 09	1.71E + 12
X_2	2.92E + 09	8.41E + 08	2.08E + 09
Y_1	2.25E + 11	9.2E + 08	2.24E + 11
Y_2	4.70E + 11	1.03E + 08	4.70E + 11
Y_3	6.39E + 12	5.35E + 11	5.86E + 12
Y_4	1.87E + 12	3.55E + 11	1.52E + 12
Y_5	4.72E + 10	3.23E + 09	4.40E + 10
Y_6	5.44E + 10	0	5.44E + 10
Y_7	6.28E + 12	4.81E + 10	6.23E + 12

Table 5: Distance between DMU1 and its benchmark

Inputs and outputs	Benchmark	DMU1	Difference
X_1	3.81E + 09	3.81E + 09	0
X_2	1.46E + 09	1.46E + 09	0
Y_1	7.13E + 09	7.13E + 09	0
Y_2	3.31E + 09	3.31E + 09	0
Y_3	7.12E + 11	7.12E + 11	0
Y_4	1.35E + 12	1.35E + 12	0
Y_5	9.14E + 10	9.14E + 10	0
Y_6	8.32E + 09	8.32E + 09	0
Y_7	6.60E + 11	6.60E + 11	0

REFERENCES

1. Athanassopoulos AD, Curram SP (1996) A comparison of data envelopment analysis and artificial neural networks as tool for assessing the efficiency of decision making units. J Oper Res Soc 47(8):1000–1016
2. Athanassopoulos AD, Giokas D (2000) The use of data envelopment analysis in banking institutions: evidence from the commercial bank of Greece. Interfaces 30(2):81–95
3. Azadeh A, Ghaderi SF, Anvari M, Saberi M (2006) Measuring performance electric power generations using artificial neural networks and fuzzy clustering. In: Capolino GA, Franquelo LG (eds) Proceedings of the 23nd annual conference of the IEEE industrial electronics society. IECON, Paris

4. Azadeh A, Ghaderi SF, Anvari M, Saberi M (2007a) Performance assessment of electric power generation using an adaptive neural network algorithm. Energy Policy 35(6):3155–3166
5. Azadeh A, Ghaderi SF, Anvari M, Saberi M, Izadbakhsh H (2007b) An integrated artificial neural network and fuzzy clustering algorithm for performance assessment of decision making units. Appl Math Comput 187(2):584–599
6. Azadeh A, Saberi M, Tavakkoli Moghaddam R, Javanmardi L (2011) An integrated data envelopment analysis–artificial neural network-rough set algorithm for assessment of personnel efficiency. Expert Syst Appl 38(3):1364–1373
7. Banker RD, Charnes A, Cooper WW (1984) Some models for estimating technical and scale inefficiencies in data envelopment analysis. Manag Sci 30(9):1078–1092
8. Bashiri M, Farshbaf-Geranmayeh A, Mogouie H (2013) A neuro-data envelopment analysis approach for optimization of uncorrelated multiple response problems with smaller the better type controllable factors. J Ind Eng Int 9(1):1–10
9. Berger AN, Humphrey DB (1991) The dominance of inefficiencies over scale and product mix economies in banking. J Monet Econ 28(1):117–148
10. Berger AN, Humphrey DB (1997) Efficiency of financial institutions: international survey and directions for future research. Eur J Oper Res 98(2):175–212
11. Berger AN, Hancock D, Humphrey DB (1993) Bank efficiency derived from the profit function. J Bank Finance 17(2/3):317–348
12. Chang KP (1999) Measuring efficiency with quasiconcave production frontiers. Eur J Oper Res 115(3):497–506
13. Clark JA (1996) Economic cost, scale efficiency, and competitive viability in banking. J Money Bank Credit 28(3):342–364
14. Deyoung R (1997) A diagnostic test for the distribution-free efficiency estimator: an example using US commercial bank data. Eur J Oper Res 98(2):243–249
15. Deyoung R (1998) Management quality and X-inefficiency in national banks. J Financ Serv Res 13(1):5–22
16. Golany B, Storbeck JE (1999) A data envelopment analysis of the operation efficiency of bank branches. Interfaces 29(3):14–26
17. Gutierrez E, Lozano S (2010) Data envelopment analysis of multiple response experiments. Appl Math Model 34(5):1139–1148
18. Hao J, Hunter WC, Yang WK (2001) Deregulation and efficiency: the case of private Korean banks. J Econ Bus 53(2/3):237–254
19. Kaparakis EI, Miller SM, Noulas AG (1994) Short-run cost inefficiency of commercial banks: a flexible stochastic frontier approach. J Money Credit Bank 26(4):875–894
20. Rahimi I, Behmanesh R (2012) Improve poultry farm efficiency in Iran: using combination. Int J Appl Oper Res 2(3):69–84

21. Sharda R (1994) Neural networks for the MS/OR analyst: an application bibliography. Interfaces 24(2):116–130
22. Sherman HD, Gold F (1985) Bank branch operating efficiency: evaluation with data envelopment analysis. J Bank Finance 9(2):297–316
23. Soteriou A, Zenios SA (1999) Operations, quality, and profitability in the provision of banking services. Manag Sci 45(9):1221–1238
24. Tulkens H (1993) On FDH efficiency analysis: some methodological issues and applications to retail banking, courts and urban transit. J Product Anal 4(1/2):183–210
25. Wang S (2003) Adaptive non-parametric efficiency frontier analysis: a neural network-based model. Comput Oper Res 30(2):279–295
26. Wu D, Yang Z, Liang L (2006) Using DEA-neural network approach to evaluate branch efficiency of a large Canadian bank. Expert Syst Appl 31(1):108–115

13
CHAPTER

E-BANKING FUNCTIONALITY AND OUTCOMES OF CUSTOMER SATISFACTION: AN EMPIRICAL INVESTIGATION

Dr. Ala`Eddin Mohd Khalaf Ahmad and Dr. Hasan Ali Al-Zu'bi

Keywords: E-banking, Customer satisfaction, Loyalty, WOM, Jordan

INTRODUCTION

One of the most recent channels of distribution to be used in the financial services organizations is electronic banking; this method was established in the mid 1990s, thereafter steadily becoming more important (Allen et al, 2001). The term electronic banking refers to "the provision of information or services by a bank to its customers, via a computer or television"(Allen et al, 2001). A more developed service is one that provides customers with the opportunity to gain access to their accounts and execute transactions or to buy product online via the internet (Daniel, 1999). Compatible with the revolutionary components of the electronic marketplace, Jordan has actively developed e-banking services since 2004 (Central Bank of Jordan, 2009). Moving towards an industrialization nation with knowledge economy as the backdrop, the personal computer and online approach of life is growing in Jordan. Public awareness of e-banking among users has been increased and thus people are ready to migrate to technology applications. With the population of approximately 6 million in Jordan (General Statistics Bureau, 2009), it is vital for bankers to understand the current usage trend of e-banking system.

Some scholars have shown that many international internet users demonstrate similar behaviors and preferences across nations (Quelch and Klein, 1996). Other researchers have studied the internet in the context of traditional cultures, and yet delimited by national borders (Park and Jun, 2003). Some studies have examined the issues on the evolution of e-banking (Sohail and Shanmugham, 2003) and investigated

Citation: Ala`Eddin Mohd Khalaf Ahmad, Hasan Ali Al-Zu'bi, E-banking Functionality and Outcomes of Customer Satisfaction: An Empirical Investigation, DOI: http://dx.doi.org/10.5539/ijms.v3n1p50.

the success factors in various e-delivery channels in banking scenario (Ong and Cheng, 2003). Some have investigated customer preferences of e-banking (Suganthi et al., 2001; Sohail and Shanmugham, 2003).

This study examines the factors which contributes and enhances the adoption of e-banking in Jordan, and the impact of e-banking functionality on the satisfaction outcomes for Jordanian banks customers. Also, this research assesses whether the adoption of e-banking customers in Jordan is constrained by the technology, particularly on the basis of different demographic characteristics, such as different age groups, educational level, income level and etc. Findings of this research are useful for the banking sector in formulating appropriate strategies to build customer satisfaction, loyalty, and positive WOM.

LITERATURE REVIEW

Definition of the e-Banking

The concept of electronic banking has been defined in many ways. Daniel (1999) defines electronic banking as the delivery of banks' information and services by banks to customers via different delivery platforms that can be used with different terminal devices such as a personal computer and a mobile phone with browser or desktop software, telephone or digital television.

Pikkarainen et al (2004) define internet banking as an "internet portal, through which customers can use different kinds of banking services ranging from bill payment to making investments". With the exception of cash withdrawals, internet banking gives customers access to almost any type of banking transaction at the click of a mouse (De Young, 2001). Indeed the use of the internet as a new alternative channel for the distribution of financial services has become a competitive necessity instead of just a way to achieve competitive advantage with the advent of globalization and fiercer competition (Flavián et al, 2004; Gan and Clemes, 2006). Banks use online banking as it is one of the cheapest delivery channels for banking products (Pikkarainen et al, 2004). Such service also saves the time and money of the bank with an added benefit of minimizing the likelihood of committing errors by bank tellers (Jayawardhena and Foley, 2000). Robinson (2000) believes that the supply of internet banking services enables banks to establish and extend their relationship with the customers. There are other numerous advantages to banks offered by online banking such as mass customization to suit the likes of each user, innovation of new products and services, more effective marketing and communication at lower costs (Tuchilla, 2000), development of non-core products such as insurance and stock brokerage as an expansion strategy, improved market image, better and quicker response to market evolution (Jayawardhena and Foley, 2000). Wise and Ali (2009) argued that many banks want to invest in ATMs to reduce branch cost since customers prefer to use them instead of a branch to transact business. The financial impact of ATMs is a marginal increase in fee income substantially offset by the cost of significant increases in the number of customer transactions. The value proposition however, is a significant increase in the intangible item "customer satisfaction". The increase translates into improved customer loyalty that in result in higher customer retention and growing organization value. Internet banking is a lower-cost delivery channel and a way to increase sales. Internet banking services has become one of the most important factors in the business economy today.

Factors of Adopting e-Banking

Accessibility

Accessibility defines as the ability of users to access information and services from the web is dependent on many factors. These include the content format; the user's hardware, software and settings; internet connections; the environmental conditions and the user's abilities and disabilities (Godwin-Jones 2001; Hackett and Parmanto, 2009). The term "web accessibility" generally relates to the implementation of website content in such a way as to maximize the ability of users with disabilities to access it. For example, providing a text equivalent for image content of a web page, allows users with some visual disabilities access to the information via a screen reader. The techniques and approaches that create more accessible web pages for people with disabilities also address many other access issues such as download speed and discoverability (Godwin-Jones 2001; Hackett et al, 2004; Hackett and Parmanto, 2009).

Jun et al (1999) revealed reliable/prompt responses, attentiveness, and ease of use had considerable impacts on both customers perceived overall service quality and satisfaction. It also indicated that there is a significant positive relationship between overall service quality and satisfaction. Yang and Jun (2002) redefined the traditional service quality dimensions in the context of online services, and suggested an instrument consisting of seven online service dimensions (reliability, access, ease of use, personalization, security, credibility, and responsiveness). Joseph et al (1999) considered banking service quality with respect to technology use, such as ATMs, telephone, and the internet and identified six dimensions. They were convenience/accuracy; feedback/complaint management; efficiency; queue management; accessibility; and customization. Therefore, it is hypothesized that accessibility has positive effect on customer satisfaction.

Convenience

E-banking provides higher degree of convenience that enables customers to access internet bank at all times and places. Apart from that, the ease of access of computers is perceived as a measure of relative advantage (Daniel, 1999, Black et al, 2001; Polatoglu and Ekin, 2001; Gerrard and Cunningham, 2003). Johnston (1995) revealed that there are some service quality determinants that are predominantly satisfiers and others that are predominantly dissatisfiers with the main sources of satisfaction being attentiveness, responsiveness, care and friendliness. The main sources of dissatisfaction are integrity, reliability, responsiveness, availability and functionality.

According to Ainscough and Luckett (1996), the provision of customer interactivity is an important criterion that attracts users in the delivery of e-banking. Gerrard and Cunningham (2003) also identify other factors of paramount importance in ensuring the success of e-banking, i.e. the ability of an innovation to meet users' needs using different feature availability on the web site. For instance, the provision of interactive loan calculators, exchange rate converters, and mortgage calculators on the web sites draw the attention of both users and non-users into the bank's web site. A UK study uncovered five key service quality attributes, such as security related issues, convenience, speed and timeliness of the service, and product variety/diverse features (White and Nteli, 2004). Therefore, it is hypothesized that convenience has positive effect on customer satisfaction.

Privacy

Customers have doubts about the trust ability of the e-bank's privacy policies (Gerrard and Cunningham, 2003). Trust has striking influence on user's willingness to engage in online exchanges of money and personal sensitive information (Friedman et al, 2000; Wang et al, 2003). Privacy is an important dimension that may affect users' intention to adopt e-based transaction systems. Encryption technology is the most common feature at all bank sites to secure information privacy, supplemented by a combination of different unique identifiers, for instance, a password, mother's maiden name, a memorable date, or a few minutes of inactivity automatically logs users off the account. Besides, the Secure Socket Layer, a widely-used protocol use for online credit card payment, is designed to provide a private and reliable channel between two communicating entities; the use of Java Applet that runs within the user's browser; the use of a Personal Identification Number, as well as an integrated digital signature and digital certificate associated with a smart card system (Hutchinson and Warren, 2003). Thus, a combination of smart card and biometric recognition using fingerprints offers a more secure and easier access control for computers than the password method. Zeithaml et al (2000) developed e-SERVQUAL for measuring e-service quality, identifying 11 dimensions: access; ease of navigation; efficiency; flexibility; reliability; personalization; security/privacy; responsiveness; assurance/trust; site aesthetics; and price knowledge. Hence, it is hypothesized that privacy has a positive effect on customer satisfaction.

Security

Assurance about security relates to the extent to which the web site guarantees the safety of customers` financial and personal information, an area which has witnessed a proliferation of research interest (Kimery and McCord, 2002; Miyazaki and Krishnamurthy, 2002). Security can be assured by providing a privacy statement and information about the security of the shopping mechanisms and by displaying the logos of trusted third parties. For example, displaying trusted third party logo guarantees a certain level of security protection and has been shown to significantly influence how consumers regard the trustworthiness of e vendors (Jiang et al, 2008).

Internet banking was made possible by the creation of Web browsers. In this mode of online banking, consumers do not have to purchase additional software (all they need is the browser), store any data on their computer, backup any data, or wait for software upgrades or new versions (Kolsaker and Payne, 2002; Dong-Her et al, 2004). All transactions occur on a secure server of a bank via the internet. The bank has all of the required data and software to execute the transactions. Customers go the bank's Web site, log in, and then take advantage of the bank's internet services. Typical bank services are account access and review, transfers of funds between accounts, bill payment, and then a widening variety of new services and products. Security plays an important role in internet banking and so there are several protocols for internet security of encrypted data packets (Kolsaker and Payne, 2002; Dong-Her et al; 2004). Customers are not aware of the encryption, however, only certain versions of popular internet browsers are acceptable to some banks due to their security limitations (Kolsaker and Payne, 2002; Dong-Her et al; 2004). Therefore, it is hypothesized that privacy has a positive effect on customer satisfaction.

Design

The goal of aesthetic design is to make a web site visually attractive and enjoyable. Proctor et al (2002, 2003) discussed content preparation in a broad sense and identified its four aspects: knowledge elicitation, information organization and structure, information retrieval, and information presentation. During design, and prior to implementation, it is strongly recommended that users of different ages, and with a range of capabilities and limitations be engaged to trial the new service and provide feedback. Financial institutions should test accessibility of their customer websites with both automated tools and user accessibility trials. Therefore, it is hypothesized that design has a positive effect on customer satisfaction.

Content

Jayawardhena and Foley (2000) and Pikkarainen et al (2004) claim that content on online banking on the web site is one of the factors influencing online-banking acceptance. On the other hand, quality designs, graphics or colors and the propensity to portray good image of the bank would enhance efficient use of navigation. In the context of internet banking, there is a growing body of research that has looked at influences on customer satisfaction. Jayawardhena and Foley (2000) illustrated that such web site features as speed, web site content and design, navigation, interactivity and security all influence user satisfaction whereas Broderick and Vachirapornpuk (2002) found that the level and nature of customer participation had the greatest impact on the quality of the service experience and issues such as customers' zone of tolerance, the degree of role understanding by customers and emotional response potentially determined, expected and perceived service quality.

Yang and Fang (2004) found that ease of use and usefulness are important factors in evaluating online service quality. Earlier Doll and Torkzadeh (1988) identified five quality dimensions that have an impact on "end-user" satisfaction in an online environment: content, accuracy, format, ease of use, timeliness. Thus, it is hypothesized that content has positive effect on customer satisfaction.

Speed

Hoffman and Novak (1996) find that there is a significant correlation between download speed and user satisfaction. Speed of download depends on the nature of the site downloaded content, the computing hardware and method of connection used to download information (Jayawardhena and Foley, 2000). Most sites demonstration is small snapshots, and some users have to download the program in order to view the demonstration. Most people perceive downloading may import unwanted viruses, and consume hard disk space. Very often, slow response time after any e-interaction leads to a delay of service delivery and makes consumers unsure about whether or not the transaction is completed (Jun and Cai, 2001). Johnston (1997) illustrates that certain actions, such as increasing the speed of processing information and customers, are likely to have an important effect in terms of pleasing customers; however other activities, such as improving the reliability of equipment, will lessen dissatisfaction rather than delight customers and suggests that it is more important to ensure that the dissatisfiers are dealt with before the satisfiers. Thus, it is hypothesized that speed has positive effect on customer satisfaction.

Fees and Charges

Service quality attributes in e-banking industry are important since human-internet interaction is the main service delivery and communication channel. Offering high quality services to satisfy consumers' needs, at lower costs, are potential competitive advantage of e-banking. Some studies show that e-banking has successfully reduced operating and administrative costs (Devlin, 1995; Siriluck and Speece, 2003). Cost savings have helped e-based banks offer lower or no service fees, and offer higher interest rates on interest-bearing accounts than traditional banks (Gerlach, 2000; Jun and Cai, 2001). Therefore, it is hypothesized that fees and charges have positive impact on customer satisfaction.

Customer Satisfaction and Outcomes of Satisfaction

In this section the research spotlights on the relevant literature on the concept of satisfaction, its consequences (loyalty and WOM).

Satisfaction

Satisfaction has been considered as one of the most important theoretical as well as practical issues for most marketers and customer researchers (Jamal, 2004). Oliver (1981, p. 29) firstly defined it in the consumption context as "the summary psychological state resulting when the emotion surrounding disconfirmed expectations is coupled with the customer's prior feelings about the consumption experience". In other words, we may say that satisfaction reflects a post-purchase evaluation of product quality given pre-purchase expectations (Kotler, 1991). On one hand, within literature on services marketing, satisfaction has traditionally been defined as a cognitive-based phenomenon (Westbrook, 1987). Cognition has been studied mainly in terms of the expectations/disconfirmation paradigm; also known as the confirmation/disconfirmation paradigm, which states that expectations originate from the customer's beliefs about the level of performance that a product/service would provide (Oliver, 1980). Many marketing scholars (Tse and Wilton, 1988 Anderson and Sullivan, 1993; Patterson et al, 1997), indicate that customer satisfaction is related to the size and direction of disconfirmation, which is defined as the difference between the post-purchase and post-usage evaluation of the performance of the product/service and the expectations held prior to the purchase (Sharma and Ojha, 2004).

On the other hand, other studies (Dube-Rioux, 1990; Homburg et al, 2006) have recognized that the affect experienced during the acquisition and consumption of the product or service can also have a significant influence on satisfaction judgments (Homburg et al, 2006). Dube-Rioux (1990) points out that a consumer affective response can be used to predict satisfaction more accurately than cognitive evaluation. Therefore, it is hypothesized that customer satisfaction has positive impact on customer loyalty.

Loyalty

Oliver (1999, p. 34) defines loyalty as "a deeply held commitment to re-buy or repatronize a preferred product/service consistently in the future, thereby causing repetitive same brand or same brand-set purchasing, despite situational influences and marketing efforts having the potential to cause switching behavior". Broadly, loyalty development has been an objective traditionally aimed at by managers (Andreassen, 1999) since it enables higher future purchase intention. In particular, loyalty may be defined as a customer's intention or predisposition to purchase from the same organization again (Edvardsson et al, 2000), that result from the conviction that the value received from one seller is greater than the value available from other alternatives (Hallowell, 1996). As a consequence, loyalty has been considered to be a key factor in order to achieve company success and sustainability over time (Flavián et al, 2006; Keating et al, 2003), and several authors have proposed that loyalty also favors higher intensity in positive WOM (Hallowell, 1996), lower price sensibility (Lynch and Ariely, 2000) and more stable and bigger incomes (Knox and Denison, 2000). Therefore, it is hypothesized that loyalty has positive impact on WOM.

WOM

Word-of-mouth (WOM) is an informal mode of communication between private parties concerning the evaluation of goods and services (Singh, 1988). Marketing literature has consistently shown its powerful role in influencing consumers' attitudes. For example, WOM is found to have more influence on product judgments than less vivid printed information (Herr et al, 1991). In general, WOM may be defined as an informal type of communication between private parties concerning the evaluation of goods and services and it has been considered to be one of the most powerful forces in the market place (Bansal and Voyer, 2000).

To be precise, the importance of WOM resides in the fact that consumer choice is usually influenced by WOM, especially when the purchase in important. This is explained due to the fact that consumers prefer to rely on informal and personal communication sources in making purchase decisions instead of on formal and organizational sources such as advertising campaigns (Bansal and Voyer, 2000).

The specific references only partially covered the e-banking and outcomes of satisfaction. Therefore, the present research attempts to fill a gap in the subject of e-banking in Jordanian commercial banks. The study addressed some of the shortcomings in the literature such as looking at the e-banking functionality factors from the point of view of accessibility, convenience, security, privacy, content, design, speed, fees and charges, to investigating the influences of e-banking on outcomes of satisfaction in the Jordanian commercial banks. It was established that no previous research had been conducted at Jordanian commercial banks, which investigated the relationship between the e-banking and the outcomes of satisfaction namely loyalty and positive WOM in the Jordanian commercial banks.

RESEARCH OBJECTIVES

Based on the research questions and relevant literature of the e-banking, customer satisfaction, loyalty and WOM, the research objectives are:

1). To reveal the adoption of e-banking factors in the Jordanian commercial banks.

2). To determine the factors which constitute e-banking functionality in the Jordanian commercial banks?

3). To examine the effect of e-banking on customer satisfaction.

4). To examine the effect of customer satisfaction on outcomes of satisfaction namely (loyalty and WOM).

RESEARCH METHODOLOGY

Population and Sample

Our research population is all the banks that are operating in Jordan and are registered with the Central Bank of Jordan. There are 24 commercial banks operating in Jordan (Central Bank of Jordan, 2009).

The research population consisted of all the customers who have an account at any commercial banks in the Hashemite Kingdom of Jordan. Therefore, all the banks customers were called and invited to participate in the research survey. Since all their headquarters are located in Amman, the whole population was invited to participate in the survey. The researchers gathered 185 questionnaires, yielding a response rate of 74 per cent. Finally, 179 (71.6 per cent) questionnaires were fully and correctly completed. All data collection procedures were designed to ensure the anonymity. Respondents typically held purposive sample.

It should be noted that every questionnaire was personally handed and instructions were given to each customers before completing the questionnaire. In terms of demographic findings, (70.4%) of respondents were males, and the remaining (29.6%) were females. In terms of the age group of respondents, it is interested to note that (27.4%) of them are less than (26) years, whereas (29.1%) fell into the (26-30) age group, whereas (15.1%) fell into the (31-35) age group, whereas (12.3%) fell into the (36-40) age group, whereas (8.4%) fell into the (41-45) age group, only (7.8%) are above this group. As for the educational levels of those customers, the majority (60.9%) were university degree holders, and some those (10.1%) of these, have postgraduate degree. As for the computer literacy of those customers, were all of them (100 %) were computer literacy, As for the internet accessibility at home/office of these customers, the majority (89.9%) were internet accessibility at home/office. See table (1).

Table 1: Characteristics of the Sample (N=179)

Characteristics		Frequency	Percent
Gender:			
	Male	126	70.4
	Female	53	29.6
Age:			
	< 26	49	27.4
	26 – 30	52	29.1
	31 – 35	27	15.1
	36 – 40	22	12.3
	41 - 45	15	8.4
	> 45	14	7.8
Education level:			
	High School or Less	15	8.4
	Community College Diploma	37	20.7
	Bachelor	109	60.9
	Postgraduate	18	10.1
Computer literacy:			
	Yes	179	100
	No	---	---
Internet accessibility at home/office:			
	Yes	161	89.9
	No	18	10.1

Data Collection

The research questionnaire was designed based on previous empirical literature. The questionnaire design was pre-tested and redesigned through personal interviews with bank managers and banks customers by undertaking the pilot study work (Aaker et al, 2001).

The research questionnaire was used as primary data collection method as shown in (Table 2, 3, 4). The components of e-banking and outcomes of customer satisfaction items were measured on 5-point Likert- scale ranging from 5 (strongly agree) to 1 (strongly disagree). For the e-banking and outcomes of customer satisfaction dimensions, the research respondents were asked to indicate the degree of agreement or disagreement on the ebanking items that banks used e-banking technique in order to achieve customer satisfaction. For the outcomes of satisfaction, the respondents were asked to indicate how important they believed of customer satisfaction. Multiple items were used to assess their measurement properties. Consistent with the literature, the scale items selected for the dependent variable were direct measures of customer satisfaction with influences received from adoption of e-banking functionality as independent variables. This format has been recommended for marketing and banking surveys. Both the independent and dependent variable(s) deployed in the research are explained in Table 2, 3and 4 according to the proposed hypotheses.

Table 2: adoption of e-banking factors: Independent variables

Accessibility (independent variable)

Hypothesis 1: accessibility has a positive significant influence on customer satisfaction.

Accessibility in the Jordanian commercial banks was measured on:

Internet accessibility, site has details when the bank charges apply, site has details of overdraft facilities, site has details on how to fund transfer between accounts, site has details on competitors' interest rates, exchange rate and foreign exchange, details on security arrangements, site has a search engine.

Convenience (independent variable)

Hypothesis 2: Convenience has a positive significant influence on customer satisfaction.

The measure for this factor consists of: access anytime and anywhere, no queue, save time as compared to conventional banking, e-banks transaction is easy to use, user friendly, easy login, check transaction details and statement regularly, computer literate keeps me using e-banking services.

Security (independent variable)

Hypothesis 3: security accessibility has a positive significant influence on customer satisfaction.

The authorized username and password are important, saving login number and password on the computer, leaving computer unattended, while connected to the e-banking services, Trust affects the demand for e-banking services, Pins obtain by fraud may allow hackers to access to customers' account, don't mind registering before supplying information, Banks' reliability in correcting erroneous transactions, Trust the bank will compensate for losses due to security reasons, satisfying with the security system.

Privacy (independent variable)

Hypothesis 4: privacy has a positive significant influence on customer satisfaction.

Privacy influences consisted of evaluating: Confidential information is delivered safely from banks to customers, Customers' financial information may be passed on to other companies among the banks, third parties are able to assess customers' financial details, Banking institutions keep customers information private and confidential, trust the bank's privacy protection to the users, Continuous improvement on online systems.

Content (independent variable)

Hypothesis 5: Content has a positive significant influence on customer satisfaction content influences consisted of evaluating: clear and easy guidance screen, clear and simple help menus allow me to perform e-banking transaction easily, Information credibility, willing to seek helps from the customer services when I encounter problems, E-banking services have been upgraded compared to, I first started using the services.

Design (independent variable)

Hypothesis 6: design has a positive significant influence on customer satisfaction

The role of design was assessed by measuring: Attractiveness screen layout and design, Site has flashy graphics and color configuration, Web site design is important.

Speed (independent variable)

Hypothesis 7: speed has a positive significant influence on customer satisfaction

This factor measured by: Frequent connection breakdown, Easy to navigate the bank site due to smooth speed, Transition is efficient/no waiting time, Response speed to complaint is satisfactory, Speed of e-transactions flow is faster than traditional banking channels.

Fees and charges (independent variable)

Hypothesis 8: fees and charges have a positive significant influence on customer satisfaction

The role of fees and charges were assessed by measuring: Prices of computer are reasonable and affordable, Fee of internet connection is affordable, E-banks charge lower transaction fees, Continue using although need to pay low subscription fees, I won't terminate services even if bank charges annual fee, E-banks charge annual fee, Time saving using e-banking services, Price of service fees is acceptable.

Table 3: Customer Satisfaction: dependent variable/ independent variable (mediation).

Customer satisfaction (dependent variable)

Hypothesis 9: customer satisfaction has a positive significant influence on customer loyalty

The measurement of performance was assessed by: customer made the correct decision to use this website, the experience that had with this website has been satisfactory, and customer satisfied with the way that this website has carried out transactions, and customer satisfied with the service have received from the website.

Hypothesis 10: customer loyalty has a positive significant influence on WOM.

Table 4: customer loyalty: dependent variable/ independent variable

Customer loyalty: I have the intention to continue my relationship with this website, Based on my experience, I am very likely continuing my relationship with this website in the next months.

WOM (dependent variable): Will recommend this website to other customers, I will point out the positive aspects of this website if anybody criticizes it.

Hypothesis 11: customer satisfaction has a positive significant influence on WOM

Table 2: Results – adopting of e-banking (customer satisfaction)

E-banking factors	B	Standardized error	Beta	t-value	Significant
E-banking factors	0.800	0.432	0.197	3.157	0.004

R^2 =0.434 Adjusted R^2 =0.446 F =11.720 $P < 0.05$

Table 3: Results – Accessibility / (customer satisfaction)

E-banking factors	B	Standardized error	Beta	t-value	Significant
Accessibility	0.781	0.765	0.654	2.765	0.045

Table 4: Results – Convenience / (customer satisfaction)

E-banking factors	B	Standardized error	Beta	t-value	Significant
Convenience	0.700	0.325	0.213	2.154	0.034

RESULTS AND DISCUSSION

Our basic assumptions are that e-banking functionality factors namely (accessibility, convenience, security, privacy, content, design, speed, fees and charges) influence satisfaction and outcomes of satisfaction namely loyalty and positive word of mouth. A multiple regression modeling approach was proposed as an effective method for studying the relationships. As displayed in Table 5, the adjusted R2 is 0.446, suggesting that the eight e-banking factors explain close to 45 per cent of the variance for the dimension of satisfaction. Specifically, other Tables also act variables have a statistically significant effect on satisfaction.

Table 5: Results – Security / (customer satisfaction)

E-banking factors	B	Standardized error	Beta	t-value	Significant
Security	1.305	0.342	0.360	3.815	0.000

Of these significant variables, security, privacy, and content appear to have the greatest impact on satisfaction. In addition, it predicted that the influence of such factors (accessibility, convenience, security, privacy, content, design, speed, fees and charges) on satisfaction would differ according to the personal variables, which are personal characteristics and their experience in computers (as shown in table 5). The results of the multiple regression analysis signal that there is variation in the effect of e-banking functionality factors on satisfaction and empirical evidence in this research suggests that e-banking factors have a significant degree of influence on satisfaction and outcomes of satisfaction. This empirical evidence has provided significant support for the e-banking literature, which substantively advocates that e-banking functionality factors have an impact on outcome of satisfaction.

The results empirically substantiate that e-banking functionality factors play a fundamental role in the satisfaction among Jordanian commercial banks.

The e-banking functionality factors has a positive significant influence on customer satisfaction

Empirically, the model assumed that e-banking functionality factors positively influence customer satisfaction in the Jordanian commercial banks. In addition, it predicted that the influence of such factors on customer satisfaction would differ according to the personal variable that is gender, age, marital status, educational level, computer literacy, and internet accessibility (table 5). The results of the multiple regression analysis signal that there is variation in the effect of e-banking factors on customer satisfaction and empirical evidence in this research suggests that adoption of e- banking factors have a significant degree of influence on customer satisfaction. This empirical evidence has provided significant support for the electronic banking literature, which substantively advocates that e-banking factors have an influence on customer satisfaction (Jayawardhena and Foley, 2000; Robinson, 2000; Pikkarainen et al, 2004; Gan et al, 2006; Hua, 2009; Wise and Ali, 2009). The results empirically substantiate that using of e-banking services play a fundamental role in the customer satisfaction among Jordanian commercial banks.

Accessibility has a positive significant influence on customer satisfaction

The findings in table (6) provide significant support for the accessibility literature which advocates that accessibility have an influence upon Jordanian commercial banks. As a consequence, we are able to substantiate that accessibility has a significant influence on customer satisfaction. These findings are also consistent with other research findings (for example, Godwin-Jones 2001; Hackett and Parmanto, 2009)

Table 6: Results – Privacy / (customer satisfaction)

E-banking factors	B	Standardized error	Beta	t-value	Significant
Privacy	1.210	0.354	0.312	2.752	0.000

Convenience has a positive significant influence on customer satisfaction

Convenience is also considered to be one of the influential factors on the satisfaction of Jordanian commercial banks (table 7). Prior research has empirically found positive relationship between convenience and satisfaction as critical factors on the use of e-banking (Venkatesh and Davis, 1996; Johnson and Marakas, 2000; Hong et al, 2001; Chau, 2001; Wang et al, 2003; Pikkarainen et al, 2004).

Table 7: Results – Design / (customer satisfaction)

E-banking factors	B	Standardized error	Beta	t-value	Significant
Design	0.144	0.543	0.333	2.659	0.047

These results are not surprising as when Jordanian commercial banks consider the convenience as a competitive tool; this might impact positively on the adapting and generalize the using of e-banking in Jordan. As a result, we are able to confirm that convenience have a significant influence on customer satisfaction. These findings are also consistent with other research findings. For example, (Devlin, 1995; Daniel, 1999, Black et al, 2001; Polatoglu and Ekin, 2001; Suganthi et al, 2001; Gerrard and Cunningham, 2003) found that e-banking provides higher degree of convenience that enables customers to access internet bank at all times and places.

Privacy has a positive significant influence on customer satisfaction

Examining data appears that a pre-requisite for survival and growth is that both the banks and its customers have an interest in their joint relationship – leading to a win-win effect. Factors such as confidential information is delivered safely from banks to customers; trust the bank's privacy protection to the users should help to build effective relationships and increase the customer satisfaction in the long run.

Banks customers have doubts about the trust ability of the e-bank's privacy policies (Gerrard and Cunningham, 2003). Trust has striking influence on user's willingness to engage in online exchanges of money and personal sensitive information (Hoffman et al, 1999; Friedman et al, 2000; Wang et al, 2003). Privacy is important dimension that may affect users' intention to adopt e-based transaction systems. Privacy consider as one of the most influential factor on customer satisfaction as shown in table (8).

Table 8: Results – Content / (customer satisfaction)

E-banking factors	B	Standardized error	Beta	t-value	Significant
Content	2.640	0.440	0.519	6.006	0.000

Security has a positive significant influence on customer satisfaction

An examination of table (9) suggests that security is an influential factor on customer satisfaction in Jordanian commercial banks. The results therefore, substantiate that security has a positive bearing on customer satisfaction. These findings are also consistent with other research findings. For example, (Daniel, 1999, Black et al, 2001; Polatoglu and Ekin, 2001; Suganthi et al, 2001; Gerrard and Cunningham, 2003) found that e-banking provides higher degree of security that enables customers to trust internet banking at all times and places.

Table 9: Results – Speed / (customer satisfaction)

E-banking factors	B	Standardized error	Beta	t-value	Significant
Speed	0.812	0.306	0.259	2.651	0.009

Design has a positive significant influence on customer satisfaction

Design is also considered to be one of the influential factors on the satisfaction of Jordanian commercial banks customers (table 10). Prior research has empirically found positive relationship between banks web design and customer satisfaction as critical factors on the use of e-banking (Fang and Salvendy, 2003; Lazar and Sears, 2006). These results indicate that the web design is an important element to facilitate the using of e-banking which is reflects on the customer satisfaction. Other researches have empirically found positive relationship between bank web site design and customer satisfaction as critical factors on the use of e-banking (Fang and Salvendy, 2003; Lazar and Sears, 2006; Vu and Proctor, 2006).

Table 10: Results – Fees / (customer satisfaction)

E-banking factors	B	Standardized error	Beta	t-value	Significant
Fees	3.545	0.460	0.777	2.985	0.008

Content has a positive significant influence on customer satisfaction

Examining data in table (11), it appears that content of bank site has a positive significant influence on the acceptance of adopting this service by Jordanian commercial banks customers. Factors such as information credibility; Clear and simple help menus allow customers to perform e-banking transaction easily should help users to build effective relationships and increase the customer satisfaction in the long run. Content is important dimension that may affect users' intention to adopt e-banking systems. Other researches have empirically found positive relationship between bank web content and customer satisfaction as critical factors on the use of e-banking (Friedman et al, 2000; Hutchinson and Warren, 2003; Wang et al, 2003).

Table 11: Results- Customer Satisfaction/Loyalty

Outcomes of Satisfaction	B	Standardized error	Beta	t-value	Significant
Customer Satisfaction	0.125	0.047	0.261	2.680	0.009

Speed has a positive significant influence on customer satisfaction

Our findings in table (12) provide support for speed having a statistically significant positive effect on customer satisfaction. This finding is similar to the work of Hoffman and Novak (1996) that identified speed as a major factor influencing customer satisfaction. Other researches have empirically found positive relationship between e-banking speed and customer satisfaction as critical factors on the use of this service (Hoffman and Novak, 1996; Jayawardhena and Foley, 2000).

Table 12: Results-Loyalty/ WOM

Outcomes of Satisfaction	B	Standardized error	Beta	t-value	Significant
Loyalty	0.543	0.086	0.524	3.680	0.000

Fees have a positive significant influence on customer satisfaction

Fees are also considered to be one of the influential factors on the customer satisfaction of Jordanian commercial banks customers (table 13). Prior research has empirically found positive relationship between e-banking fees and customer satisfaction as critical factors on the use of e banking (Devlin, 1995; Gerlach, 2000; Jun and Cai, 2001; Siriluck and Speece, 2003). These results indicate that the fees determine by Jordanian banks are an important element to facilitate the using of e-banking which is reflects on the customer satisfaction. Other researches have empirically found positive relationship between fees rate and customer satisfaction as critical factors on the use of e- banking (Devlin, 1995; Gerlach, 2000; Jun and Cai, 2001; Siriluck and Speece, 2003).

Table 13: Results- Customer Satisfaction/WOM

Outcomes of Satisfaction	B	Standardized error	Beta	t-value	Significant
Customer Satisfaction	0.511	0.081	0.513	3.213	0.000

In summary, it can be seen that all e-banking functionality factors, which accessibility, convenience, security, privacy, content, design, speed, fees and charges, have proven to positively customer satisfaction. Examining data in tables (14, 15, 16) it appear that customer satisfaction has a positive significant influence on customer loyalty of adopting e-banking service by Jordanian commercial banks. This result generalized on the other research outcomes (loyalty on positive WOM and also customer satisfaction on positive WOM). Loyalty and WOM were explained at a similar level in the proposed model (R2 loyalty=0.375, R2 SAT influence WOM=0.362). Generally speaking, we can conclude that satisfaction is a key mediating factor in the loyalty and positive WOM in the e-banking services in Jordanian commercial banks.

IMPLICATIONS

The theoretical underpinning of this research is based on literature from the e-banking relating to commercial banks within the banking industry. Service marketing scholars have long since recognized the crucial characteristics of service intangibility, inseparability, heterogeneity, fiduciary, and perishability, lack of transfer of title (Zeithaml et al, 1985; Harrison, 2000). The recognition of such characteristics has led researchers to recognize the key role played by service marketers in improving service delivery and accessibility to shed light on the important role of marketing within service sectors, especially in the provision of banking services. The empirical conclusions drawn from this research are multifaceted and as a result, it is vitally important that banks managers pay attention to the influences of customer satisfaction. Researchers are therefore encouraged to place more focus on the impact influences stemming from the e-banking functionality and its impact on customer satisfaction within Jordanian commercial banks. In addition, adoption of e-banking has not been previously identified as crucial inputs for satisfaction by banks managers operating within the commercial banks sector.

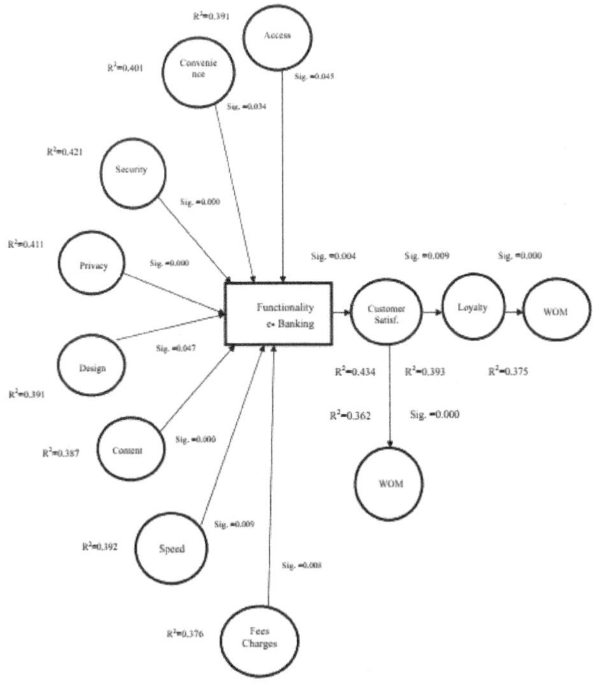

Figure 1: Research Model

CONCLUSION

This research seeks to make an original contribution to knowledge by investigating the impact of e-banking factors on outcomes of customer satisfaction in the commercial banks industry in Jordan. This research contributes to the services marketing discipline in finding out the role of the e-banking in enhancing customer satisfaction and loyalty. Factors pertaining to accessibility, convenience, security, privacy, content, design, speed, fees and charges were a focus of this study as they have an influence on customer satisfaction. Contributions found will be beneficial for both academics and managers alike. Academically, this work aims to focus academic attention upon a much neglected domain – the marketing and information technology of banking services in Jordan. There is currently a distinct lack of studies in academia relating to research in the Middle East. This is somewhat surprising when considering that Jordan has been at the forefront of the banking services industry in the Middle East. In fact, the banking services industry is an important and vibrant sector in Jordan and banks are considered as an important segment of the financial services provider where customers can receive a wide range of financial services.

Although this research has provided valuable insights into a somewhat scant area of research, it has been subject to some limitations. To begin with, there were some difficulties in the distribution of the research questionnaire within the customers of Jordanian commercial banks, possibly leading to some inconsistencies in the data collection process. For example, a portion of banks opted to distribute the instrument to respondents themselves, where in other cases the researcher delivered the survey to respondents individually. In addition, this research has been conducted within a single service industry and exclusively in the Jordanian commercial banks sector, thus limiting the generalisability of the research results to the foreign banks and other financial organizations in Jordan. Future research is therefore required to extend these results in other geographical areas and among managerial employees at these banks. For example, the concept could be extended to other Arab countries in order to validate the model and findings. By studying other service and financial services (for example, specialty banks, money transfer services, insurance companies) a model could be developed to better represent the service sector in more general, rather than focusing on the commercial banks alone. The inclusion of employees at all service levels would allow for more insight to be gathered on employees' viewpoints, attitudes, perceptions and overall satisfaction of outcomes of satisfaction.

Future research should also investigate whether the model could be used for a comparative study between the service sector and the industrial sector, testing for the differences and effects of electronic functionality factors in both sectors. By doing so, it would be interesting to test whether the model could hold across a range of industries and service sectors apart from banking industry.

REFERENCES

1. Aaker, D., V. Kumar, and G. Day. (2003). Marketing research. 800 p. 7th ed., John Wiley and Sons, New York, USA.
2. Ainscough, T.L., & Luckett, M.G. (1996).The internet for the rest of us: marketing on the World Wide Web. Journal of Consumer Marketing, 13 (2), 36-47

3. Allen, F., McAndrews, J., & Strahan, P. (2001). E-finance: An Introduction, Working Paper No. 01-36. Financial Institutions Center, Wharton University, Philadelphia, PA, 7 October,

4. Anderson, E.W., & Sullivan, M.W. (1993). The antecedents and consequences of customer satisfaction for firms. Marketing Science, 12, (2), 125-43.

5. Andreassen, T.W. (1999). What drives customer loyalty with complaint resolution?. Journal of Service Research, 1, (4), 324-32

6. Bansal, H., & Voyer, P. (2000). Word-of-Mouth Processes Within a Service Purchase Decision Context. Journal of Service Research, 3, (2), 166-77.

7. Black, N.J., Lockett, A., Winklhofer, H., & Ennew, C. (2001). The adoption of Internet financial services: A qualitative study. International Journal of Retail &Distribution Management, 29(8), 390-398.

8. Broerick, A Vachirapornpuk, S. (2002). Service quality in Internet banking: the importance of customer role. Marketing Intelligence & Planning, 20, (6), 327 – 335.

9. Central Bank of Jordan. (2009). Annual Report, HKJ.

10. Daniel, E. (1999). Provision of electronic banking in the UK and the Republic of Ireland. International Journal of Bank Marketing, 17(2), 72-82.

11. Devlin, J.F. (1995). Technology and innovation in retail banking distribution. International Journal of Bank Marketing, 13, (4), 19-25.

12. DeYoung, R. (2001). The financial performance of pure play Internet banks. Economic Perspectives, 25, (1), 60-75.

13. Doll, W.J., & Torkzadeh, G. (1988). The measurement of end-user computing satisfaction. MIS Quarterly, 12, (2), 259-74.

14. Dong-Her, S., Hsiu-Sen, C., Chun-Yuan, C., Lin, B. (2004). Internet security: malicious e-mails detection and protection. Industrial Management & Data Systems, 104,(7), 613-23.

15. Dube-Rioux, L. (1990). Power of affective reports in predicting satisfaction judgments. in Goldberg, M., Gorn, G.,Pollay, R. (Eds). Advances in Consumer Research,17, 571-6.

16. Edvardsson, B., Johnson, M.D., Gustafsson, A., & Strandvik, T. (2000). The effects of satisfaction and loyalty on profits and growth: products versus services. Total Quality Management, 11, 917-27.

17. Flavián, C., Guinalíu, M., & Gurrea, R. (2006). The role played by perceived usability, satisfaction and consumer trust on website loyalty. The International Journal of Information Systems Applications, 43, (1), 1-14.

18. Flavian, C., Torres, E., and Guinaliu, M. (2004). Corporate image measurement: a further problem for the tangibilization of internet banking services. International Journal of Bank Marketing, 22 (5), 366-84.

19. Friedman, B., Kahn, P.H. Jr, & Howe, D.C. (2000). Trust online. Communications of the ACM, 43, (2),34-40.

20. Gan, C and Clemes, M. (2006). A logit analysis of electronic banking in New Zealand. International Journal of Bank Marketing, 24 (6), 360-383.
21. General Statistic Bureau. (2009). Annual Report, HKJ.
22. Gerlach, D. (2000). Put your money where your mouse is. PC World, .March, 191-9.
23. Gerrard, P., & Cunningham, J. (2003). The diffusion of internet banking among Singapore consumers. International Journal of Bank Marketing, 21, (1), 16-28.
24. Goodwin-Jones, B. (2001). Emerging technologies – accessibility and web design why does it matter?. Language Learning and Technology, 5, 11-19.
25. Hackett, S., Parmanto, B., & Zeng, X. (2004). ASSETS'04. ACM, Atlanta, GA, .18-20 October, 32-9.
26. Hackett, S., B. Parmanto and X. Zeng. (2004). Accessibility of Internet Websites through Time. Association for Computing Machenary, Atlanta, USA.
27. Hackett, S & Parmanto, B. (2009). Homepage not enough when evaluating web site accessibility. Internet Research, 19, (1),78 – 87.
28. Hallowell, R. (1996). The relationships of customer satisfaction, customer loyalty, and profitability: an empirical study. International Journal of Service Industry Management, 7, (4), 27-42.
29. Harrison, T. (2000). Financial services marketing. Prentice Hall.
30. Herr, P., Kardes, F., and Kim, J. (1991). Effects of Word-of-Mouth and Product Attribute Information on Persuasion: an Accessibility-Diagnocisticity Perspective. Journal of Consumer Research, 17, 454-462.
31. Hoffman, D.L., Novak, T.P., & Peralta, M. (1999). Building consumer trust online. Communications of the ACM, 42, (4), 80-5.
32. Homburg, C., Koschate, N., & Hoyer, W.D. (2006). The role of cognition and affect in the formation of customer satisfaction: a dynamic perspective. Journal of Marketing, 70, July, 21-31.
33. Hutchinson, D., & Warren, M. (2003). Security for internet banking: a framework. Logistic Information Management, 16, (1), 64-73.
34. Jamal, A. (2004). Retail banking and customer behaviour: a study of self concept, satisfaction and technology usage. The International Review of Retail, Distribution and Consumer Research, 14, (3), 357-379.
35. Jayawardhena, C., & Foley, P. (2000). Changes in the banking sector – the case of Internet banking in the UK. Internet Research: Electronic Networking Applications and Policy, 10, (1), 19-30.
36. Jiang, Pingjun, David B. Jones, and Sharon Javie. (2008). How Third-Party Certification Programs Relate to Consumer Trust in Online Transactions: An Exploratory Study. Psychology & Marketing, 25 (9), 839-858.
37. Johnston, R. (1995). The determinants of service quality: satisfiers and dissatisfies. International Journal of Service Industry Management, 6, (5), 53-71.

38. Joseph M, McClure C & Joseph B. (1999). Service quality in the banking sector: the impact of technology on service delivery. International Journal of Bank Marketing, 17(4), 182-191.

39. Jun, M., & Cai, S. (2001). The key determinants of internet banking service quality: a content analysis. International Journal of Bank Marketing, 19, (7), 276-91.

40. Jun, M., Peterson, R., Zsidisin, G., & Daily, B. (1999). Service quality perceptions in the banking industry: major dimensions. Journal of Business Strategies, 16, (2), 170-88.

41. Keating, B., Rugimbana, R., & Quazi, A. (2003). Differentiating between service quality and relationship quality in cyberspace. Managing Service Quality, 13, (3), 217-32.

42. Kimery, K.M., & McCord, M. (2002). Third-party assurances: mapping the road to trust in e-retailing. Journal of Information Technology Theory and Applications, 4, (2), 63-82.

43. Knox, S.D., & Denison, T.J. (2000). Store loyalty: its impact on retail revenue. An empirical study of purchasing behaviour in the UK. Journal of Retailing and Consumer Services, 7, (1), 33-45.

44. Kolsaker, A Payne, C. (2002). Engendering trust in e-commerce: a study of gender-based concerns. Marketing Intelligence & Planning, 20 (4), 206 – 214.

45. Lynch, J.G., & Ariely, D. (2000). Wine online: search costs affect competition on price quality and distribution. Marketing Science, 19, (1), 83-103.

46. Miyazaki, A.D., & Krishnamurthy, S. (2002). Internet seals of approval: effects on online privacy policies and consumer perceptions. The Journal of Consumer Affairs, 36, (1), 28-49.

47. Oliver, R.L. (1999). Whence consumer loyalty?. Journal of Marketing, 63, 33-44.

48. Oliver, Richard L. (1980). A Cognitive Model of the Antecedents and Consequences of Satisfaction Decisions. Journal of Marketing Research, 17, (September), 460-469.

49. Oliver, Richard, L. (1981). Measurement and Evaluation of Satisfaction Process in Retail Setting. Journal of Retailing, 57, (Fall), 25-48.

50. Ong, H.B., & Cheng, M.Y. (2003). Success factor in e-channels: the Malaysian banking scenario. International Journal of Bank Marketing, 21, (6), 369-77.

51. Park, C., & Jun, J.K. (2003). Effects of internet usage, perceived risks, and innovativeness. International Marketing Review, 20, (5), 534-53.

52. Patterson, P.G., Johnson, L.W., & Spreng, R.A. (1997).Modeling the determinants of customer satisfaction for business-to-business professional services. Journal of the Academy of Marketing Science, 25, (1), 4-17.

53. Pikkarainen, T., Pikkarainen, K., Karjaluoto, H., and Pahnila, S. (2004). Consumer acceptance of online banking: an extension of the technology acceptance model. Internet Research, 14, (3).

54. Polatoglu, V.N., & Ekin, S. (2001). An empirical investigation of the Turkish consumers' acceptance of Internet banking services. International Journal of Bank Marketing, 19(4), 156-165.

55. Proctor, R.W., Vu, K., & Salvendy, G., et al.. (2002). Content Preparation and Management for Web Design: Eliciting, Structuring, Searching, and Displaying Information. International Journal of Human-Computer Interaction, 14, (1), 25-92.

56. Quelch, J.A., & Klein, L.R. (1996). The internet and international marketing. Sloan Management Review, spring, 60-75.

57. Robert W. Proctor, Kim-Phuong L. Vu, Lawrence J. Najjar, Misha W. Vaughan, & Gavriel Salvendy. (2003). Content preparation and management for e-commerce Web sites. Communications of the ACM, .46, (12), December.

58. Robinson, T. (2000). Internet banking: still not a perfect marriage. Informationweek.com, April 17, pp.104-106.

59. Sharma, N., & Ojha, S. (2004). Measuring service performance in mobile communication. The Service Industries Journal, 24, (6), 109-28.

60. Singh, J. (1990). Voice, Exit and Negative Word of Mouth Behaviours: An Investigation Across Three Service Categories. Journal of the Academy of Marketing Science, 18, 1-15.

61. Siriluck, R., & Speece, M. (2003). Barriers to internet banking adoption: a qualitative study among corporative customers in Thailand. International Journal of Bank Marketing, 21, (6), 312-23.

62. Sohail,M.S., & Shanmugham, B.E-b. (2003). E-banking and customer preferences in Malaysia: an empirical investigation. Information Sciences, 150,207-17.

63. Suganthi, S., Balachandher, K.G., & Balachandran, S. (2001). Internet banking patronage: an empirical investigation of Malaysia. Journal of Internet Banking and Commerce, [Online] Available: www.arraydev.com/commerce/JIBC/0103_01.htm, 6, (1).

64. Tse, D.K., & Wilton, P.C. (1988). Models of customer satisfaction formation: an extension. Journal of Marketing Research, 25, (2), 204-12.

65. Tuchila, R. (2000). Servicii bancare prin Internet. E-finance Romania, 3, (3), 23.

66. Wang, Y.S., Wang, Y.M., Lin, H.H., & Tang, T.I. (2003). Determinants of user acceptance of internet banking: an empirical study. International Journal of Service Industry Management, 14, (5), 501-19.

67. Westbrook, R.A. (1987). Product/consumption-based affective responses and post-purchase processes. Journal of Marketing Research, 24 , (3), 258-70.

68. White, H., & Nteli, F. (2004). Internet banking in the UK: why are there not more customers?. Journal of Financial Services Marketing, 9, 49-57.

69. Wise, Victoria and Ali, Muhammad Mahboob. (2009). Customer Relationship Management in Banks with special reference to Bangladesh. Southwest Review of International Business Research, 19, (1), March.

70. Yang, Z., and Fang, X. (2004). Online service quality dimensions and their relationships with satisfaction: A content analysis of customer reviews of securities brokerage services. International Journal of Service Industry Management, 15(3), 302-326.

71. Yang, Z., & Jun, M. (2002). Consumer perception of e-service quality: from internet purchaser and non-purchaser perspectives. Journal of Business Strategies, 19 (1), 19-41.

72. Zeithaml, V.A., Parasuraman, A., & Malhotra, A. (2000). A conceptual framework for understanding e-service quality: implications for future research and managerial practice. Marketing Science Institute and Dell star, working paper.

14
CHAPTER

E-BANKING IN EMERGING ECONOMY

Mahdi Salehi and Mehrdad Alipour

Keywords: Banking sector, E-banking, Iran

INTRODUCTION

Financial services industry has recently been open to historic transformation, it can call e-developments are emerging and advancing rapidly in all areas of financial intermediation and financial markets: e-finance, e-money, electronic banking (e-banking), e-brokering, e-insurance, e-exchanges, and even e-supervision. The new information technology (IT) is turning into the most important factor in the future development of banking, influencing banks' marketing and business strategies. In recent years, the adoption of e-banking began to occur quite extensively as a channel of distribution for financial services due to rapid advances in IT and intensive competitive banking markets. The driving forces behind the rapid transformation of banks are influential changes in the economic environment: innovations in information technology, innovations in financial products, liberalization and consolidation of financial markets, deregulation of financial inter-mediation etc. These and other factors make it complicated to design a bank's strategy, which process is threatened by unforeseen developments and changes in the economic environment and therefore, strategies must be flexible to adjust to these changes. The financial services market is continuing to change rapidly, which brings into question whether traditional banks, as they are now structured, will actually continue to exist by the end of the decade or even survive through the next five years. Competition has been increasing for some years within traditional financial centers, amongst the banks themselves. A significant challenge comes from international banks

Citation: Mahdi Salehi and Mehrdad Alipour, E-Banking in Emerging Economy, ISSN 1916-971X.

offering technology-based financial services across geographical boundaries and thereby competing with traditional banks for their best business within their own back yard.

Indeed, there is a growing concern that e-banking is not yielding the anticipated results, creating a gap between the actual returns and the proposed objectives and thereby losing a large amount of investment. This especially concerns the interaction with clients and thereby increased and more rapid access to new markets. This has thrown the spotlight onto the problem of change from one particular delivery channel to another. This is highly important since the implementation of e-banking may have radical implications on a bank's structures, business processes, products and services and value flows with clients and other parties.

A strong banking industry is important in every country and can have a significant affect in supporting economic development through efficient financial services. In Iran the role of the banking industry needs to change to keep up with the globalization movement, both at the procedural level and at the informational level. This change will include moving from traditional distribution channel banking to electronic distribution channel banking. Given the almost complete adoption of e-banking in developed countries, the reason for the lack of such adoption in developing countries like Iran is an important research that will be addressed by this paper. In other words, despite this growth of IT worldwide, Iranian banks continue to conduct most of their banking transactions using traditional methods. Understanding the reasons for the lack of such technological innovation in developing countries such as Iran will develop a fruitful research. The aim of the paper is to look at the emergence, advantages and acceptance of e-banking in Iran.

DEFINITION OF E-BANKING

E-banking is the newest delivery channel for banking services. Banks have used electronic channels for years to communicate and transact business with both domestic and international corporate customers. With the development of the Internet and the World Wide Web (WWW) in the latter half of the 1990s, banks are increasingly using electronic channels for receiving instructions and delivering their products and services to their customers. This form of banking is generally referred to as e-banking or Internet banking, although the range of products and services provided by banks over the electronic channel vary widely in content, capability and sophistication. E-banking is defined as the automated delivery of new and traditional banking products and services directly to customers through electronic, interactive communication channels. The definition of e-banking varies amongst researches partially because electronic banking refers to several types of services through which bank customers can request information and carry out most retail banking services via computer, television or mobile phone (Daniel, 1999; Mols, 1998; Sathye, 1999). Burr (1996), for example, describes it as an electronic connection between bank and customer in order to prepare, manage and control financial transactions. Electronic banking can also be defined as a variety of following platforms:

(a) Internet banking (or online banking), (b) telephone banking, (c) TV-based banking, (d) mobile phone banking, and e-banking (or offline banking).

As online Internet banking and mobile phone banking are the fastest developing areas, in the present paper the focus is mainly on the development and the future of these platforms.

E-banking includes the systems that enable financial institution customers, individuals or businesses, to access accounts, transact business, or obtain information on financial products and services through a public or private network, including the Internet or mobile phone. Customers access e-banking services using an intelligent electronic device, such as a personal computer (PC), personal digital assistant (PDA), automated teller machine (ATM), kiosk, or Touch Tone telephone. While some literature restricts the use of the term to internet banking (i.e. Daniel 1999), elsewhere the term is limited to retail banking (Aladwani 2001) or both retail and corporate banking (Simpson 2002). The common definition for e-banking, and the one used in this paper, comes from the Basel Committee Report on Banking Supervision (1998, 3), 'e-banking refers to the provision of retail and small value banking products and services through electronic channels. Such products and services can include deposit-taking, lending, account management, the provision of financial advice, electronic bill payment, and the provision of other electronic payment products and services such as electronic money.'

E-BANKING BENEFITS

E-banking serves several benefits to any societies which are summarized as below:

Benefits from the banks' point of view

From the banks' view point, the first benefits for the banks offering e-banking services is better branding and better responsiveness to the market. Those banks that would offer such services would be perceived as leaders in technology implementation. Therefore, they would enjoy a better brand image. The other benefits are possible to measure in monetary terms. The main goal of every company is to maximize profits for its owners and banks are not any exception. Automated e-banking services offer a perfect opportunity for maximizing profits. According to a survey an estimated cost providing the routine business of a full service branch in USA is $1.07 per transaction, as compared to 54 cents for telephone banking, 27 cents for ATM (Automatic Teller Machine) banking and 1.5 cents for Internet banking (Nathan 1999; Pyun et al., 2002).

Benefits from the customers' point of view

The main benefit from the bank customers' point of view is significant saving of time by the automation of banking services processing and introduction of an easy maintenance tools for managing customer's money. The main advantages of e-banking for corporate customers are as follows (Gurău, 2002). Reduced costs in accessing and using the banking services. According to their idea the main benefits of e-banking are as flow:

1) Increased comfort and timesaving — transactions can be made 24 hours a day, without requiring the physical interaction with the bank, without requiring the physical interaction with the bank.
2) Quick and continuous access to information. Corporations will have easier access to information as, they can check on multiple accounts at the click of a button.
3) Better cash management. E-banking facilities speed up cash cycle and increases efficiency of business processes as large variety of cash management instruments is available on Internet sites of banks.
4) Private customers seek slightly different kind of benefits from e-banking. In the study on online banking drivers Aladwani (2001) has found, that providing faster, easier and more reliable services to customers were amongst the top drivers of e-banking development. The main benefits from e-banking for private customers are as follows (BankAway, 2001):
    - Reduced costs: This is in terms of the cost of availing and using the various banking products and services.
    - Convenience: All the banking transactions can be performed from the comfort of the home or office or from the place a customer wants to.
    - Speed. The response of the medium is very fast; therefore customers can actually wait till the last minute before concluding a fund transfer.
    - Funds management. Customers can download their history of different accounts and do a "what-if" analysis on their own PC before affecting any transaction on the web. This will lead to better funds management.

Economical benefits

The impact of the New Economy on the entire economic growth has been studied in several research projects. For example Pohjola (2002) shows, that the contribution of the use of information communication technology to growth of output in the Finnish market sector has increased from 0.3 percentage points in early 1990s to 0.7 points in late 1990s. However, unlike the US, there has been no acceleration in the trend rate of labor productivity in Finland. According to the recent research conducted in Estonia (Aarma and Vensel, 2001), bank customers use bank office services on average 1.235 times per month, and wait in queue in bank office on average for 0.134 hours. In nutshell, E-banking serves so many benefits not only to the bank it self, but also to the society at whole. Accordingly From bank's side, e-banking makes finance economically possible:

(1) Lower operational costs of banks
    - Automated process
    - Accelerated credit decisions
    - Lowered minimum loan size to be profitable

(2) Potentially lower margins
    - Lower cost of entry

- Expanded financing reach
- Increased transparency

(3) Expand reach through self-service

- Lower transaction cost
- Make some corporate services economically feasible for society
- Make anytime access to accounts and loan information possible
- From society perspective

E-banking business makes access to finance from banks attractive. Society have benefited from the development of Efinance and gradually stepped out of the informal sector. In particular, E- finance offers the following attractive benefits for society:

- Ease of use
- Lower costs of financing
- Convenience
- Time savings
- Operational efficiency

HISTORY OF BANKING IN IRAN

La Porta et al., (2002) documents that government ownership of banks is pervasive worldwide. In 1995 state ownership in the banking industry around the world averaged about 41.6% percent (38.5% if we exclude former socialist countries). Mayer (1990) shows that bank financing is the main source of outside financing in all countries. Yet despite the prevalence of government-owned banks in many countries, the prominent role of bank financing, and the importance of efficient financial markets for growth, there is very little evidence on how government ownership affects bank lending.

Banking operations had been carried out in Iran by temples and princes before the advent of Achaemenid dynasty by government. In that period, trade boomed in the country, thus giving a boost to banking. Before a bank in its present form was established in the country, banking operations had been carried out in traditional forms in the form of money changing. Money changing began to decline with the establishment of New East Bank, an originally British owned bank in the country in 1850. Bank Sepah was the first bank to be established with Iranian capitals in 1925 under the name of Bank Pahlavi Qoshun, in order to handle the financial affairs of the military personnel and set up their retirement fund. The primary capital of the bank was 388,395 Tomans. In the spring of 1979, all Iranian banks were nationalized and banking laws changed with the approval of the new interest free Islamic banking regulations. Before a bank in its present form was established in Iran, banking operations had been carried out in traditional form, or in other words in the form of money changing. Simultaneous with promotion of trade and business in the country, more people chose money changing as their occupation.

Following a boost in trade and use of bank notes and coins in trade during the Parthian and Sassanian eras, exchange of coins and hard currencies began in the country. Some people also managed to specialize in determining the purity of coins. Bank notes and gold coins were first used in the country following the conquest of Lidi by Achaemenid king Darius in 516 B.C. At that time, a gold coin called Derick was minted as the Iranian currency. During the Parthian and Sassanian eras, both Iranian and foreign coins were used in trade in the country. However, with the advent of Islam in Iran, money changing and use of bank notes and coins in trade faced stagnation because the new religion forbade interest in dealing. In the course of Mongol rule over Iran, a bank note which was an imitation of Chinese bank notes was put in circulation. The bank notes, called Chav bore the picture and name of Keikhatu. On one side of the bank notes there was the following sentence: "Anybody who does not Besides Chav, other bank notes were used for a certain period of time in other Iranian cities and then got out of circulation. Before the printing of first bank notes by the Bank Shahanshahi (Imperial Bank), a kind of credit card called Bijak had been issued by money dealers. As mentioned before, money changing got out of fashion with the advent of Islam under which usury is strictly forbidden.

The New East Bank establishment 1850 and it was in fact the first banking institute in its present form established in Iran. It laid the foundation of banking operations in the country. It was a British bank whose headquarters was in London. The bank was established by the British without receiving any concession from the Iranian government. The New East Bank allowed individuals to open accounts, deposit their money with the bank and draw checks. It was at this time that people began to draw checks in their dealings. In order to compete with money dealers, the bank paid interest on the fixed deposits and current accounts of its clients. The head office of the bank in Tehran issued five `qeran' bank notes in the form of drafts. According to a concession granted by the Iranian government to Baron Julius De Reuter in 1885, Bank Shahanshahi (Imperial Bank) was established. This bank purchased the properties and assets of the New East Bank, thus putting an end to the baking operations of the former. The activities of Bank Shahanshahi ranged from trade transactions, printing bank notes, and serving as the treasurer of the Iranian government at home and abroad in return for piecework wage. In return for receiving this concession, Reuter obliged to pay six percent of the annual net income of the bank, providing that the sum should not be less than 4,000 pounds, and 16 percent of incomes from other concessions to the Iranian government. The legal center of the bank was in London and it was subject to the British laws but its activities were centered in Tehran.

In 1209 (lunar hejira), the right of printing bank notes was purchased from Bank Shahanshahi for a sum of 200,000 pounds and ceded to the Bank Melli of Iran. Bank Shahanshahi continued its activities until 1948 when its name was changed into Bank of Britain in Iran and Middle East. The activities of the bank continued until 1952. In 1269 (l.h.), a Russian national by the name of Jacquet Polyakov, received a concession from the then government of Iran for establishment of Bank Esteqrazi for 75 year. Besides, banking and mortgage operations, the bank had an exclusive right of public auction. In 1898 the Tzarist government of Russia bought all shares of the bank for its political ends. Under a contract signed with Iran, the bank was transferred to the Iranian government in 1920. The bank continued its activities under the name of Bank Iran until 1933 when it was incorporated into the Bank Keshavarzi (Agriculture Bank).

Bank Sepah was the first bank to be established with Iranian capitals in 1925 under the name of Bank Pahlavi Qoshun, in order to handle the financial affairs of the military personnel and set up their retirement fund. With Bank Sepah opening its branches in major Iranian cities, the bank began carrying financial operations such as opening of current accounts and transfer of money across the country. The Iran-Russia Bank was formed by the government of the former Soviet Union in 1926 with an aim of facilitating trade exchanges between the two countries.

The headquarters of the bank was in Tehran with some branches being inaugurated in northern parts of the country. The bank dealt with financial affairs of institutes affiliated to the government of the former Soviet Union and trade exchanges between the two countries. The activities of this bank, which were subject to Iranian banking regulations, continued until 1979. In that year, this bank along with 27 other state-owned or private banks was nationalized under a decision approved by the Revolutionary Council of the Islamic Republic of Iran.

The proposal to establish a national Iranian bank was first offered by a big money dealer to Qajar king Nasereddin Shah before the Constitutional Revolution. But the Qajar king did not pay much attention to the proposal. However, with the establishment of constitutional rule in the country, the idea of setting up a national Iranian bank in order to reduce political and economic influence of foreigners gained strength and at last in December 1906 the establishment of the bank was announced and its articles of association compiled. In April 1927, the Iranian Parliament gave final approval to the law allowing the establishment of Bank Melli of Iran. But, due to some problems the Cabinet ministers and the parliament's financial commission approved the articles of association of the bank in the spring of 1928. The Central Bank of Iran was established in 1928, tasked with trade activities and other operations (acting as the treasurer of the government, printing bank notes, enforcing monetary and financial policies and so on). The duties of the CBI included making transactions on behalf of the government, controlling trade banks, determining supply of money, foreign exchange protective measures and so on.

In June 1979, Iranian banks were nationalized and banking regulations changed with the approval of the Islamic banking law (interest free), and the role of banks in accelerating trade deals, rendering services to clients, collecting deposits, offering credits to applicants on the basis of the CBI's policies and so on was strengthened. In short now days there are currently around seventeen commercial banks in Iran, of which eleven are state-owned and six are privately owned which all the banks must follow Islamic banking principles whereby usury is forbidden and, rather than AIRs, profit rates are set on deposits and expected rates of profit on facilities are set on loans. In terms of both assets and capital, the banking sector is dominated by Bank Melli Iran (National Bank of Iran). In recent years, six privately owned banks, Bank Kafarin, Bank Parsian, Bank Eqtesad-e-Novin Bank Saman, Bank Pasargad and Bank Sarmaye have commenced operations in Iran for the first time since the nationalization of the Iranian banking sector in 1952.

REVIEW OF LITERATURE

Costs of transactions in e-banking can be as low as a tenth of the cost of banking through conventional means. A further very telling factor is that Internet banking clients generate twice the revenue of a bank's traditional customers and we already know that the cost of their transactions is one-tenth of the cost of transactions through conventional banking; and access to e-banking is becoming easier all the time. Banking industry, locally as much as internationally, is becoming a tougher business to run and grow, given the increasing competition in a shrinking globe. Bankers are looking more and more into solutions to better reach out to their customers, improve customer's loyalty, gain competitive advantage, and provide better services, while reducing their running cost and generating more revenues.

Daniel (1999) described e-banking as the provision of banking services to customers through new technology. Other researches (Daniel, 1999; Karjaluoto et al., 2002) indicated that banks have the choice to offer their banking services through various electronic distribution channels technologies such as Internet technology, video banking technology, telephone banking technology, and WAP technology. Karjaluoto et al. (2002) also indicated that Internet technology is the main electronic distribution channel in the banking industry. In other words, e-banking as an online banking that involves the provision of banking services such as accessing accounts, transferring funds between accounts, and offering an online financial service. Wang et al. (2003) claim that in the 1990s e-banking was under-utilised as business organisations used it only to market their products and services. Thornton and White (2001), who examined customer orientations and usage of financial distribution channels in the Australian financial industry, found that more recently most financial institutions, faced with competitive pressure after the introduction of deregulation in 1983, have rethought their strategies to take full advantage of Internet technology. Tan and Teo (2000) note that the challenge to expand and maintain banking market share has influenced many banks to invest more in making better use of the Internet. The emergence of e-banking had made many banks rethink their Information Technology (IT) strategies in competitive markets.

They suggest that the banks that fail to respond to the emergence of e-banking in the market are likely to lose customers and that the cost of offering e-banking services is less than the cost of keeping branch banking. This notion was also confirmed in a study conducted by Jasimuddin (2004) who examined the role of e-banking in Saudi Arabia. He indicated that the majority of Saudi banks had taken advantage of Internet technology to establish web sites but few offered e-banking services. He suggested that if the Saudi Arabian banking industry wished to be successful in the global economy it would need to integrate Internet technology into its banking strategy.

Chiemeke et al. (2006) conducted an empirical investigation on adoption of e-banking in Nigeria. The study identified the major inhibiting factors to Internet banking adoption in Nigeria such as, insecurity, inadequate operational facilities including telecommunications facilities and electricity supply, and made recommendations on how Nigeria banks can narrow the digital divide. Also, the report revealed that Internet banking is being offered at the basic level of interactivity with most of the banks having mainly information sites and providing little Internet transactional services.

Similarly, Agboola (2006) investigated electronic payment systems and tele-banking services in Nigeria. The findings revealed that there has been a very modest move away from cash. Payments are now being automated and absolute volumes of cash transactions have declined. The result of the study revealed that tele-banking is capable of broadening the customer relationship, retain customer's loyalty and enable banks to gain commanding height of market share if their attendant problems such as, ineffectiveness of telecommunications services, epileptic supply of power, high cost, fear of fraudulent practices and lack of facilities necessary for their operation were taken care of. Ayo (2006) investigated the prospects of e-commerce based on ability, motivation and opportunities (AMO) model and observed that virtually all companies have online presence. The paper reported the motivation and opportunities for e-commerce as low based on lack of e-Payment infrastructure and access to ICT facilities.

Also, in an empirical assessment of customer acceptance of m-Commerce carried out in Germany, and reported by Buse and Tiwari (2006) as follows:

1) The highest mobile users are top management, followed by self employed, salaried class, students and others. Government employees were found not to patronize mobile banking.
2) The most favored reason for carrying out mobile banking is ubiquity, next is overview of bank account, followed by immediacy.
3) The highest fear of customers about mobile banking is that of insecurity, next is cost, and uncomfortably.

Research questions and hypotheses

According to the above literature e-banking caused so many advantages, so the research questions are as below:

Q1: does e-banking cause advantages to Iranian banks?

Q2: are there some barriers for using e-banking in Iran?

According to the above research questions the hypotheses of the study as follow:

H1: from the view points of customers, e-banking cause higher advantages to Iran;

H2: e-banking leads to increase of volume of transactions in Iran;

H3: e-banking leads to increase in using ATM among the banks' customers in Iran; and

H4: non-existing of enough knowledge have led to decrease in using e-banking in Iran.

RESEARCH METHODOLOGY

Two research tools were employed. The first is an exploratory research based on secondary data obtained through the Net, books and related journals.

Secondly, Survey questionnaire was administered to empirically assess the level of adoption of e-banking in Iran. A survey questionnaire was completed by the banks customers, at the end of 2008. The questionnaire contains two parts namely (A) bio-data and (B) this section includes several questions regarding to the e-banking services which rendering in Iran. Five-Point Likert Scale questionnaire was employed in this research. The Five-Point Likert's scale having the ratings of "strongly disagree" (1) and "strongly agree" (5) were used. For analyzing data X2 is employed which is the most relevant test to this kind of study. A total of eight hundred (800) questionnaires were randomly administered to business men and customers in the general public. Six hundred (600) were returned, which represents 75% of the total respondents. The bio data of participants is summarized in Table. 1

Table 1: Bio data of participants

Variable	Category	Frequency	Percentage
Gender	Male	275	45.83
	Female	325	54.17
Age	20-30	98	16.34
	31-40	309	51.50
	41-50	99	16.50
	50 and upper	94	15.66
Education	Diploma	111	18.50
	B.S	281	46.83
	M.S/M.A	201	33.50
	PhD	7	1.17
Job position	Businessman	122	20.33
	Clerk	207	34.50
	Self employed	189	31.50
	Others	82	13.67

As Table 1 shows, out of 600 participants 325 (54.17%) are female and 275 are male. It means that the majority of participants are female. Majority of the respondents were between ages 31 to 50 years, which represent 51.5% followed by ages 41 to 50 years with 16.50%. Regarding to educational background, out of 600 respondents 281 had bachelor degree which represent 46.83% followed by master degree of 201 participants in percentage 33.50%. The least number of participants had PhD degree (1.17%). Related to job position, majority of the respondents were clerk, which represent 34.50% followed by Businessman with 20.33%. Out of 600 participants 189 were self employed in percentage 31.50%. The least number of participants fall in the category of others (teacher, student and housewife).

Analysis and interpretation of data

In order to analyzing data, as it is mentioned before, X2 test is employed. The results of testing hypotheses is summarized in Table.2

The first hypothesis postulated in this study is:

H1: from the view points of customers, e-banking cause higher advantages to Iran.

According to table 2 the first hypothesis is accepted and null hypothesis is rejected. In other words, Iranian banks enjoy highly from e-banking in Iran. In this condition Jayawardhena and Foley (2000) explore the e-banking as a new delivery channel arguing that e-banking may help to overcome the inherent disadvantages of traditional banks.

Table 2. The results of testing hypotheses

Hypotheses	X2 Table amount	Mono-sample X2 amount	D.f	Alpha P-value	Results
Hyp. No. 1	7.814	8.162	3	0.043	Accepted
Hyp. No. 2	5.991	17.10	2	0.002	Accepted
Hyp. No. 3	3.841	6.00	1	0.014	Accepted
Hyp. No. 4	6.002	18.08	3	0.001	Accepted

The second hypothesis is:

H2: e-banking leads to increase of volume of transactions in Iran.

Table 2 shows that this hypothesis is also accepted and a null hypothesis is rejected.

It is very clear that if e-banking conducted successfully it leads to big volume of transactions, further Birch and Young (1997) argue that the internet may be exploited as a new delivery channel by the financial services industry to completely reorganize the structure of banks.

The third hypothesis is:

H3: e-banking leads to increase in using ATM among the banks' customers in Iran.

With reference to table 2 this hypothesis also accepted. It means that conducting e-banking in Iran leads more usage of ATM in Iran. The authors came to conclusion that the active ATM in banking sectors will cause cash circulation decreases , the efficiency of banking sector will increase, as:

a. client banking costs decreases (less cash fees to pay),

b. shop keeper / service provider costs will decrease, and

c. bank costs decrease (cash storage, less checking and processing costs)

The fourth hypothesis is:

H4: non-existing of enough knowledge have led to decrease in using e-banking in Iran.

With regard to table 2 the results of this study show that this hypothesis is also accepted, in other words, the Iranian costumers have not enough knowledge related to e-banking in Iran. Accordingly the null hypothesis is rejected also. The authors believe that the lack of enough information on e-banking in Iran may cause less efficiency of Iranian banks. To achieving high efficiency both bankers as well as Iranian legislators should introduce e-banking services at mass level. By the way, improving society knowledge through out TV, bulletin, etc will improve the knowledge of society at whole.

CONCLUSION

A strong banking industry is important in every country and can have a significant affect in supporting economic development through efficient financial services (Salehi and Azary, 2008, Salehi et al. 2008). Iranian banks have rapidly introduced innovative banking technologies and e-banking services in recent years. Almost all banks have invested in expanding and improving the IT systems and a number of new e-banking services have been developed. All major banks have declared e-business as one of the core strategies for the future developments. At the same time, e-banking acceptance depends probably on bank service quality, customer preferences and satisfaction. One of the main reasons for the growth of e-banking is that, if handled correctly, it can significantly lower the cost of delivering products and services. The results of this study showed that the customers also strongly agree with e-banking in Iran.

However, with banking customers growing increasingly comfortable with the digital lifestyle, their expectations from financial service providers have undergone a significant transformation but Iranian customers are not aware about e-banking in Iran. They are not fully understand the power of technology and seek to leverage it to enjoy better control over their banking operations. According to this condition we are at on the middle of the way. Bankers and practitioners should try to introduce e-banking very well in Iran. To conclude that e-banking may also provide other benefits. For instance, creating new markets, and reducing operational costs, administrative costs and workforce are increasingly important aspects for the banks' competitiveness, and e-banking may improve these aspects as well. So, Iranian banks should take these advantages of e-banking in Iranian economics as early as possible.

REFERENCES

1. Aarma, August; Vensel, Vello. (2001). Banks' Retail Customer Satisfaction and Development of Bank-Customer relationships, in Vello Vensel; Clas Wihlborg, eds. Estonia on the Threshold of the European Union: Financial Sector and Enterprise Restructuring in the Changing Economic Environment, Tallinn: Tallinn Technical University, 2001, pp. 85–106.
2. Agboola A. A. (2006). Electronic Payment Systems and Tele-banking Services in Nigeria, Journal of Internet Banking and Commerce, December 2006, vol. 11, no.3 (http://www.arraydev.com/commerce/jibc/)
3. Aladwani, Adel. (2001). Online Banking: A Field Study of Drivers, Development Challenges, and Expectations, International Journal of Information Management, 21, pp. 213–225.
4. Aladwani, Adel. (2001). Online Banking: A Field Study of Drivers, Development Challenges, and Expectations," International Journal of Information Management, 21, pp. 213–225.
5. Ayo Charles K. (2006). The Prospects of e-Commerce Implementation in Nigeria, Journal of Internet Banking and Commerce, December 2006, vol. 11, no.3 (http://www.arraydev.com/commerce/jibc/)

6. BankAway (2001). Net Banking Benefits! Sheer Acceleration, Electronic Banking: The Ultimate Guide to Business and Technology of Online Banking, Edited by SCN Education B.V.

7. Basel Committee Report on Banking Supervision. (1998). Risk management for electronic banking and electronic money activities, Switzerland: Bank of International Settlements

8. Birch D., M. Young. (1997). Financial services and the internet-what does the cyberspace mean for the financial services industry? Internet Research: Electronic Networking Applications and Policy, vol.7, n.2, pp. 120-128.

9. Burr, W. (1996). Wie Informationstechnik die Bankorganisation verändern könnte," Bank und Market, 11, pp. 28–31.

10. Buse S., R. Tiwari. (2006). Mobile Banking stages a remarkable come back, Press Release, [Online], Retrieved Feb, 2007 http://www1.uni-hamburg.de/m-commerce/banking/index_e.html.

11. Chiemeke S. C., A. Evwiekpaefe and F. Chete. (2006). The Adoption of Internet Banking in Nigeria: An Empirical Investigation, Journal of Internet Banking and Commerce, December 2006, vol. 11, No.3 (http://www.arraydev.com/commerce/jibc/)

12. Daniel, E. (1999). Provision of electronic banking in the UK and the Republic of Ireland, International Journal of Bank Marketing, 17, 2, , pp. 72–82.

13. Gurău, Catalin. (2002). E-banking in Transition Economies: the Case of Romania, Journal of Financial Services Marketing, 6, 4, pp. 362–379.

14. Jasimuddin, S. (2004). Saudi Arabia Banks on the Web, Retrieved 15 November 2004, from www.arraydev.com/commerce/jibc/0103-02.htm.

15. Jayawardhena C., P. Foley. (2000). Changes in the banking sector-the case of internet banking in the UK, Internet Research: Electronic Networking Applications and Policy, vol.10, N.1, pp. 19-30.

16. Karjaluoto, Heikki; Mattila, Minna; Pento, Tapio. (2002). Electronic Banking in Finland: Consumer Beliefs and Reactions to a New Delivery Channel, Journal of Financial Services Marketing, 6, 4, , pp. 346–361.

17. La Porta, R., F., Lopez-de-Silanes and Shleifer. A. (2002). Government Ownership of Banks, Journal of Finance, Vol. 57, No. 1, pp: 256–301.

18. Mayer, C. (1990). Financial Systems, Corporate Finance, and Economic Development, In: Hubbard, R.G. (Ed.), Asymmetric Information, Corporate Finance and Investment. University of Chicago Press, Chicago, pp. 307–332.

19. Mols, Niels. (1998). The Behavioral Consequences of PC banking, International Journal of Bank Marketing, 16, 5, , pp. 195–201.

20. Nathan, L. (1999). Www.your-community-bank.com: community banks are going online, Community and Banking, Federal Reserve Bank of Boston.

21. Pohjola, Matti. (2002). The New Economy: Facts, Impacts and Policies, Information Economics and Policy, 14, pp. 133–144.

22. Pyun, Chong Soo; L. Scruggs, N. Nam. (2002). Internet banking in the US, Japan and Europe, Multinational Business Review, fall, pp. 73– 81.

23. Salehi, Mahdi and Zhila Azary. (2008). Fraud Detection and Audit Expectation Gap: Empirical Evidence from Iranian Bankers, International Journal of Business and Management, Vol. 3, No. 10, pp. 65-77.

24. Salehi, Mahdi, Ali Mansouri and Zhila Azary. (2008). Islamic Banking Practice and Satisfaction: Empirical Evidence from Iran, ACRM Journal of Business and Management Research, Vol. 3, No.2, pp. 35-41.

25. Sathye, Milind. (1999). Adoption of Internet Banking by Australian Consumers: An Empirical Investigation, International Journal of Bank Marketing, 17, 7, , pp. 324–334.

26. Simpson, J. (2002). The impact of the Internet in banking: Observations and evidence from developed and emerging markets, Telematics and Informatics, Vol. 19. No. 4, 315–330.

27. Tan, M. and T. Teo. (2000). Factors Influencing the Adoption of Internet Banking, Journal of the Association for Information Systems 1(5): 1-42.

28. Thornton, J. and L. White. (2001). Customer Orientation and Usage of Financial Distribution Channels, Journal of Services Marketing 15(3): 168-185.

29. Wang, Y.S., Y.M. Wang, H.H. Lin, and T.I. Tang. (2003). Determinants of User Acceptance of Internet Banking: an Empirical Study, International Journal of Service Industry Management, Vol. 14 No. 5, pp. 501-19.

15
CHAPTER

THE REASONS TO LACK OF ELECTRONIC BANKING ACHIEVEMENT

Dr. Mohsen Rasoulian and Monire Safari

Keywords: Electronic banking, management obstacles, financial obstacles, technical obstacles, cultural obstacles

INTRODUCTION

Electronic banking has many advantages and interesting diversities including more number of customers, services in higher quality and lower price, preservation and enhancement of share in market, unlimited space for market, concentration in new distribution, making competition between commercial brands, concentration on expenses and improvement of revenue, providing extensive services, improvement in management system, decreasing the expenses of contractions, close intra banking connection, controlling ecological pollution, etc.

The implementation of article 44 of constitutional law and manifestation of electronic government can make electronic banking much more serious. Also electronic trade requires electronic banking. Besides, in recent years sanctions have influenced all current issues and electronic banking can be affective in breaking suctions. (But also suctions can be effective communication with foreign banks…). Also in recognizing financial operation of competitors it can be very useful. Existence of a comprehensive electronic banking system can prevent the process of launder in the country and can minimize tax violation, fabrication of banking documents and monetary theft. Electronic banking has different models like internet banking, telephone banking, cell phone banking and related technologies like ATM, POS, electronic links, etc.

Citation: Dr. Mohsen Rasoulian and Monire Safari, The Reasons to Lack of Electronic Banking Achievement, DOI : 10.5121/ijmit.2011.3305.

OVER VIEW OF STUDIES

Alireza Moghali (1386) considers the importance of electronic banking and discusses its advantages in an article titled "the acceptance of electronic banking in customers in Shiraz." The education of customers is of real importance in this regard as well. Atousa Goudaezi and Vahid Zobeidi (1387) discussed the influence of electronic banking in profits made by the banking system. Hamide Amade and Mahmoud Jafarpour (1388) studied the 4 groups of obstacles in a research titled "the study of obstacles and strategies to improve electronic banking in perspective of Iran 1404." These obstacles include cultural-social, management, financial and technical ones and the first two are accepted and the second two are rejected at the end of the study. In another article written by Mohammadreza Hamidizadeh and Manije Ghareche and Abdolhamid Abdolbaghi (1386) some other factors such as decrease in service expenses, managers and experts are taken into account as influencing on electronic banking system. They also introduce factors like lack of Internet foundation and lack of experts as the important challenges in the field of electronic banking.

METHODS

First part- Comparative study

In this part it is tried to compare the actions taken in Turkey and Malaysia with Iran. Malaysia is the model of our Islamic country in the field of banking so taking it into consideration can be very helpful. Turkey is a country with a similar religion and culture and is located near our country so that we can study this country in respect of similar affordability of the people in Turkey and Iran.

The comparison of electronic banking in Iran and Turkey

The banking industry of Turkey started in 1990. In 1992 CBT was established to organize the transformations related to this issue. In 2000 a new round was started in Turkey in the field of electronic banking by introducing new operations and alterations in signatures in software and hardware systems (electronic signature). EST (Electronic Securities Transfer) is used for purchasing and other system were implemented for other purposes like EFT. These items were protected by the government.

In Iran, the commencement of electronic banking turns back to 1381-1391. From 2001 the comprehensive paying system is defined and its operational levels are under construction. By the end of implementation levels all banking operations will be done by the use of electronic system. The comprehensive paying system includes: 1- Shetab system that has been implemented in 2001. 2- SATNA system that has been established in 2006. 3- Paya system. 4 -TABA systems. 5- the providers of paying services. 6- Sheba System 7- NAMAD systems

In this part Iran and Turkey are compared form different perspectives: Internet: based on a plan designed by the Turkey government, most residents of big cities in this country are connected to Internet with the speed of 32 MB per second. Based on a report issued by a site named InternetWorldStats, Iran stands in 34/9 place in regard of Internet use in the middle east. Zionist regime has allocated the 74th stand and has won the first place. After that, Emirates stands in 48/9th place, Qatar stands in 42/6th place and Lebanon stands in 39/5th place respectively. The amount of influence in Turkey is 35 and it stands in 26/5th place that is higher than the position of Iran.

The fundamental investments: This country is making the largest optical cable in the region and a consortium of 7 operators from 5 countries is involved in the project. The fiber optics is able to transfer 12.8 terabytes of data per second. Based on this plan VDSL2 will be delivered to the customers and it increases the speed of Internet in Turkey 8 as much. The expense of 16 MB service is 105 Dollars per month and the expense of 32 MB service is 138 Dollars per month. VDSL2 Internet lines are established in 73 cities of Turkey and this plan will be finished within a few months.

In Iran the similar plans are not predicted by any related organizations yet.

The Internet expense: The organization for Radio connections has designed the below table to show the expenses of Internet with a 20% discount (1389).

The width of band (Byte per second)	The rlated rade (Toman)
64 KB	86800 Tomans
128 KB	173600 Tomans
256 KB	260400 Tomans
512 KB	434000 Tomans
1024 KB	781200 Tomans
2048 KB	1388800 Tomans
4 MB	2343600 Tomans
8 MB	2906000 Tomans

These prices are 12 times higher than the prices in Turkey. (The Tomans is a super unit of the official currency of Iran, the rial)

Credit cards: Based on a report issued by The Nilson Report Magazine more than 50% of Debit card exporters are categorized as Credit card exporters and only 25% of Credit exporters are categorized under the group of Debit exporters. So that it can be concluded superior card exporters are more into exporting credit cards and about 90% of the transactions are because of credit transactions. Also it is important to know that the average amount of exporters' transactions in Asia is 22.9 milliard dollars for credit cards and 3 milliard dollars for debit cards. This issue shows the attraction of credit cards for its exporters so for this comparison only credit cards are used. The total amount of credit card issuance in Iran was 0.0006% until 2010, May and it was 63% in Turkey which means 45 million and 65 thousand credit cards were issued in Turkey when there were only 442139 thousand cards in Iran.

The comparison of electronic banking in Iran and Malaysia

In 1975 the electronic banking activities started in Malaysia. In the first round that last until 1970, the complementary operations were done to open the financial sectors. Then in 1980, ATM was established as the first manifestation of electronic banking. In 1997 CDMs (Cash Deposit Machines) were provided that completed ATM systems. In later rounds in 1990 Tele -banking started its activity that enjoyed AVR technology and was provided with equipments such as checking the account, intra bank transactions, trust fund, credibility, bill payment card and monetary transactions. After that PC-Banking started its activity in 1995 and it was welcomed by giant companies. Finally, internet banking was established in 1998 and was completed in 2002 (electronic wallet that was cheaper that credit card). The banks in Malaysia had the chance to use different channels to use services including: PC-Banking, Tele -banking, BSN, ATM, EBC (Electronic Banking Center) and virtual stands.

The virtual branches including EBC and stands can be seen in shopping centers and administrations. Virtual stands include: PALPHONE, PALPOINT, PALWORLD and PALTELLER that use a touch screen for its operations and it can talk to the customer and see him at the same time. In 1996 SFNB systems were established for the security of banking system. The supports of Malaysia: In 1994 the Malaysian government started to encourage customers to pay fewer taxes in this regard. Privatization of banks in this country was a big step in the way of electronic banking. Association of Banks in Malaysia (ABM) was established in 1973 to make an order in AMB systems by having a connection with credit card exporters (installation of security chips on credit cards) and also being pioneer in modernization of its banks and introducing new banking strategies to the people of Malaysia.

The instruments of electronic banking in Malaysia have much more considerable diversity as they do in Iran. In Iran many machines are capable of only a few tasks like telephone bank and ATM. Some electronic banking instruments that are used in Malaysia are not even introduced in Iran like electronic wallet, stands, and conference video that increase the safety of users but such things are not possible in Iran.

Internet: The speed of Internet in this Islamic country is 160 times more than Iran and its expense is 3000 Tomans per Megabyte and in many places people are provided with wireless system for free. Wimax Internet service is delivered to people for 23000 Tomans per Megabyte in this country. The users pay only 1/58 dollars per month for 224 MB Internet (about 1500 Tomans). It can be concluded that the expense of Internet in this country is 16 times more than Iran.

Section 2- The reasons to lack of electronic banking system in Iran:

First assumption: the cultural elements are the most important ones in this regard. Second assumption: the financial elements are the most important ones in this regard. Third assumption: the technical elements are the most important ones in this regard. Fourth assumption: the management elements are the most important ones in this regard. Fifth assumption: the safety elements are the most important ones in this regard. Standard measures are used to discuss the influence of all above mentioned elements.

A) Cultural obstacles

Before we go to cultural obstacles it should be mentioned that culture is acquired so the elements that are discussed hereunder are due to lack of education and information. These elements include: lack of information among electronic bank users, the resistance of beneficiaries toward electronic banking, lack of the culture to use electronic bank system and IT. In order to study the influence of this element, we can use the statistics provided by central bank and the statistics center of Iran. Based on the declaration of Iran's statistics organization, the population of each province is listed in following:

5 populated provinces of Iran are: Tehran ,Razavi Khorasan, Isfahan, Fars and Khouzestan and on the other hand Ilam, Semnan, Kohkiluye and Boyer Ahmad, Southern Khorasan and Northern Khorasan are less in population. The central bank did not provide statistics regarding the amount of transactions of other banking models like internet transactions and it only provided information about the transactions in ATMs and POS. It seems like other types are not very popular in the country yet. As a result we just discuss ATM and POS in this study (until2011/2/19): The result of the study is summarized in below table:

Ratio	The highest ratio	The lowest ratio
Population to ATM	Semnan(2347.678), Tehran(2679.60) Ilam(3094.71),Boushehr(3406.26), Zanjan(3811.61), Isfahan(396081)	Sistanbalouchestan(8594.98), W.Azarbayjan(6336.77),Khuzastan(5696.16), Lorestan(5960.09),Golestan(5549.62), E.Azarbayjan(5525.85)
Population to POS	Ardebil(0.005619),Isfahan(06773), Boushehr(2.7169), S.Khorasan(7.1333), N.Khorasan(21.5448), Yazd(33.1878)	R.Khorasan(597.1819),Kermanshah(334.64), Fars(264.6861),Khuzestan(234.9458), W.Azarbayjan(157.3941), E.Azarbayjan(151.8979)
Population to issued cards	Tehran(0.4368),semnan(0.5893), Yazd(0.649),Markazi(0.7712) ,Qom(0.7924), Isfahan(0.8146)	Sistanbaluchestan(1.7749), W.Azarbayjan(1.4536),Hamedan(1.2631), N.Khorasan(1.1908),Lorestan(1.1858), Kordestan(1.1615)
Population to ATM transaction	Tehran(0.4119),Yazd(0.4748) Ilam(0.5096),Boushehr(0.5100), Semnan(0.5380), Isfahan(0.5739)	W.Azarbayjan(1.1262) ,Sistanbaluchestan(1.0884),Hamedan(0.9790), Golestan(0.8529),N.Khorasan(0.8368), Ardebil(0.8231)
Population to POS transactions	Boushehr(0.1190), S.Khorasan(0.2848),Ardebil(0.7), N.Khorasan(0.8061), Kohkiluye and BoyerAhmad(1.4257),Zanjan(1.4830)	Tehran(93.608),Isfahan(53.2491), R.Khorasan(25.9525),Fars(15.4452), Khuzestan(15.0435), Kermanshah(13.6592)

B) Financial obstacles

Every alteration requires foundation, support and expertise. The possibility to have suitable foundations, updated equipments and support groups requires a considerable amount of money. In fundamental changes of the society such as electronic banking this issue is of even more importance. Lack of investment in the field of telecommunication, expenses regarding web connection, satellite expenses, the expenses for up grading webs are some examples in this regard.

The average speed of Internet is 128 Kb per second and it costs 20000 Tomans monthly. About using ATM and POS machines it should be said that the banks keep receiving commissions. Telecommunication center is not faced with serious financial problems in this regard.

C) Technical obstacles

Electronic banking is dependant to updated and useful technology. Lots of are required in this regard at the same time like telecommunication, information technology, etc. The influencing factors on electronic banking are: access to web, internet speed, ISP centers, number and width of internet bands, lack of IT and electronic banking experts, lack of quality, ICI expansion, disqualified electronic banking services, etc.

In order to discuss this issue we need the statistics issued by telecommunication center and central bank. The below chart is used in the site of telecommunication center to show the operations of the said organ:

Row	Index	1384	1385	1386	1387	1388	1389 (May)
1	telephone division	20340060	22626944	23952089	24709447	25410361	24972645
2	Telephone influence	2971	3257	3345	3395	3404	3360
3	Cell phone division	8510513	15385289	24509714	31423104	35427101	35554812
4	Cell phone influence	1243	2220	3420	4320	4790	4792
5	Connected villages	47955	51058	52784	52459	52596	52600
6	ICT villages	963	2287	5590	8200	9812	9900
7	Public phone	141912	167366	186198	218719	22800	229000
8	Public toll call	64774	89460	124314	162055	176800	177000
9	Data ports	14897	16392	36806	50818	91016	98547
10	Internet users	8800000	12000000	12800000	21000000	26500000	26800000
11	Info transfer web	716	956	1182	1220	1223	1223

Fiber optics are about 47000 Km in Iran. By comparing the internet users to the population of the country it can be concluded that the number of internet users is very few in Iran. Based on the ranking of countries in respect of personal internet speed in first half of 2010, 152 countries were studied and Iran has the 144th place after Venezuela, Nigeria, Bolivia, Iraq, Prague, Turkey and kayaks with the speed of 0.61 MB per second. The width of imported international internet band: 1705 Mbps, The width of exported international internet band: 1705 Mbps, number ISP: t 1370, the capacity of information transfer: 106000 MB, Fiber optics: 56000 Km. About the speed of problem solving no statistics have been issued.

About the number of IT-EB experts it should be mentioned that from 1381 the university acceptance in the field of IT MA and BA is started and in the field of EB there's no official training course and the problem of IT graduates is lack of experience due to its new nature. The telecommunication center is expected to provide the needs of banks but no statistics have been delivered in this regard. But based on the issued statistics by central bank about the transactions it can be understood that the banks are improving their electronic bank services all over the country and it's a sign of telecommunication services to the banks.

D) Management obstacles

There are many reasons to lack of electronic banking from the perspective of management role and the most important ones are: tendency to previous processes, low risk ability, changes made in board of managers, the existence of many decision making organs, long term management, the amount of knowledge, lack of familiarity with electronic banking and vague policies. In recent years central bank and some other banks witnessed the changes made in board of high ranking managers. First of all we are going to discuss the actions taken by Sheibani, Mazaheri, Bahmani and Nourbakhsh in regard of electronic banking.

Nourbaksh was the chairman of central bank in 1994-2003 and he took the first steps in the field of electronic banking. After him Sheibani started his career as the chairman of central bank from 2003-2007 and his important actions were listed in the report of 2006 as: the daily liquidation of Shetab centers, SATNA establishment, and the expansion of credit and debit cards. After him Mazaheri provided services such as fast monetary transactions, ATM, PINPAD, SATNA and issuance of credit cards during 2007-2008. Then Bahmani started his job from 2008 and his services include: SHEBA, Card to card transaction, Mirror and DR supporting sites, etc. you can see no considerable changes can be observed in management methods of all mentioned managers. Based on by laws of banking system enacted on 2004, the central bank is responsible for determination of strategies and foundations of electronic banking system.

Due to the adherence of all banks all over the country from the central bank it can be concluded that the actions taken by the managers of different banks is toward electronic banking so the existence of many decision making organs does not seem to be true. But the different services provided in different banks with similar banking policies is because of the different actions of middle ranking managers so middle ranking managers can be influential in this regard.

E) Safety obstacles and acceptance of risks

Regarding this item we first discuss all possible risks in banking system: In evaluation of risk in electronic banking system we can use the below items: 1 the recognition of risk by customer. 2 the ability of customer to analyze the capabilities of the system 3 sensitivity to information preservation by bank and customer Regarding the discussed issues, safety measurements and risking in electronic banking include: lack of legal encounter with violations made in the field of electronic banking, the use of multi functional factors by banks, lack of enough attention to preservation of information by customer and bank, the passive attitudes of banks towards the safety issues, the risks caused by cheating, etc. In order to determine the amount of influence of the above mentioned factors we used the statistics provided by the Police and central bank:

Based on a report issued by the police, the most electronic crimes occur in banking system. Based on a report issued by the deputy special crimes officer, 33% of cases are about illegal access to systems and computer data by using bank cards and electronic devices.

Central bank stated that this issue is because of lack of attention of people in preserving their passwords. This problem can be solved by the use of electronic signatures. In 1388 central bank started its activity in regard of electronic signature. So it can be concluded that abuses are because of ignorance of people about safety issues and banking system itself is provided with enough security measurement.

FINDINGS

Based on the result of this study cultural factors can be categorized in this way: 1. the dispersal of ATM, POS is not related to the population of each city. 2. This issue can also be seen in card issuance by the banks as well. 3. The number of issued cards is more harmonic with ATM than it is with POS. 4. The provinces with large amounts of ATM, POS have the highest amount of transaction. 5. The provinces with small amounts of ATM, POS have lower amount of transaction. 6. Commissions exist in both items so financial issues are not influential in this regard. Generally, it can be concluded that cultural issues are very influential. ATM was used before POS and that's why people are much more familiar with that. So the influence of issued cards can be seen in ATM transaction and provinces such as Tehran and Isfahan have a suitable proportion of POS but because people are not familiar with that it has a low transaction amount (while it was expected to have the highest transactions). In financial elements we can conclude that financial obstacles affect the use of people from banking services but the custodian organizations are not faced with this problem in the field of electronic banking. Regarding technical obstacles it can be said that because of the importance of internet in this regard this can be an influential factor but its influence is fading away due to the actions under operation. Regarding management obstacles only middle ranking managers can be influential. About safety obstacles it should be said that it is affected by cultural elements because it can be reduced by instruction so safety obstacles are not very serious for electronic banking in Iran.

CONCLUSION

From the first section it can be concluded that internet is a very important element in this regard. Reduction in its price, increasing its speed, paying attention to the expansion of credit cards, expansion ofbanking services and paying attention to foundations especially privatization can encourage people to take advantage o this system. In the second section this issue is stressed as well (confirmation of first assumption). Also Ghareche and Abdolbaghi introduce Internet foundation and decrease in service expenses and Moghali also confirm culture as effective parameter (indirectly). Second assumption: financial elements affect the way people use these services so after cultural elements, they take the second place. Third assumption: because of the current improvements the influence of this factor is fading away. Fourth assumption: only middle ranking managers are considered as influential. Amade and Jafarpour introduce culture-social, management and reject financial and technical parameters, that this study only confirms culturesocial parameters as effective parameter. Fifth assumption: these obstacles do not play an important role in electronic banking system and are influenced by cultural factors. Totally it can be said that cultural, financial, management and technical obstacles are influential respectively.

REFRENCES

1. Authentication in an internet banking environment- federal financial institutions examination council- 2000- http://www.ffiec.gov (2…).
2. Effective of electronic banking facilities, employment sector and age group on customers' choice on banking Nigeria- journal of internet banking and commerce- jibca 2010, vo. 152, No. 1. http://www.ayardev.com/commerce/gibc
3. Connel Fullenkamp & Saleh M. Nsouli, "six puzzles in electronic money and banking".
4. Payment systems in Turkey- Bulletin central bank of the republic of Turkey- September 2008.
5. Committee on payment and settlement system- CPSS- payment system in Turkey- www.bis.org.
6. E. Anguelov. Marianne A.hilgert Jeanne M. Hogarth2004- U.S consumers and electronic banking 1995-2003
7. Electronic banking in Malaysia: a note on evolution of services and customer reactions. Balachandher Krishnan Guru, Santa Vaithilingam, Norhazlin Ismail, Rajendra Prasad JIBC.
8. Suganthi, Balavhandher & Balachandran- internet banking patronage: an empirical investigation of Malaysia. GHBC-2000.
9. Classifying Users and Non-Users of Internet Banking in Northern Malaysia ,T. Ramayah, Fauziah Md. TaibKoay Pei Ling : Journal of Internet Banking and Commerce, August 2006, vol. 11, No.2
10. Imtiyaz Al-Sabbagh & Alemayehu Molla , Adoption and Use of Internet Banking in the Sultanate of Oman : An Exploratory Study
11. JOSHUA ABOR ,Technological Innovations and Banking in Ghana: An Evaluation of Customers' Perceptions
12. Suganthi, Balachandher, Balachandran , Internet Banking Patronage: An Empirical Investigation of Malaysia. Journal of Internet Banking and Commerce ,2001.
13. Hamid Amade, Mahmoud Jafarpour,(1388), "The strategies to expand electronic banking system, Iran "1404", danesh and tose'e magazine, No. 26.
14. Alireza Moghali (1386), "The acceptance of electronic banking in customers in Shiraz" ,management science of Iran Journal , No.7
15. Atousa Goudaezi & Vahid Zobeidi (1387), "Review effect of expansion of electronic banking on commercial banks", Economic Research of Iran Journal. No35 -1387

16. Hamide Amade & Mahmoud Jafarpour (1386), "the study of obstacles and strategies to improve electronic banking in perspective of Iran 1404", Humanities and social sciences, especially management journal .No27
17. Ali Akbar Goy Ababdi (1386) ," Electronic Banking A selection or a requirement take accordance with access and technology" , export development Bank magazine

16
CHAPTER

APPLYING LOGISTIC REGRESSION TO E-BANKING USAGE

Kwame Annin, Maurice Omane-Adjepong & Sonita Sarpong Senya

Keywords: socioeconomic, binary regression, e-banking, Ghana

INTRODUCTION

Globalisation and rapid technological advancement in Information and Communication Technology (ICT) has generally brought vigorous transformation and competition into the banking industry. According to Tandrayen-Ragoobur and Ayrga (2011), with rising globalisation, as well as fierce competition and technological developments, the trading and investment environment have changed dramatically over the years. This progress in ICT has directly or indirectly affected the way every organization performs its business. Gallivan (2004) stated that changes in technology do affect the routine activities of professionals, managers and everyone in the structural setup of organizations. A number of studies have concluded that information technology has appreciable positive effects on bank's productivity; cashiers' work, banking transaction, bank patronage, and bank services delivery to customers (Hunter & Stephen, 1991; Yasuharu, 2003). The banking industry in Ghana has seen a dynamic change in recent years, not only in the minimum set-up capital for the banks, but also in the way the banks transact businesses. The banking industry is constantly responding to changes in customer preferences and needs; increasing competition from non-banking institutions, changes in demographic and social trends, information technology advancement, channel strategies, and government deregulations of the financial service sector (Giannakoudi, 1999; Byers & Lederer, 2001).

Citation: Annin, Maurice Omane-Adjepong & Sonita Sarpong Senya, Applying Logistic Regression to E-Banking Usage in Kumasi Metropolis, Ghana, doi:10.5539/ijms.v6n2p153.

The continual development or advancement in technology has brought a new way of transacting businesses in the banking industry through electronic means. This act of banking via electronic channels is popularly termed as electronic banking or simply put, e-banking. The evolution of e-banking into the banking industry has fundamentally transformed the means by which banks traditionally conduct their businesses, and has also redirect the manner in which consumers transact their banking activities (Sayar & Wolfe, 2007; Eriksson et al., 2008;). E-banking can be simply defined to mean a process where banks create platform for its customers to generally access information and to transact businesses electronically through an electronic device without necessarily being present at the bank. The concept of e-banking has been defined by (Daniel, 1999; Karjaluoto, 2002) to also mean the delivery of banks' information, as well as new and traditional banking products to customers via different delivery platforms that can be used with different terminal devices such as personal computers and mobile phones with browser or desktop software, telephone or digital television. Daniel (1999) further advances the use of e-banking by ascribing that it provides alternative channels for routine banking services that readily allow customers the opportunity to gain access to their accounts, execute transactions or buy products online, or via other electronic means such as TV, telephone and automated teller machines (ATM). Examples of these e-banking services include Automated Teller Machine (ATM), Credit card, Debit card, Internet banking, Mobile or Telephone banking, etc.

Currently, most banks in Ghana are offering at least one of these e-banking services; namely ATM, Debit card, E-Zwich (National Switch Card), Internet banking, Mobile or Telebanking. According to Abor (2004), the first bank in Ghana to have introduced any form of e-banking service was The Trust Bank (TTB). The bank pioneered the provision of ATM services to the Ghanaian banking industry in 1995. This was later adopted by several banks across the length and breadth of the country. In collaboration with the Agriculture Development Bank (ADB), the Ghana Commercial Bank (GCB) also started the provision of ATM services in 2001. From the early 2000's to date, several kinds of e-banking services have been increasingly introduced into the Ghanaian banking industry. However, Abor (2004) identified ATM as the most revolutionary electronic innovation in Ghana and the world over. The introduction of e-banking in the Ghanaian banking industry has increasingly changed business transactions from the orthodox paper base of transacting business to the paperless base; all aimed at reducing the waiting time by customers in the banking halls for transacting businesses such as shopping, withdrawals, deposits, etc.

Generally, the benefits of e-banking are well-spelt in many multi-country studies around the globe. Paper cheques are gradually being supplemented with electronic images, permitting greater storage capacity, reducing costs and improving customer services (Rose & Hudgins, 2005). E-banking is intended to speed operations, reduce cost and human factor, and to make available twenty-four hour service for transacting businesses. It is being asserted that a simple transaction cost for a non-cash payment at a branch is likely to cost a bank as much as eleven (11) times more than the same transaction over the internet (Jayawardhena & Foley, 2000). From the customers' point of view, e-banking allows them easier access to financial services and offers them a leeway of time saving, in terms of managing their financial transactions (Tan & Teo, 2000; Almazari & Siam, 2008).

With the numerous transaction benefits derived from e-banking services, the question one may then ask is, how well are people adopting these services? Several works (Akinci et al., 2004; Laforet & Li, 2005; Wan et al., 2005, Hernandez & Mazzon, 2007) have attempted to identify factors that possibly influence peoples' adoption of e-banking services. For example, Gan et al. (2006) employed a logit model to examine consumers' choices between electronic banking and non-electronic banking in New Zealand. Cairo and Staten (1999) also used a logistic regression model to investigate the preferences of consumers using debit cards, credit cards, and cash for gasoline purchases.

In Ghana, not much has been done on e-banking and its adoption. The few works that exist includes the work carried out by Abor (2004), who examined the perception of bank customers pertaining to the effects of technological innovations on banking services in Ghana. In a similar work, Marfo-Yiadom and Ansong (2012) assessed customers' perception of innovative banking products in a metropolis in Ghana. Other existing works have much concentrated on the use of ATM, by either assessing its intended objective of increasing effectiveness of customer service provision and reducing workload of bank tellers (Sanda & Arhin, 2011), or by measuring the standard and service quality of ATM's (Asabere et al., 2012). To the best of our knowledge, none of these works has attempted to investigate the factors that may possibly influence the decision of people to use e-banking in the Ghanaian banking market.

Despite increases in studies about e-banking in Ghana, no work has been identified that attempts to ascertain whether socioeconomic classification or grouping of people based on socioeconomic characteristics, explicitly affects adoption of technological innovations in the banking markets for developing economies such as Ghana. Socioeconomic as used in this context is a classification or grouping of people based on key variables such as education, income, employment, etc. The core objective of this study is to ascertain whether usage of e-banking within urban communities in the Kumasi Metropolis, is influenced by socioeconomic status of bank customers. The study again seeks to identify the kinds of e-banking services being offered by the banks. Lastly, the study examines the most frequently used e-banking services among bank customers in the metropolis.

MATERIALS AND METHOD

The data used for this study was obtained through a well-structured questionnaire (accessible from the author upon request), administered to customers at the banking hall of three selected commercial retail banks. The study purposely considered state-owned commercial retail banks that operate in urban communities in the Kumasi Metropolitan Area. The metropolis readily serves as a haven for the rapid urbanization in Ghana. Several categories of people; skilled and non-skilled, educated and non-educated, rapidly drift from the northern part and the coastal areas of Ghana to seek real or perceived better economic opportunities in urban communities within the metropolis. With its highly commercialized communities, it is best described as one of the few most economically vibrant metropolis in Ghana. The Kumasi Metropolis was chosen to fairly represent all manner of people or group of people, based on varied socioeconomic statuses. Moreover, the main reason for the use of state-owned commercial retail banks was as a result of their broad base customer population. A second reason was a widely held perception of state banks' ability to provide greater security to customers on all transactions. The state-owned commercial retail banks considered for the study had altogether sixteen (16) branches within the metropolitan area. Out of this, Ghana Commercial Bank Ltd (GCB) had nine (9) branches, Agriculture Development Bank (ADB) with five (5) branches and National Investment bank Ltd (NIB) with two (2) branches. A branch each of GCB, ADB and NIB was randomly selected for the study. Some of the customers who were found within the banking hall of each selected branch at the time of the survey were used as sample for the study. At the banking halls, customers were engaged whiles they were in queues to access various services within the service points in the halls. Questionnaires were administered to every third (3rd) person in respective queues at the banking halls of the selected branches. The survey was conducted in April, 2013. It lasted for three (3) weeks within the said month. In all, 300 questionnaires were administered to customers in the three (3) selected branches of the banks. Out of the 300 administered questionnaires, 241, representing 80.3% were completed. The successfully completed questionnaires were initially considered for the analysis. However, further checks on the completed questionnaires indicated that only 188, representing 62.7% were fully completed and could be used for the final analysis. The unusable percentage of questionnaires (37.3%) in this study was not significantly higher than the reported thirty-four percent (34%) in a similar study on electronic service delivery in the UK retail banking sector (Ibrahim et al., 2006). The survey questionnaires generally sought to gather information on the usage and non-usage of e-banking among bank customers within urban communities in the Kumasi Metroplis. To ascertain whether the usage or non-usage of e-banking by customers is influenced by their socioeconomic groupings, the survey questionnaire gathered information on customers, with respect to their formal educational attainment level, monthly income, customer's operational bank and occupational status. Other variables included customer's account preference, duration as a customer to a bank, ICT educational status and easy internet access by customers. Some demographic characteristics (age, gender, marital status) were also collected. Customers' responses were mainly analyzed using a binary logistic regression.

The binary logistic regression is a special case of generalized linear models (McCullagh & Nelder, 1989). It is generally used to model binary responses. It was employed in this study to assess whether a customer's decision to use or not to use e-banking is influenced by the customer's socioeconomic groupings and some demographic characteristics. This statistical technique was used because of the dichotomous response to customer's decision to the usage or non-usage of e-banking. Agresti (2007) defined a binary logistic regression model with multiple explanatory variables as:

$$Logit[P(Y=1)] = \alpha + \beta_1 x_1 + \beta_2 x_2 + \ldots + \beta_k x_k \tag{1}$$

In this study, we specified the binary logistic regression model as:

$$Log\left[\frac{P(Y=1)}{1-P(Y=1)}\right] = Log\left(\frac{\pi}{1-\pi}\right) = Logit(\pi) = \alpha + \beta_1 x_1 + \beta_2 x_2 + \ldots + \beta_k x_k, 0 \leq \pi \leq 1 \quad (2)$$

where a is the constant term of the model, b 's denote the regression coefficients of the covariates and x's represent a set of covariates or independent variables. The covariates in any regression model can either take the form of categorical, continuous or both. From equation (2), P(Y =1) or p describes the probability of the usage of e-banking by customers, while 1- P(Y =1) or (1–p) denotes probability of non-usage of e-banking. This binary response by customers was modeled using a log transformation, Logit(p) of the probabilities and by incorporating a set of categorical covariates. Here, the set of covariates or independent variables comprises an earlier specified socioeconomic groupings and some demographic characteristic of the customers. For easy interpretation of each covariate effect on the response variable, an exponential transformation of the estimated coefficients was undertaken. This transformation of the regression coefficients is popularly known as odds ratio. The odds ratio reported in this study gives an indication of the likelihood of a customer to use e-banking with emphasis on a chance in the covariates incorporated in the specified logit model.

RESULTS

Sampled Characteristics of E-Banking Usage

Out of the 188 bank customers who participated in this study, 99 (52.7%) were using some form of e-banking services, whereas 89 (47.3%) do not use any of the e-banking services in their banking transactions. Among the users of e-banking, it was realized that ATM was the most frequently used (62.6%) service. This was followed by mobile phone banking (18.2%). E-Zwich banking (17.2%) took the next position, while internet banking recorded the lowest (2%) patronage by bank customers.

Table 1: Descriptive statistics of e-banking usage

Variables	Users		Non-Users		
	N	(%)	N	(%)	Total
Age					
Below 40	87	(53.4)	76	(46.6)	163
40 and Above	12	(48.0)	13	(14.6)	25
Gender					
Male	68	(53.5)	59	(46.5)	127
Female	31	(50.8)	30	(49.2)	61
Marital Status					
Single	67	(54.9)	55	(45.1)	122
Married	32	(48.5)	34	(51.5)	66
Highest Educational Level					
No Formal Education	3	(33.3)	6	(66.7)	9
Basic level	2	(18.2)	9	(81.8)	11
Second Cycle Level	25	(55.6)	20	(44.4)	45
Tertiary Level	69	(56.1)	54	(43.9)	123
Occupational Status					
Student	51	(60.0)	34	(40.0)	85
Employed	37	(59.7)	25	(40.3)	62
Unemployed	3	(23.1)	10	(76.9)	13
Trader	8	(28.6)	20	(71.4)	28
Monthly Income Level					
Non-Income Earner	31	(32.6)	64	(67.4)	95
Below 500	18	(48.6)	19	(51.4)	37
500-999	19	(57.6)	14	(42.4)	33
1000-1499	5	(41.7)	7	(58.3)	12
1500 and Above	6	(54.5)	5	(45.5)	11
Customer's Bank					
ADB	28	(65.1)	15	(34.9)	43
GCB	57	(55.3)	46	(44.7)	103
NIB	14	(33.3)	28	(66.7)	42
Customer's Account					
Savings	80	(51.9)	74	(48.1)	154
Current	15	(57.7)	11	(42.3)	26
Others	4	(50.0)	4	(50.0)	8
Period as a Customer					
1-3yrs	54	(50.9)	52	(49.1)	106
4-6yrs	28	(51.9)	26	(48.1)	54
7-9yrs	7	(58.3)	5	(41.7)	12
10yrs and Above	10	(62.5)	6	(37.5)	16
ICT Educational Status					
ICT Illiterate	20	(46.5)	23	(53.5)	43
ICT Literate	79	(54.5)	66	(45.5)	145
Easy Internet Access					
Never	62	(48.4)	66	(51.6)	128
Always	37	(61.7)	23	(38.3)	60
	99	(52.7)	89	(47.3)	188

The results in Table 1 present descriptive statistics on e-banking users, as well as non-users with respect to some demographic characteristics and socioeconomic groupings of customers. From the table, users of e-banking were highly recorded among customers below age 40 (53.4%), unmarried customers (54.9%), and male customers (53.5%). In terms of educational attainment, bank customers who had no formal education were found to have less (33.3%) patronized e-banking services, compared to customers who attain second cycle (55.6%) and tertiary (56.1%) levels of education. Results from the table clearly indicate that traders (28.6%) and unemployed (23.1%) bank customers recorded lower percentages in the usage of e-banking services than those employed (59.7%) and students (60%). This later finding might not be much surprising as Lewis et al., (1994) ascribed that banks and building societies regard young people as key market for financial services. The group of unemployed customers comprises of people who were not actively engaged in any kind of job at the time of the survey. Furthermore, it was realized that lower income earners (Below GH¢ 500) fairly patronizes e-banking services than that of the moderately higher income earners (GH¢ 1000 and 1499). In a sharp contrast, middle income earners (GH¢ 500–999) were to be the majority users (57.6%) of e-banking services in the metropolis, relative to the percentage of usage recorded by other monthly income groupings. However, non-income earners recorded the lowest percentage of patronage. With respect to the banks, ADB recorded the highest (65.1%) users of e-banking among its customers. This was followed by GCB (55.3%). NIB had the lowest (33.3%) patronage of e-banking users among its numerous customers. From the customer's account preference, it can be deduce that current account users had higher percentage (57.7%) of using e-banking services. It could further be inferred from Table 1 that, the longer a customer stays with a bank, the higher the percentage of such a customer to adopt its newly introduced innovative services; for this case, e-banking services. In terms of ICT background, customers with no knowledge in ICT recorded lower percentage (46.5%) of e-banking usage, whereas those classified as ICT literates had greater percentage (54.5%) of e-banking usage. Similarly to this situation, customers with easy internet access recorded high rate (61.7%) of e-banking usage than among their colleague customers (46.5%) who generally have difficulties in accessing internet.

Bivariate Analysis of E-Banking Usage

To examine significant association between each socioeconomic or demographic variable, and usage of e-banking by bank customers, the likelihood-ratio chi-squared test of association was employed for this bivariate analysis. In testing for association in any (I x J) contingency table, the likelihood-ratio statistic is given as:

$$G^2 = 2\sum n_{ij} \log\left(\frac{n_{ij}}{\hat{\mu}_{ij}}\right) \tag{3}$$

where n_{ij} are the observed cell counts or frequencies (row and column totals) and $\hat{\mu}_{ij}$ are the estimated expected frequencies. The test statistic has approximately a chi-squared distribution with (I–1) (J–1) degrees of freedom. The evidence of association is clearly seen if the test statistic (G^2) gives a value which can be observed at the far end of the chi-squared distribution ($p < 0.05$).

Table 2: Likelihood ratio Chi-squared test of association

Dependent Variable: E-Banking Usage			
Independent Variable	**Value**	**DF**	**Sig.**
Age	0.251	1	0.617
Gender	0.123	1	0.726
Marital Status	0.711	1	0.399
Highest Educational Level	7.696	3	0.053
Occupational Status	14.518	3	0.002
Monthly Income Level	1.535	4	0.820
Customer's Bank	9.394	2	0.009
Customer's Account	0.319	2	0.852
Period as a Customer	0.864	1	0.353
ICT Educational Status	0.844	1	0.358
Easy Internet Access	2.890	1	0.089

Generally, Table 2 presents the chi-squared values, degrees of freedom for the cell counts and the statistical significance of each socioeconomic and demographic variable, as associated or otherwise with usage of e-banking. From the table, none of the selected demographic characteristics (age, gender, marital status) of customers were significantly associated with their choice to use e-banking. With respect to the socioeconomic variables, grouping of people based on their respective banks of operation (customer's bank) and occupational status were found to have significantly influenced the choice to use e-banking among bank customers in urban communities in Kumasi Metropolis.

Analysis of the Specified Logistic Regression Model

The results of the specified logistic regression model, with multiple categorical independent variables are presented in Table 3. The table shows the estimated regression coefficients, the standard errors of the coefficients and the statistical significance of each covariate. It also shows an exponential transformation of the regression coefficients (odds ratio) and some diagnostic tests on the fit of the regression model. The fit of the final model over the null model was examined using the likelihood-ratio test. From the table, the final fitted logit model significantly far improves upon the null model.

To assess the fit of the final logit model against actual outcomes, the Hosmer and Lemeshow test results, with χ^2 (7) of 5.809 and $p > 0.05$, suggest clearly that the data fit the model quite well. In building the logit model, covariates with 0.25 significant levels were initially considered using the purposeful selection of variables, which was proposed by Hosmer and Lemeshow (2000). In all, eight (8) covariates and confounders were selected for the final logit model. These entirely accounted for about twenty-one percent (21%) of the decision to use e-banking. The finally selected variables included customer's age, marital status, occupation, monthly income and duration or period as a customer. Others include customer's operational bank, account preference and easy internet access. However, only significant covariates, based on 0.05 (5%) level have been reported in Table 3.

Table 3: Parameter estimates for the logit model

Variable	Coefficients	Standard Error(S.E)	Sig.	Odds ratio(OR)	95% CI(OR) Lw	Up
Constant	-1.352	0.536	0.012	*****	*****	*****
Occupational Status						
Student **[Ref]**	*****	*****	*****	*****	*****	*****
Unemployed	-0.705	0.589	0.231	0.494	0.156	1.567
Employed	2.027	0.771	0.009	7.588	1.673	34.419
Trader	0.853	0.576	0.139	2.346	0.759	7.250
Monthly Income Level						
Non-income **[Ref]**	*****	*****	*****	*****	*****	*****
Below 500	0.975	0.564	0.084	2.652	0.879	8.003
500-999	0.738	0.574	0.199	2.092	0.679	6.447
1000-1499	2.012	0.881	0.022	7.476	1.330	42.023
1500 and Above	1.071	0.817	0.190	2.917	0.588	14.468
Customer's Bank						
ADB **[Ref]**	*****	*****	*****	*****	*****	*****
GCB	0.915	0.488	0.061	2.497	0.959	6.500
NIB	1.596	0.544	0.003	4.935	1.698	14.347
			χ^2	**DF**	**Sig.**	
Overall Model Evaluation						
Likelihood Ratio Test			32.892	15	0.005	
Goodness-of-fit Test						
Hosmer and Lemeshow			5.809	7	0.562	
Nagelkerke $R^2 = 0.214$						

The results of the logit model, as reported in Table 3, clearly indicate that customer's operational bank, occupational status and monthly income level were the socioeconomic factors that significantly influence bank customers' decision use e-banking. With the exception of customer's monthly income, these findings confirm an earlier bivariate analysis which also revealed statistical significance for customer's operational bank and occupational status, on the choice to use e-banking. From the table, traders and employed customers in the urban communities are respectively 2.346 and 7.588 times more likely to use e-banking in their banking transactions, than students. Moreover, customers who are unemployed are 0.494 times less likely to use e-banking in their banking operations than students. With respect to classification by customer's monthly income, it was evident that customers who earn low incomes (below GH¢ 500) are 2.652 times more likely to use e-banking than non-income earners. Also, middle income earners (GH¢500–999) in the metropolis are 2.092 times more likely to use e-banking than non-income earners. Customers classified as moderately higher income earners (GH¢1000–1499), are more likely (OR: 7.476, CI: 1.330–42.023) to use e-banking than those classified as non-income earners. Compared to non-income earners, higher income earners (GH¢1500 and above) are 2.917 times more likely to be users of e-banking. In terms of classifying customers by their operational banks, customers who transact businesses with GCB are 2.497 times more likely to use e-banking, as compared to their counterpart customers of ADB. It can further be observed from the table that, customers of NIB are 4.935 times more likely to use e-banking than customers of ADB.

DISCUSSION

From the descriptive statistics, it was generally observed that moderate proportion of the sampled customers (52.7%) uses e-banking in their banking transactions. Although, e-banking is believed to provide transaction related benefits such as easy transfer, relatively less cost, speedy transaction and time saving from long queues, quite a huge proportion (47.3%) of the customers still uses only the traditional banking services. This relatively high rate of non-adoption of e-banking services by bank customers in developing countries has been reported by several studies (Njuguna et al., 2012; Al-Smadi, 2012; Mughal et al., 2012) around the globe. Among the e-banking services, ATM was the most frequently patronized service, followed in that order by mobile phone banking, E-Zwich and internet banking. In a work by Abor (2004) and Marfo-Yiadom and Ansong (2012), ATM was again discovered as the most popular innovative product in the Ghanaian banking market. However, Marfo-Yiadom and Ansong (2012) discovered a very low patronage for telephone and internet banking usage. The foregoing situation was much similar in a study to evaluate customers' use of e-banking systems in Nigeria (Okechi and Kepeghom, 2013). This adoption trait is usually common among bank customers in many developing countries. With respect to gender, greater proportion of male customers in urban communities in Ghana uses e-banking, compared to female customers. The aspect of gender differences to e-banking adoption is much shown in a study by Olalekan (2011). It was again realized from the descriptive statistics that, the proportion of e-banking users fairly increases as customer's formal educational attainment level increases. This was also the same for customers with knowledge in ICT. In a write-up on customer behaviour, Schiffman and Kanuk (2009) asserted that, the young and educated cohorts in society are usually the first to adopt new technological products. Furthermore, it was evident that the longer customers stay with a bank, the higher the proportion of such customers to adopt the e-banking services offered by the bank. This finding is similar to a study by Bowen and Chen (2001), which established that customers who are loyal readily consume more products. Also, the study revealed greater proportion of e-banking adoption among bank customers who easily have internet access at either their work or places of abode.

From the logit model, the study generally identified occupational status, monthly income and customer's operational bank as the dominant socioeconomic variables that significantly influence customers' choice of e-banking adoption. In consonance to these findings, different studies on adoption of e-banking have also reported employment or occupational status (Gan et al., 2006) and level of income (Adapa et al., 2009) as significant factors that influence the use of e-banking services. In contrast to the study's findings, other works (Izogo et al., 2012; Polasik & Wisniewski, 2009) have identified variables such as age, gender, religion, marital status, ethnic groupings, education, etc., and behavioural factors (Singh, 2012) as major contributing factors that influence the adoption of several e-banking services. In addition to these already identified variables, this study have demonstrated that the grouping of customers according to their respective banks of operation also have significant influence on customer's decision to use e-banking.

CONCLUSION AND RECOMMENDATIONS

The study identified internet banking, ATM, E-Zwich and mobile phone banking as the commonly offered e-banking services by GCB, ADB and NIB. From the 188 sampled bank customers, a little above 50% were found to be users of e-banking. This obviously suggests that, quite a huge number of bank customers have still not embraced the usage of e-banking. Among the popularly identified e-banking services, ATM was realized to have been the most patronized service, whereas internet banking recorded the least frequency of patronage. With respect to the bivariate analysis, customer's operational bank and occupational status were statistically significant socioeconomic classification variables that influence the choice to use e-banking. This was further confirmed by the logit model, which in addition, added customer's monthly income level, as yet, another significant socioeconomic classification variable that influence the choice to use e-banking in urban communities in Kumasi Metropolis.

Based on the findings of this study, we recommend the banks to sensitize and generally educate customers to widely embrace the use of e-banking, as innovative alternative to the over reliance on the traditional banking services through media advertisement, the use of screens at the banking halls and setting up personnel-assisted unit to easily manage customers' challenges or difficulties towards e-banking usage. Seeing to an extensive adoption of e-banking may help bank customers and tellers to transact business with ease and as a result, reduce unproductive hours and unnecessarily long queues at banking halls. In a quest to meet the changing technological trends in the banking industry, we again recommend the banks to broaden the scope of the e-banking services they offer, so as to attract and maintain present and future customers.

ACKNOWLEDGEMENTS

Sincere appreciation goes to the Branch Managers/Manageress of GCB (Tech Branch), NIB (Adum Branch) and ADB (Adum Branch) for willingly allowing us to undertake this piece of work using their respective branches. We again express a deserving thump up to Dr. Z.K. M Batse for proof reading the entire article.

REFERENCES

1. Abor, J. (2004). Technological innovation and banking in Ghana. Accra: Ghana Universities Press.
2. Adapa, S., Rindfleish, J., Cooksey, R., & Valenzuela-Abaca, F. (2009). An Empirical Investigation of Frequency of Internet Banking Usage by Australian Consumers. Proceedings of the Australian and New Zealand Marketing Academy (ANZMAC) Conference. Melbourne. Retrieved from http://duplication.net.au/ANZMAC09/papers/ANZMAC2009-549.pdf
3. Agresti, A. (2007). An Introduction to Categorical Data Analysis (2nd ed.). Hoboken, New York: John Wiley & Sons Inc.
4. Akinci, S., Aksoy, S., & Atilgan, E. (2004). Adoption of Internet banking among sophisticated consumer segments in an advanced developing country. International Journal of Bank Marketing, 22(3), 212–232. http://dx.doi.org/10.1108/02652320410530322
5. Almazari, A. A. K., & Siam, A. Z. (2008). E-Banking: An Empirical Study on the Jordanian Commercial Banks. Journal of King Abdul-Aziz University, 22(2), 3–26.

6. Al-Smadi, M. O. (2012). Factors Affecting Adoption of Electronic Banking: An Analysis of the Perspectives of Banks' Customers. International Journal of Business and Social Science, 3(17), 294–309.

7. Asabere, N. Y., Baah, R. O., & Odediyah, A. A. (2012). Measuring Standards and Service Quality of Automated Teller Machines (ATMs) in the Banking Industry of Ghana". International Journal of Information and Communication Technology Research, 2(3), 216–226

8. Bowen, J. T., & Chen, S. L. (2001). The relationship between customer loyalty and customer satisfaction. International Journal of Contemporary Hospitality Management, 13(4), 213–7. http://dx.doi.org/10.1108/09596110110395893

9. Byers, R., & Lederer, P. J. (2001). Retail bank services strategy: a model of traditional, electronic, and mixed distribution choices. Journal of Management Information Systems, 18(2), 133–56. Retrieved from http://www.jstor.org/stable/40398532

10. Carow, K. A., & Staten, M. E. (1999). Debit, credit, or cash: Survey evidence on gasoline Purchases. Journal of Economics and Business, 41, 409–421. http://dx.doi.org/10.1016/S0148-6195(99)00016-8

11. Daniel, E. (1999). Provision of electronic banking in the UK and the Republic of Ireland. International Journal of Bank Marketing, 17(2), 72–82. http://dx.doi.org/10.1108/02652329910258934

12. Eriksson, K., Kerem, K., & Nilsson, D. (2008). The adoption of commercial innovations in the former Central and Eastern European markets. The case of internet banking in Estonia. International Journal of Bank Marketing, 26(3), 154–169. http://dx.doi.org/ 10.1108/02652320810864634

13. Gallivan, M. J. (2004). Examining IT professionals' adaptation to technological change: The influence of gender and personal attributes. The Data Base for Advances in Information Systems, 35(3), 28–49. http://dx.doi.org/10.1145/1017114.1017119

14. Gan, C., Clemes, M., Limsombunchai, V., & Weng, A. (2006). A logit analysis of electronic banking in New Zealand. International Journal of Bank Marketing, 24(6), 360–38. http://dx.doi.org/10.1108/02652320610701717

15. Giannakoudi, S. (1999). Internet banking: the digital voyage of banking and money in cyberspace. Information and Communications Technology Law, 8(3), 205–43. http://dx.doi.org/10.1080/13600834.1999.9965811

16. Hernandez, J. M. C., & Mazzon, J. A. (2007). Adoption of internet banking: proposition and implementation of an integrated methodology approach. International Journal of Bank Marketing, 25(2), 72–88. http://dx.doi.org/10.1108/02652320710728410

17. Hosmer, D. W., & Lemeshow, S. (2000). Applied Logistic Regression (2nd ed.). New York: John Wiley & Sons Inc.

18. Hunter, W. C., & Stephen, G. T. (1991). Technological change in large commercial Banks. Journal of Business, 64(3), 331–362.

19. Ibrahim, E. E., Joseph, M., & Ibeh, K. I. N. (2006). Customers' perception of electronic service delivery in the UK retail banking sector. International Journal of Bank Marketing, 24(7), 475–493. http://dx.doi.org/10.1108/02652320610712094

20. Izogo, E. E., Nnaemeka, O. C., Onuoha, O. A., & Ezema, K. S. (2012). Impact of Demographic Variables on Consumers' Adoption of E-banking in Nigeria: An Empirical Investigation. European Journal of Business and Management, 4(17), 27–39.

21. Jayawardhena, C., & Foley, P. (2000). Changes in the banking sector—the case of internet banking in the UK. Internet Research, 10(1), 19–31. http://dx.doi.org/10.1108/10662240010312048

22. Karjaluoto, H. (2002). Selection criteria for a mode of bill payment: empirical investigation among Finnish bank customers. International Journal of Retail and Distribution Management, 30(6), 33–339. http://dx.doi.org/10.1108/09590550210429540

23. Laforet, S., & Li, X. (2005). Consumers' attitudes towards online and mobile banking in China. International Journal of Bank Marketing, 23(5), 362–380. http://dx.doi.org/10.1108/02652320510629250

24. Lewis, B. R., Orledge, J., & Mitchell, V. W. (1994). Service Quality: Students' Assessment of Banks and Building Societies. International Journal of Bank Marketing, 12(4), 3–12. http://dx.doi.org/10.1108/02652329410057978

25. Marfo-Yiadom, E., & Ansong, A. (2012). Customers' Perception of Innovative Banking Products in Cape Coast Metropolis, Ghana. International Journal of Business and Management, 7(3), 162–172. http://dx.doi.org/10.5539/ijbm.v7n3p162

26. McCullagh, P., & Nelder, J. A. (1989). Generalized Linear Models (2nd ed.). London: Chapman and Hall.

27. Mughal, M. M., Farhan, M., Ali, K., & Khan, A. J. (2012). Accepting of E-banking among Banking Customers of Pakistan. Information Management and Business Review, 4(6), 332–339.

28. Njuguna, P. K., Ritho, C., Olweny, T., & Wanderi, M. P. (2012). Internet Banking Adoption in Kenya: The Case of Nairobi County. International Journal of Business and Social Science, 3(18), 246–252.

29. Okechi, O., & Kepeghom, O. M. (2013). Empirical Evaluation of Customers' Use of Electronic Banking Systems in Nigeria. Afr J. of Comp & ICTs., 6(1), 7–20.

30. Olalekan, A. (2011). E-Banking patronage in Nigeria: An exploratory study of gender difference. Business Intelligence Journal, 4(2), 243–252.

31. Polasik, M., & Wisniewski, T. P. (2009). Empirical analysis of internet banking adoption in Poland. International Journal of Bank Marketing, 27(1), 32–52. http://dx.doi.org/10.1108/02652320910928227

32. Rose, P. S., & Hudgins, S. C. (2005). Bank Management and Financial Services (6th ed.). Mcgraw Hill.

33. Sanda, M. A., & Arhin, E. (2011). Using ATMs as Workload Relievers for Ghanaian Bank Tellers: The Customer Behavioral Challenge. Journal of Economics and Behavioral Studies, 3(1), 13–21.
34. Sayar, C., & Wolfe, S. (2007). Internet banking market performance: Turkey versus the UK. The International Journal of Bank Marketing, 25(3), 122–141. http://dx.doi.org/10.1108/02652320710739841
35. Schiffman, L., & Kanuk, L. (2009). Consumer Behaviour (10th ed.). Prentice Hall PTR.
36. Singh, S. (2012). An Empirical Investigation of the Determinants of Users Acceptance of E-Banking in Singapore (A Technology Acceptance Model). Int. J. Manag. Bus. Res., 2(1), 69–84.
37. Tan, M., & Teo, T. S. H. (2000). Factors influencing the adoption of Internet banking. Journal of the Association for Information Systems, 1(5), 1–42.
38. Tandrayen-Ragoobur, V., & Ayrga, A. (2011). Is Mauritius Ready to E-Bank? From A Customer and Banking Perspective. Journal of Internet Banking and Commerce, 16(1), 1–15.
39. Wan, W. W. N., Luk, C. L., & Chow, C. W. C. (2005). Customers' adoption of banking channels in Hong Kong. International Journal of Bank Marketing, 23(3), 255–272. http://dx.doi.org/10.1108/02652320510591711
40. Yasuharu, U. (2003). The effects of information system investment in banking industry, Research Center of Socionetwork Strategies, the Institute of Economic and Political Studies. Journal of Economic Literature, 12, 30–41.

17

CHAPTER

THE IMPACT OF E-BANKING ON THE PROFITABILITY OF BANKS

Sana Haider Sumra, Mohammad Khurram Manzoor, Hassan H. Sumra and Momina Abbas

Keywords: E-Banking, Public sector banks, Profitability, Information technology

INTRODUCTION

The revolution of information technology has influenced almost every facet of life, among them is the banking sector. The introduction of electronic banking has revolutionized and redefined the ways banks were operating. As technology is now considered as the main contribution for the organizations' success and as their core competencies. So the banks, be it domestic or foreign are investing more on providing on the customers with the new technologies through e banking. PC banking, mobile banking, ATM, electronic funds transfer, account to account transfer, paying bills online, online statements and credit cards etc. are the services provided by banks. Also the feature which is commonly unique to internet banking includes importing data into personal accounting software. Some online banking platforms support account aggregation to allow the customers to monitor all of their accounts in one place whether they are with their main bank or with other institutions. Banking through internet is considered as a complimentary delivery channel for the services rather than a substitute for the brick and mortar banking branches.

This research paper aims at examining the impact of electronic banking on the profits of Pakistani banks. E banking has increased the competition among the banks and both domestic and foreign banks are offering more and more modern ways of e-banking. The study investigates the services provided by the banks and their impact on their profitability in particular. It is significant due to the proliferation of the service

Citation: Sana Haider Sumra, Mohammad Khurram Manzoor, Hassan H. Sumra and Momina Abbas, The Impact of E-Banking on the Profitability of Banks, DOI: 10.5296/jpag.v1i1.692.

sector and its importance in the economy. It also discusses about the services provided by the banks to its customers and also reveals the major rationales for the banks to use internet and other electronic mediums as the means to providing services to their customers. It is a distinguished one because it reveals the factors which lead to the success of the operations, giving more profits and the ability to manage risks of using electronic means and using the electronic services for the benefit of the bank and how they differentiate through these services in the market and the factors which lead to the increased profitability of banks, be it public or private.

The objectives of this research are to measuring and comparing of the effect of the introduction of new technologies through e banking on the profitability of domestic and foreign banks, how much the provision of these services effect the service quality of the banks and hence their efficiency, to assess the impact of changing from the traditional banking to the electronic banking on the banks and on the customers as well and also to examine the main motive or aim of the banks to provide these services to the customers and it also discusses the effect of customers' literacy on the provision of their services and hence their profits.

LITERATURE REVIEW

Electronic banking is referred to as using of the internet as delivery mode for the provision of services like opening a deposit account, electronic bill payments, and online transfers. These services can either be provided by the banks having physical offices and by creating a website and providing services through that or services can be provisioned through a virtual bank as well. Internet is used as a strategic and differentiating channel to offer high valued financial services complex products at same or improved quality at lower costs without physical boundaries and to cross sell products like credit cards and loans. Apart from the poorly developed systems and structures, the developing countries may benefit from the technologies offered by today's world while building up their financial intermediation infrastructure. These technologies are provided through electronic banking.

Allen et al (2002) gave the definition of E-finance as "the provision of financial services and markets using electronic communication and computation". The use of electronic communication in finance has the history further back than 1970s. Earlier, the payments between the banks resolved electronically over the telegraph. However, for payments let it be large or small are done effectively and efficiently over the electronic communication mechanisms. Boundaries between different financial institutions have been removed, due to electronic means for transactions the services and the product are now offered with more efficiency and quality.

Claessens et al (2001) presented the openings e-finance furnishes to the developing world. "E-finance can allow countries to establish a financial system without first building a fully functioning financial infrastructure. Because e-finance is much cheaper, since it lowers processing costs for providers and search and switching costs for consumers, providers can market financial services involving smaller transactions to lower-income borrowers, even in remote areas. To further this, government's main role will be to enhance the enabling environment."

The most significant policy issue is regarding providing an environment facilitating e-finance, providing regulatory and other reformatory frameworks for enforcing contracts, privacy, information communication, security, telecommunications and infrastructure for e-transactions.

E-finance can benefit financial sector development of emerging countries by lowering costs, increasing the breadth and quality and widening access to financial services. Birch and Young (1997) analyzed the consumer side for e-banking and the results showed that consumers basically seek for transactional efficiency, choice for core and non-core banking products and access to competitive prices and returns.

Onay et al (2008) in their research on Turkish banks concluded that e-banking has a positive impact on the profits of banks. According to their study, "Internet has changed the dimensions of competition in the retail banking sector. It has also provided opportunities for emerging countries to build up their financial intermediation infrastructure. Investment in e-banking is a gradual process. The internet banking variable has had a positive effect on the performance of the banking system in Turkey." Also, Siam (2006) examined the impact of e-banking on Jordanian banks and concluded that majority of the banks are providing services on internet through their websites and his findings show that the attention is more to achieving e-banking as satisfying and fulfilling customers' needs. He also concluded that there should be a well articulated strategy to achieve success and profits in the long run.

In their research, De Young et al (2007) analyzed the effect of e-banking on the performance of banks by studying US community banks markets and compared the performance of virtual click and mortar banks with brick and mortar banks. Their findings concluded that e-banking improved the profitability of banks hence increasing their revenues. Also, E-banking is largely driven by the factors of minimizing the operating costs and maximizing operating profit, suggests Simpson (2002). According to Centeno (2004), the e-banking adoption factors are divided into two categories:1). Factors relating to the infrastructure and accessing technology, 2). Factors that are related to retail banking factors. The prior factors include skills on the part of consumers in using internet and other related technologies, attitudes towards technologies, internet penetration rate, privacy and security concerns. Later involves factors like banking culture, e-banking culture, trust in banking institutions and internet banking push. However, lack of PC and internet penetrations serve as barriers for development of e-banking. Also, in their study conducted in Turkish retail banking sector Polatoglu and ekin (2001) concluded that e-banking decreases operational costs and it amplifies customers' satisfaction and retention.

The usage of e-banking induces many risk factors to firms' overall risk profile. The Basel committee has issued Risk Management Principles for Electronic Banking in July 2003, it has recognized the related risk factors and its purpose is to enhance and promote safety of services offered by e-banking while maintaining flexibility keeping in regard the changing technologies due to dynamic environment.

RESEARCH METHODOLOGY

The study is conducted assessing the qualitative factors in determining the impact of e-banking. It is descriptive and exploratory in nature. Survey is conducted by interviewing the managers of banks which include Habib Bank Limited, United Bank Limited, National Bank of Pakistan, Muslim Commercial Bank, Bank Al-Falah, Askari Bank Limited, Faysal Bank Limited, Saudi Pak Bank, Meezan Bank, Silk Bank, Khushali Bank and Bank Al-Habib Limited from three cities; Bahawalpur, Lahore and Islamabad. A common way to examining performance of banks' is through the level of banks' profitability.

Interviews were conducted from the managers of banks including Habib Bank Limited, United Bank Limited, National Bank of Pakistan, Muslim Commercial Bank, Bank Al-Falah, Askari Bank Limited, Faysal Bank Limited, Saudi Pak Bank, Meezan Bank, Silk Bank, Khushali Bank and Bank Al-Habib Limited. The electronic services provided by the banks' are ATM, Credit Cards, Phone banking, PC banking, SMS banking, Funds Deposit, Local Funds Transfer, Bill payment, Cheque payment, Balance enquiry, Statement of Account, Demand Draft, Pay Order, Remittance, Insurance and call Centers.

FINDINGS

Managers affirmed that e-banking has changed the business environment. Manual banking has been reduced; the culture of keeping ledgers and recording transactions by hand has diminished by the advent of electronic banking. Now, banking has become real fast, customers get the services more quickly and reliably, the local and international transactions require a very less time as compared to before. It has also increased the competition and now all the banks tend to provide these services and facilities to the customers also, the environment and ambiance provided by the banks is a factor which complements their clientage, loyalty and banks' profits. At first, the customers had to follow a long and agonizing procedure even for account opening but now, owing to e-banking this procedure has become a "one window operation" where the authority is localized to the cashier which serves as convenience for customers. The funds can be transferred from account to account, bank to bank and even internationally in a very less period of time as compared to before which took days for the purpose. Banks are linked with each other within the country and also a few are linked with banks with other countries, this has increased the accessibility of the customers and also the number of customers for the banks. Visa cards have made it possible to make transactions globally. E-banking has opened new scenarios, increased service quality and more customers. Customers seek all the facilities under one roof and banks are devising more and more electronic banking techniques to cater their customers and for their retention. Call center facility has been provided by many banks in order to answer to their needs and problems. The relationships with the customers have enhanced due to these measures undertaken by banks for better customer services.

The main motive for e-banking identified by the all bank managers was their customers, to amplify their clientage, to increase customer satisfaction, retention and business expansion which would eventually gain them more profits. E-banking enables banks to achieve efficiency; it has reduced the requirements of manual maintaining as now the transactions and activities are recorded automatically on computers which in turn reduces human errors hence, increasing the accuracy, it saves time, labor costs as now less labor is required to do same amount of work, and it also has resulted in improvement in the services provided.

Another objective of this study is to assess the effect of customers' literacy. According to the bank managers, literacy is not a major hurdle for provision of e-banking services. Customers in the big cities are more educated and have more awareness and exposure than customers in small cities. They also added if the customers experience difficulties in using facilities provided to them due to their illiteracy, the bank employees help them and make them aware how to use the services by showing procedures by themselves and by educating them. So, literacy is not an issue in providing the usual electronic services. However, customers' literacy tends to be problem in utilizing the services of PC banking and mobile banking where customers in large cities have greater proportion of educated customers than those of small cities.

Lastly, the objective of the study was to examine the impact of e-banking on the profitability of banks. The managers confirmed e-banking as contributing to the profits of their businesses. They added that however, the banks have borne considerable costs for implementing e-banking; its infrastructure, for the training of their employees and creating the environment which would increase their service quality, image, brand value and goodwill. These implementation costs have been well covered by the banks in a few months time. The managers said that banks do not have to wait for years to cover up their costs rather, these are met in short run and even they start achieving profits.

Managers have shown a positive attitude towards e-banking; they concluded that e-banking is enhancing profitability and financial positions of banks and banks are striving hard to provide more and more services to their customers and to move towards advance and modern e-banking services also developing infrastructure. They revealed that up till 2013 the banks will completely adopt e-banking and it all dimensions.

CONCLUSION AND DISCUSSION

As now the scope is transferring to plastic money, the electronic banking is gaining more importance by the passing time. The electronic banking services provided by the banks include ATM, credit cards, funds transfer, cheque payment, funds deposit, balance enquiry, utility bills payment, statement of account, remittance, draft, pay order, phone banking, mobile banking, PC banking etc. the interviews from various bank managers have given rise to many findings about the impact of e banking on profitability, service quality and efficiency. The introduction of e banking has changed the banking environment. The manual banking was a lengthy and time consuming procedure, there was manual maintaining of the accounts and transactions for which the accuracy was damaged due to human errors, labour cost was considerable.

By the initiation of e banking, the efficiency of banks has been increased, the labour costs have decreased as now, less number of employees are required to deliver the services because of electronic means, the accuracy of transactions and maintenance has been also supplemented as computer has taken the place of humans hence, decreasing human errors, the procedures, processes and services are now fast and reliable which saves time, efforts and costs. The customers are more satisfied with the services, their accuracy and timeliness. This has in turn augmented the efficiency of banks; decreasing the costs and increasing profits.

The main motive for the banks to switch towards electronic means is to increase their clientage, to serve the customers with best of the services, to facilitate them and to boost customers' loyalty. Also, the business expansion was another motive for which the electronic medium for provision of services. Increment in the clientage, clients' satisfaction, loyalty and business expansion results in increased profits for the banks.

The transition from traditional to electronic means has not affected banks in the negative way. In fact, profits tend to augment in transition also because customers who now seek these online services get them increasing customers' satisfaction which contributes to the customer loyalty and hence profits. The banks have acquired the benefits in the short run and they meet their costs within a few years even a few months time. Customers seek all he facilities, fast banking and a good environment; this is generating more and more competition day by day which banks are meeting through electronic means and ambiance.

According to the turn out from the interviews, customer literacy is not considered as a hindrance in banks' objectives to seek customer generation, satisfaction and profitability. The banks tend to generate customer awareness if they are providing services to uneducated customers, the employees cater to the needs for questions and issues faced by customers, call center facilities are provided by many banks and also the employees in the banks which overcomes illiteracy to a larger extent and thence, customer literacy is not considered as a deterrent in achieving profits for the banks.

Banks are also earning from these services in a way of commission and annual deductions. The banks charge a certain amount or flat charges or a certain percentage on products and services like ATMs, funds transfer etc. In the end, interviews from the bank managers have confirmed that electronic banking has a considerable impact on the profitability of banks. If the eras of traditional banking are compared to the present e-banking eras, the results show that e-banking has contributed positively and proliferated the profits of banks. Banks are gradually transitioning from manual means to the electronic means rather than jumping to electronic banking means. Efficiency has risen as the costs have been reduced; costs of labour, provision of services, time saved, accuracy, reliability and quality of services has improved. However, the managers added that the transitional impact is seen more for the big cities as compared to small cities.

The financial statements of these banks have also been studied for the research and these statements have also shown that the profitability of banks has increased to a large extent by incorporating electronic means in provision of their products and services.

RECOMMENDATIONS

Bank managers have identified impediments on the way of transitioning to electronic banking is the flaw in infrastructure for mobile banking. The cellular service providing companies have not yet provided sufficient facilities and services for which the banks are not yet able to properly deliver mobile banking services to their customers. Also, customer illiteracy is somewhat coming on the way of advent of PC banking as infrastructure in the country for information technology is not satisfactory, people use other electronic banking services regularly but they are not much informed about how to get advantage from PC banking and mobile banking.

REFERENCES

1. Banan, M. (2008). The viewpoint of bank's staff about internet banking. 3rd international conference on E-commerce with focus on developing countries. Isfahan.
2. Jen-Her Wu, T.-L. H. (2006). Core Capabilities for Exploiting Electronic Banking. Journal of Electronic Commerce Research , 111-122.
3. John Carlson, K. F. (2001). Internet Banking:Market Developments and Regulatory Issues. Society of Government Economists Conference 2000. Washington, DC.
4. Pooja Malhotra, B. S. (2009). The Impact of Internet Banking on Bank Performance and Risk: The Indian Experience. Eurasian Journal of Business and Economics , 43-62.
5. Sabah Abdullah Al-Somali, R. G. (2007). Internet Banking Acceptance in the Context of Developing Countries: An Extension of the Technology Acceptance Model. Birmingham: Operations &Information Management Group, Aston Business School, Birmingham B47ET, UK.
6. Siam, A. Z. (2006). Role of the Electronic Banking Services on the Profits of Jordanian Banks. American Journal of Applied Sciences , 1999-2004.
7. Zwass, V., "Electronic Commerce and Organizational Innovation: Aspects and Opportunities," International Journal of Electronic Commerce, Vol. 7, No. 3: 7-37, 2003.
8. Daniel, E.M. and H.M. Wilson, "The Role of Dynamic Capabilities in E-Business Transformation," European Journal of Information Systems, Vol. 12: 282-296, 2003.
9. Baddeley, M. "Using E-cash in the New Economy: An Economic Analysis of Micropayment System," Journal of Electronic Commerce Research, Vol. 5, No. 4: 239-253, 2004.
10. Cheung, M.T. and Z. Liao, "Challenges to Internet E-Banking," Communications of the ACM, Vol. 46, No.12: 248-250, 2003.
11. Mattilia, M., Karjaluoto, H., Pento, T. (2003). Internet banking adoption among mature customers: early majority or laggards. Journal of Services Marketing, Vol.17(5), 514-28.
12. Sathye,M.(1999).Adoption of Internet banking by Australian consumer: An empirical investigation. International Journal of Bank. Vol. 17 (7), 324-334

INDEX

G

I

M

P

Q

R

S

T

V

W